27 Stunning Designs for Every Décor, Seas[illegible]vel

Best of Fons&Porter®

STAR QUILTS

LEISURE ARTS
the art of everyday living
www.leisurearts.com

Our Mission Statement
Our goal is for you to enjoy making quilts as much as we do.

Library of Congress Control Number: 2011945902
ISBN-13/EAN: 978-1-60900-378-4
UPC: 0-28906-05620-4

We're thrilled to bring you this collection of some of our very favorite star quilts! The projects we've included are among our most popular of all time. You'll find patterns for all skill levels. Enjoy the beautiful photography as you browse through the pages to find the project that's just right for you. Whether you want to make a little quilt, a bed-size one, or something in between, you'll find plenty to love. You'll also appreciate our trademarked *Sew Easy* lessons that will guide you via step-by-step photography through any project-specific special techniques. We think you'll have fun stitching these beautiful star quilts for your home or to give as gifts to family and friends.

Happy quilting, Marianne & Liz

6

20

54

84

108

136

Jewel OF THE PRAIRIE

The Jewel Box Quilters Guild of Grinnell, Iowa, made this quilt, designed by member Judy Martin, to raffle as a fund-raiser for their club. For super accurate piecing, Judy recommends trimming triangle points before joining them with other pieces to make various units. See *Sew Easy: Trimming Points* on page 11 to learn how.

PROJECT RATING: INTERMEDIATE

Size: 99⅜" × 99⅜"

Blocks: 48 (6") Star blocks, 8 (12") Star blocks, and 25 (12") Snail's Trail blocks

MATERIALS

25 fat quarters★ assorted light jewel tone prints and batiks
30 fat quarters★ assorted medium/dark jewel tone prints and batiks
1 yard purple batik for binding
9 yards backing fabric
King-size quilt batting
★fat quarter = 18" × 20"

Cutting

Measurements include ¼" seam allowances. Because there are so many pieces which are similar in size, you may want to label them as you cut.

From the assorted light fat quarters, cut a total of:

- 3 (9¾"-wide) strips. From strips, cut 5 (9¾") squares. Cut squares in half diagonally in both directions to make 20 quarter-square K triangles.
- 13 (6⅞"-wide) strips. From strips, cut 25 (6⅞") squares. Cut squares in half diagonally to make 50 half-square I triangles.
- 3 (6½"-wide) strips. From strips, cut 8 (6½") J squares.
- 2 (5⅜"-wide) strips. From strips, cut 4 (5⅜") squares. Cut squares in half diagonally to make 8 half-square E triangles.
- 9 (5⅛"-wide) strips. From strips, cut 25 (5⅛") squares. Cut squares in half diagonally to make 50 half-square H triangles.
- 6 (4¼"-wide) strips. From strips, cut 22 (4¼") squares. Cut squares in half diagonally in both directions to make 88 quarter-square C triangles.
- 12 (3⅞"-wide) strips. From strips, cut 57 (3⅞") squares. Cut squares in half diagonally to make 114 half-square F triangles.
- 12 (3½"-wide) strips. From strips, cut 60 (3½") D squares.
- 5 (3"-wide) strips. From strips, cut 25 (3") squares. Cut squares in half diagonally to make 50 half-square G triangles.
- 17 (2⅜"-wide) strips. From strips, cut 132 (2⅜") squares. Cut squares in half diagonally to make 264 half-square B triangles.
- 13 (2"-wide) strips. From strips, cut 130 (2") A squares.

From the assorted medium/dark fat quarters, cut a total of:

- 3 (9¾"-wide) strips. From strips, cut 6 (9¾") squares. Cut squares in half diagonally in both directions to make 24 quarter-square K triangles.
- 13 (6⅞"-wide) strips. From strips, cut 25 (6⅞") squares. Cut squares in half diagonally to make 50 half-square I triangles.
- 11 (6½"-wide) strips. From strips, cut 32 (6½") J squares.
- 4 (5⅜"-wide) strips. From strips, cut 10 (5⅜") squares. Cut squares in half diagonally to make 20 half-square E triangles.
- 9 (5⅛"-wide) strips. From strips, cut 25 (5⅛") squares. Cut squares in half diagonally to make 50 half-square H triangles.
- 11 (4¼"-wide) strips. From strips, cut 41 (4¼") squares. Cut squares in half diagonally in both directions to make 164 quarter-square C triangles.
- 12 (3⅞"-wide) strips. From strips, cut 57 (3⅞") squares. Cut squares in half diagonally to make 114 half-square F triangles.

- 21 (3½"-wide) strips for border.
- 5 (3"-wide) strips. From strips, cut 25 (3") squares. Cut squares in half diagonally to make 50 half-square G triangles.
- 7 (2⅜"-wide) strips. From strips, cut 50 (2⅜") squares. Cut squares in half diagonally to make 100 half-square B triangles.
- 20 (2"-wide) strips. From strips, cut 194 (2") A squares.

From purple batik, cut:

- 11 (2¼"-wide) strips for binding.

Block 1 Assembly

1. Choose 1 light D square, 8 matching light B triangles, and 1 matching set of 4 medium/dark A squares and 4 medium/dark C triangles.
2. Lay out pieces as shown in *Block 1 Assembly Diagram.* Join into rows; join rows to complete block *(Block 1 Diagram).* Make 28 Block 1.

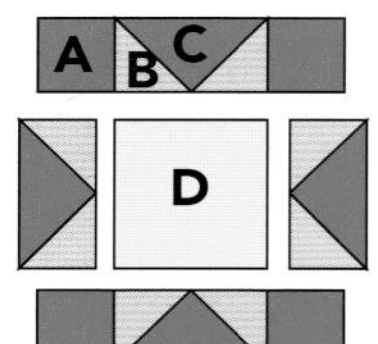

Block 1 Assembly Diagram

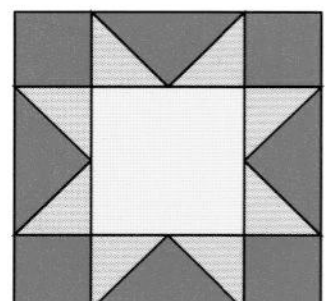
Block 1 Diagram

Block 2 Assembly

1. Choose 1 medium/dark E triangle, 1 medium/dark C triangle, 5 medium/dark B triangles, and 1 matching set of 4 light A squares and 4 light C triangles.
2. Lay out pieces as shown in *Block 2 Assembly Diagram.* Join into sections; join sections to complete light block *(Light Block 2 Diagram).* Make 20 light Block 2.
3. In the same manner, use 1 light E triangle, 1 light C triangle, 5 light B triangles, and 1 matching set of 4 medium/dark A squares and 4 medium/dark C triangles to make a dark block *(Dark Block 2 Diagram).* Make 8 dark Block 2.

Block 2 Assembly Diagram

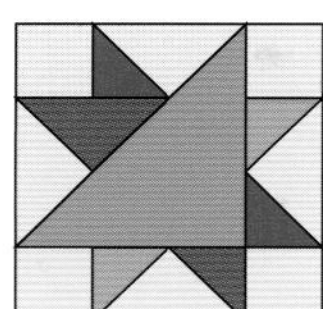
Light Block 2 Diagram

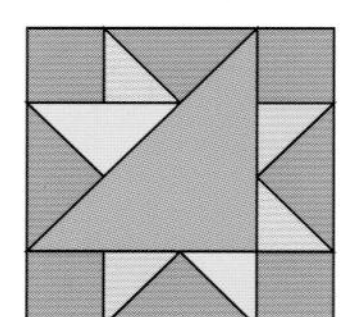
Dark Block 2 Diagram

Block 3 Assembly

1. Choose 1 dark Block 2, 8 matching medium/dark F triangles, and 4 matching sets of 2 light F triangles and 4 light D squares.
2. Lay out pieces as shown in *Block 3 Assembly Diagram.* Join pieces into rows; join rows to complete block *(Block 3 Diagram).* Make 8 Block 3.

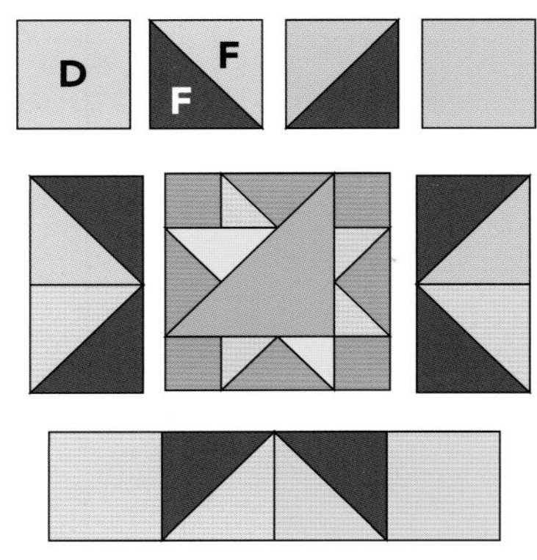

Block 3 Assembly Diagram

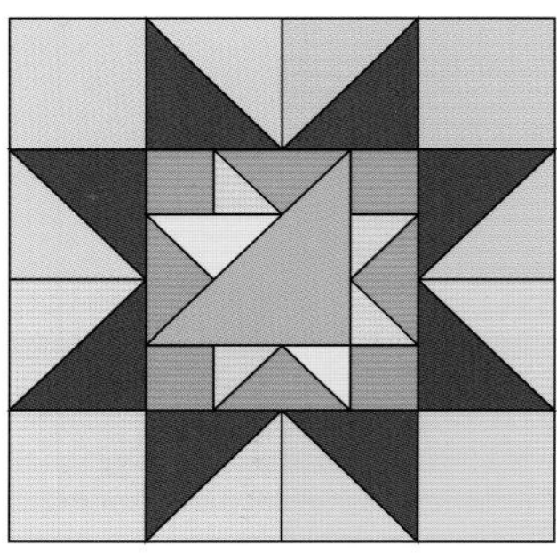
Block 3 Diagram

Block 4 Assembly

1. Choose 2 each of the following: light A squares, medium/dark A squares, light G triangles, medium/dark G triangles, light F triangles, medium/dark F triangles, light H triangles, medium/dark H triangles, light I triangles, and medium/dark I triangles.
2. Lay out pieces as shown in *Block 4 Assembly Diagram.* Join pieces as shown to complete block *(Block 4 Diagram).* Make 25 Block 4.

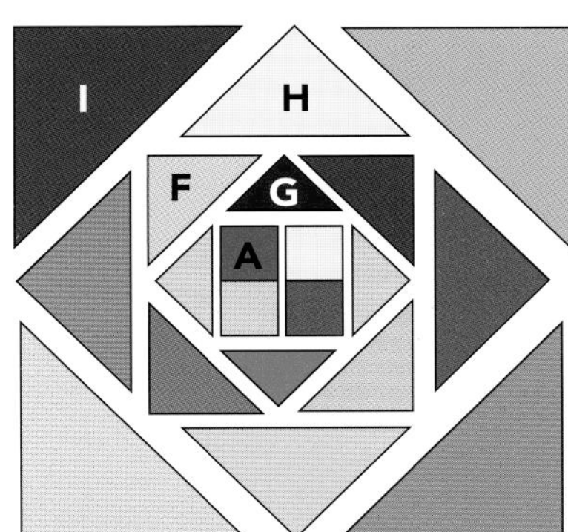

Block 4 Assembly Diagram

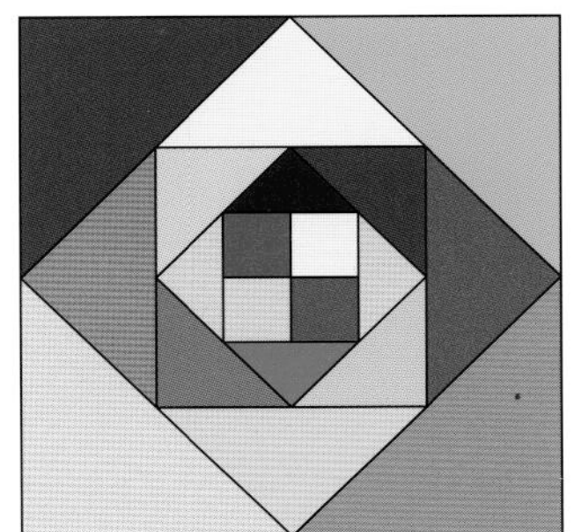
Block 4 Diagram

Quilt Top Assembly Diagram

Quilt Assembly

1. Lay out blocks, J setting squares, and K setting triangles as shown in *Quilt Top Assembly Diagram.*

2. Join into diagonal rows; join rows to complete quilt center.

3. Join random-length 3½"-wide strips to make 2 (3½" × 93⅞") side borders and 2 (3½" × 99⅞") top and bottom borders.

4. Add side borders to quilt center. Add top and bottom borders to quilt.

Finishing

1. Divide backing into 3 (3-yard) pieces. Join pieces lengthwise.

2. Layer backing, batting, and quilt top; baste. Quilt as desired. Quilt shown was quilted with an allover pattern.

3. Join 2¼"-wide purple batik strips into 1 continuous piece for straight-grain French-fold binding. Add binding to quilt.

DESIGNER

Judy Martin has been designing and making quilts for thirty-five years. She is the author of twenty-one quilting books, including her latest, *Patchwork Among Friends, From Patterns to Potlucks*. Judy buys more fabric than she will ever use and has made so many still-unquilted tops she has started saying she collects them. ⁕

Sew *Easy*™ Trimming Points

Trimming points makes pieces easier to line up. Use Judy Martin's Ultimate Point Trimmer to achieve more accurate patchwork for quilts like *Jewel of the Prairie*.

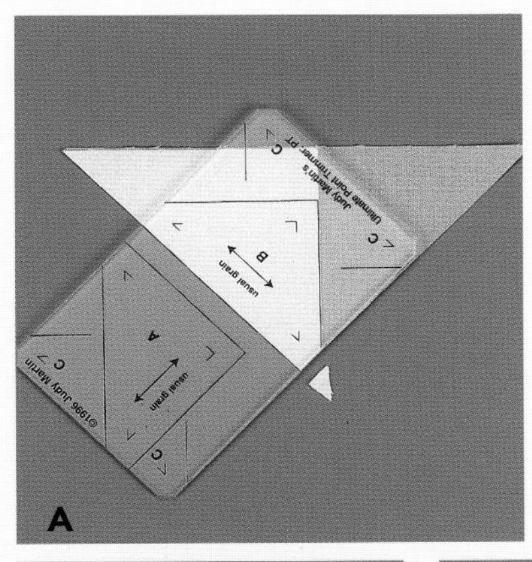
A

Trimming Points for Flying Geese Units

1. Cut large and small triangles for Flying Geese Units.
2. Align B triangle lines on Point Trimmer with edges of triangles and trim points *(Photo A)*.
3. Join small triangle to side of center triangle *(Photo B)*; press seam allowance toward side triangle.
4. Join triangle to other side of center triangle *(Photo C)*; press seam allowance toward side triangle *(Photo D)*. Trim remaining points even with edges of unit *(Photo E)*. Seam allowance will extend ¼" beyond point of center triangle.

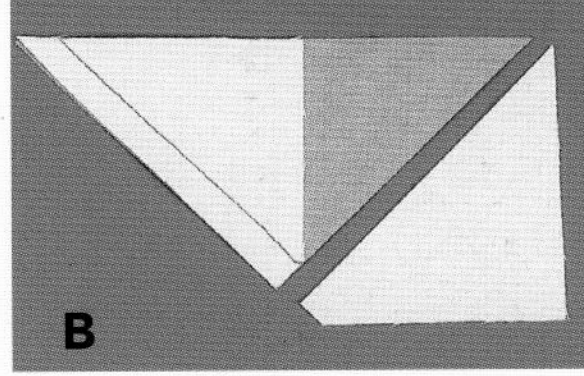
B

C

D

E

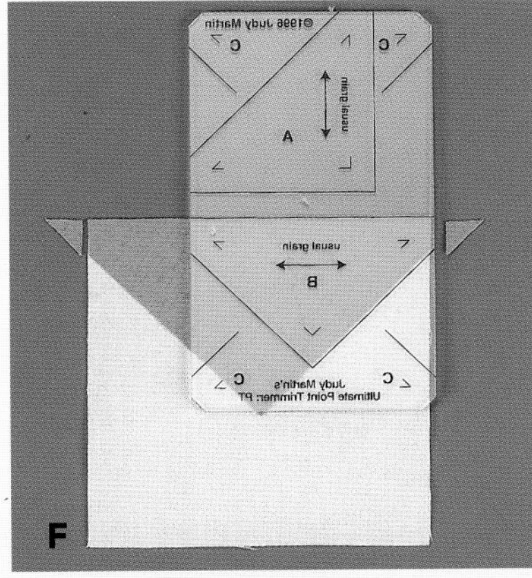
F

Trimming Points for Square-in-a-Square Units

1. Cut squares and triangles for Square-in-a-Square Units.
2. Align B lines on Point Trimmer with edges of triangles and trim both points *(Photo F)*.
3. Place triangle atop square, aligning corners of square with edges of triangle *(Photo G)*. Stitch ¼" seam; press seam allowances toward triangle *(Photo H)*.
4. Repeat to add triangles to remaining sides of center square *(Photo I)*. Trim remaining points even with sides of Square-in-a-Square Unit *(Photo J)*. Seam allowances will extend ¼" beyond points of center square.

G

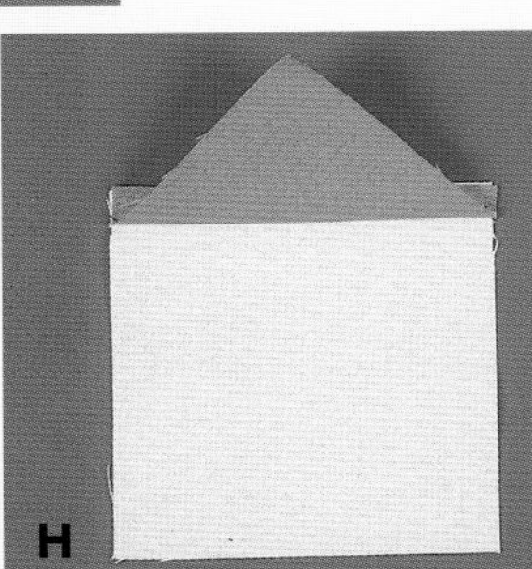
H

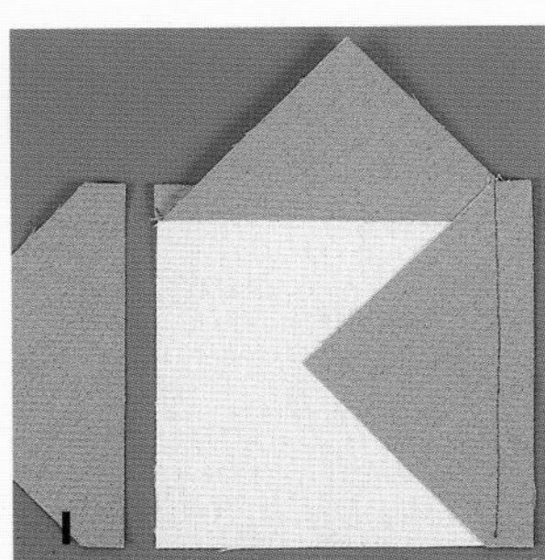
I

J

Stargazing

After designing a larger quilt for a guild challenge, Wanda Ingram had a pile of half-square triangles left over. Not one to throw scraps away, she created this little quilt by joining the triangles into Broken Dishes blocks and then sewing the blocks into the larger star pattern. "I have to do something with every little bit," she says.

PROJECT RATING: INTERMEDIATE

Size: 22½" × 28¼"

Blocks: 12 (4½") Star blocks

MATERIALS

6 fat eighths* assorted blue prints for blocks

6 fat eighths* assorted cream or light yellow prints for blocks and sashing stars

⅝ yard blue print for sashing, inner border, and binding

⅛ yard light yellow print for border accent strip

⅜ yard dark blue print for outer border

¾ yard backing fabric

27" × 33" piece quilt batting

*fat eighth = 9" × 20"

Cutting

Measurements include ¼" seam allowances. Border strips are exact length needed. You may want to make them longer to allow for piecing variations.

From each blue print fat eighth, cut:

- 2 (2"-wide) strips. From strips, cut 16 (2") squares. Cut squares in half diagonally to make 32 half-square triangles.

From each cream/yellow fat eighth, cut:

- 2 (2"-wide) strips. From strips, cut 16 (2") squares. Cut squares in half diagonally to make 32 half-square triangles.
- 1 (1¾") B square.
- 8 (1⅛") A squares.

From blue print, cut:

- 1 (5"-wide) strip. From strip, cut 17 (1¾" × 5") sashing rectangles.
- 3 (2¼"-wide) strips for binding.
- 3 (1¾"-wide) strips. From strips, cut 2 (1¾" × 22¼") side inner borders and 2 (1¾" × 19") top and bottom inner borders.

From light yellow print, cut:

- 3 (1"-wide) strips. From strips, cut 2 (1" × 24¾") side accent strips and 2 (1" × 19") top and bottom accent strips.

From dark blue print, cut:

- 4 (2½"-wide) strips. From strips, cut 2 (2½" × 24¾") side outer borders and 2 (2½" × 23") top and bottom outer borders.

Block Assembly

1. Join 1 blue print triangle and 1 cream/yellow print triangle to make a triangle-square. Make 16 triangle-squares.
2. Referring to *Quadrant Assembly Diagram*, join 4 triangle-squares to complete 1 quadrant. Make 4 quadrants.

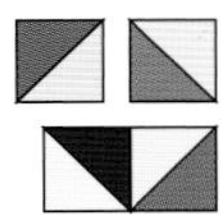

Quadrant Assembly Diagram

3. Lay out 4 quadrants as shown in *Block Assembly Diagram*. Join into rows; join rows to complete 1 Star block *(Block Diagram)*. Make 12 Star blocks.

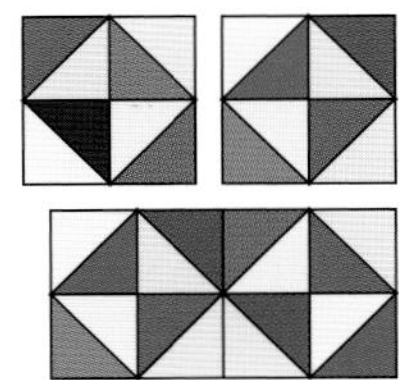

Block Assembly Diagram

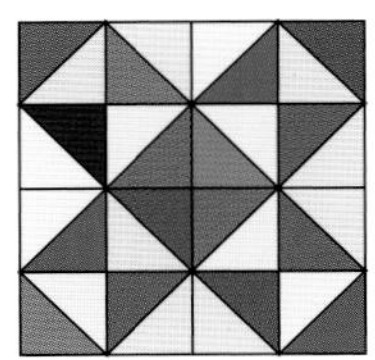

Block Diagram

Quilt Assembly

1. Referring to *Sashing Diagrams,* place 1 cream/yellow A square atop 1 sashing rectangle, right sides facing. Stitch diagonally from corner to corner. Trim ¼" beyond stitching. Press open to reveal triangle. Repeat for adjacent corner to complete 1 Sashing Unit 1. Make 10 Sashing Unit 1.

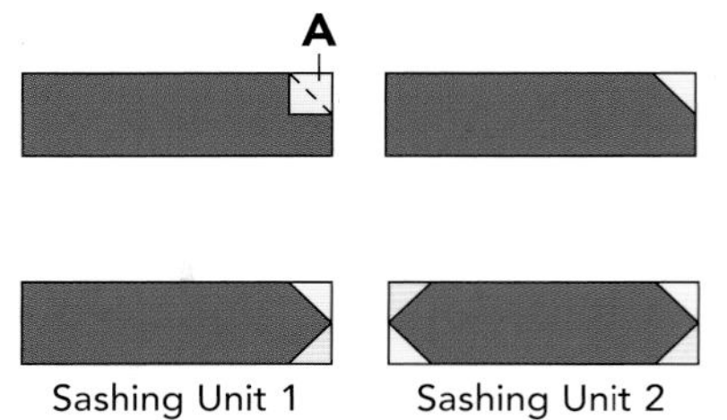

Sashing Diagrams

2. In the same manner, join 4 cream/yellow A squares and 1 sashing rectangle to make 1 Sashing Unit 2. Make 7 Sashing Unit 2.
3. Lay out Star blocks, sashing units, and B squares as shown in *Quilt Top Assembly Diagram.* Join into horizontal rows; join rows to complete quilt center.
4. Add side inner borders to quilt center. Add top and bottom inner borders to quilt.
5. Press 1 light yellow print strip in half lengthwise, wrong sides together. Align raw edges of folded strip with 1 side of quilt; baste in place. Repeat for remaining sides.

Quilt Top Assembly Diagram

6. Add side outer borders to quilt center. Add top and bottom outer borders to quilt.

Finishing

1. Layer backing, batting, and quilt top; baste. Quilt as desired. Quilt shown was quilted in the ditch around blocks, stars, and border.
2. Join 2¼"-wide blue print strips into 1 continuous piece for straight-grain French-fold binding. Add binding to quilt.

DESIGNER

Wanda Ingram of Cartersville, Georgia, has been quilting for many years. "Before quilting, I tried several other crafts," Wanda says, "but I never really enjoyed any of them. As soon as I made my first quilt, I realized that I had found my niche. I like all types of quilts, but I like traditional patterns best of all." ⁂

TRIED & TRUE

Burgundy flowers are splashed on hunter green and gold backgrounds in this block. Fabrics are prints by Kansas Troubles for Moda Fabrics.

Stars OF THE NIGHT

Designer Lynn Witzenburg used easy diagonal seam piecing in the sashing to create smaller stars that seem to float between the blocks.

PROJECT RATING: INTERMEDIATE

Size: 72" × 84½"

Blocks: 30 (10") Star blocks

MATERIALS

1⅞ yards purple batik
4¼ yards dark blue batik
3¾ yards light blue batik
5 yards backing fabric
Full-size quilt batting

Cutting

Measurements include ¼" seam allowances. Border strips are exact length needed. You may want to make them longer to allow for piecing variations.

From purple batik, cut:

- 4 (3"-wide) strips. From strips, cut 50 (3") C squares.
- 8 (2"-wide) strips. Piece strips to make 2 (2" × 73") side inner borders and 2 (2" × 63½") top and bottom inner borders.
- 19 (1¾"-wide) strips. From strips cut 400 (1¾") A squares.

From dark blue batik, cut:

- 8 (5"-wide) strips. Piece strips to make 2 (5" × 76") side outer borders and 2 (5" × 72½") top and bottom outer borders.
- 25 (3"-wide) strips. From strips, cut 240 (3") C squares and 120 (3" × 1¾") B rectangles.
- 9 (2¼"-wide) strips for binding.
- 6 (1¾"-wide) strips. From strips, cut 120 (1¾") A squares.

From light blue batik, cut:

- 4 (10½"-wide) strips. From strips, cut 49 (10½" × 3") E rectangles.
- 10 (5½"-wide) strips. From strips, cut 120 (5½" × 3") D rectangles.
- 10 (3"-wide) strips. From strips, cut 120 (3") C squares.

Block Assembly

1. Referring to *Flying Geese Unit Diagrams*, place 1 purple batik A square atop 1 dark blue batik B rectangle, right sides facing. Stitch diagonally from corner to corner as shown. Trim ¼" beyond stitching. Press open to reveal triangle. Repeat for opposite corner to complete 1 Flying Geese Unit. Make 120 dark blue/purple Flying Geese Units.

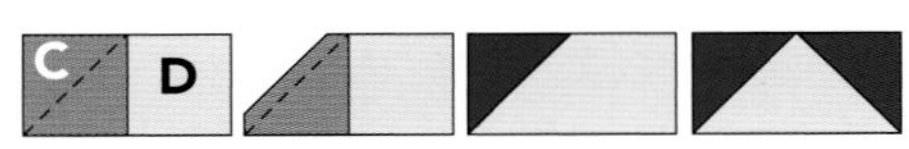

Flying Geese Unit Diagrams

2. In the same manner, make 120 light blue/dark blue Flying Geese Units using light blue batik D rectangles and dark blue batik C squares.

3. Referring to *Block Center Assembly Diagram*, lay out 1 purple batik C square, 4 dark blue/purple Flying Geese Units, and 4 dark blue batik A squares as shown. Join into rows; join rows to complete 1 Block Center *(Block Center Diagram)*. Make 30 Block Centers.

Block Center Assembly Diagram

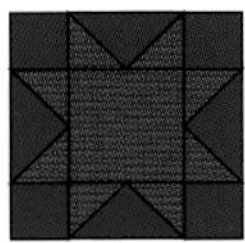

Block Center Diagram

4. Lay out 1 Block Center, 4 light blue/dark blue Flying Geese Units, and 4 light blue batik C squares as shown in *Block Assembly Diagram* on page 18. Join into rows; join rows to complete 1 Star block *(Block Diagram)*. Make 30 Star blocks.

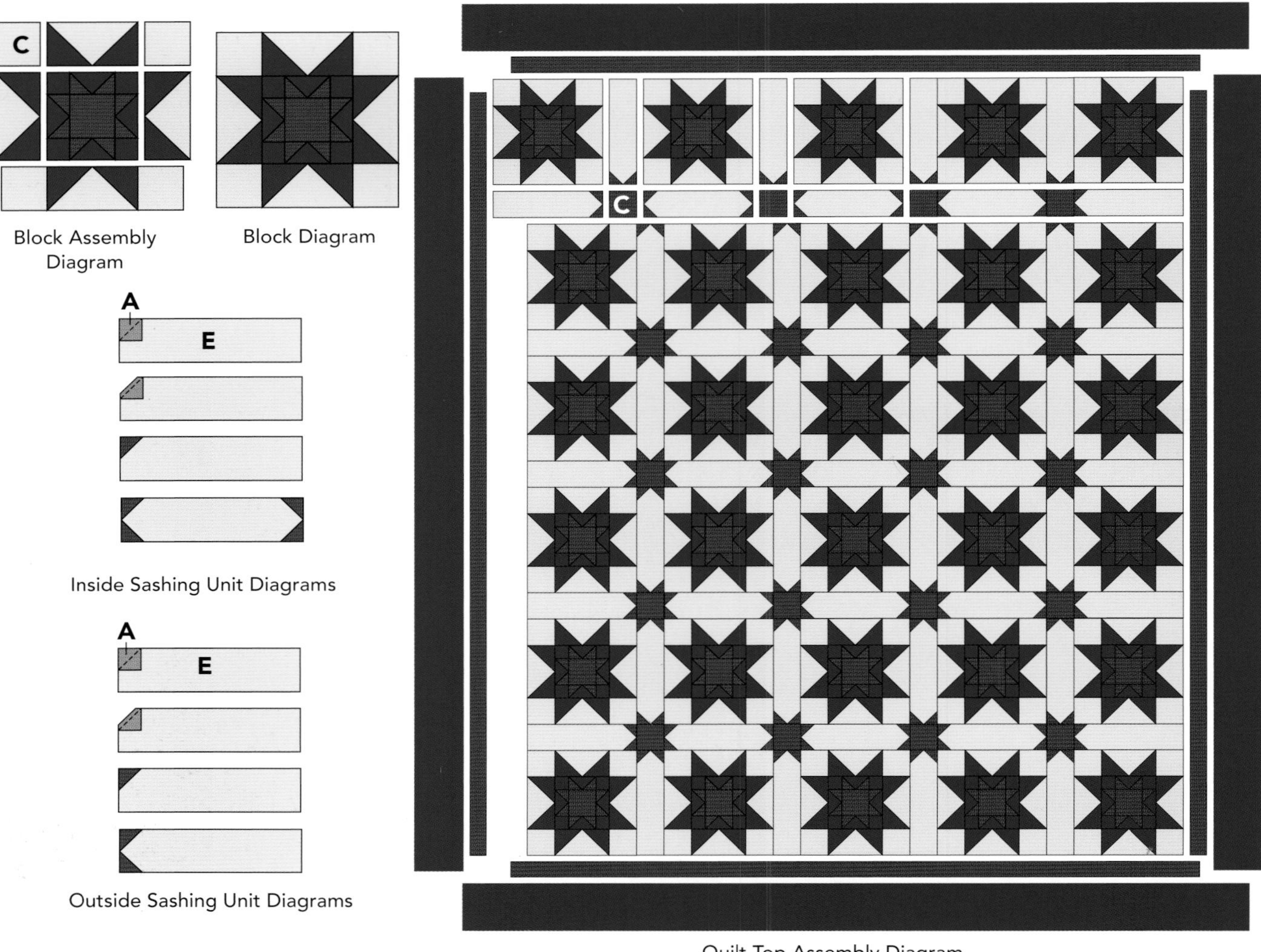

Block Assembly Diagram

Block Diagram

Inside Sashing Unit Diagrams

Outside Sashing Unit Diagrams

Quilt Top Assembly Diagram

Sashing Assembly

1. Referring to *Inside Sashing Unit Diagrams*, use the diagonal seams method to stitch 1 purple batik A square to each corner of 1 light blue batik E rectangle to complete 1 Inside Sashing Unit. Make 31 Inside Sashing Units.
2. In the same manner, make 18 Outside Sashing Units stitching purple batik A squares to two corners of light blue batik E rectangle *(Outside Sashing Unit Diagrams)*.

Quilt Assembly

1. Lay out Star Blocks, purple batik C squares, and Sashing Units as shown in *Quilt Top Assembly Diagram*. Join into rows; join rows to complete quilt center.
2. Add purple print side inner borders to quilt center. Add top and bottom inner borders to quilt.
3. Repeat for dark blue print outer borders.

Finishing

1. Divide backing into 2 (2½-yard) lengths. Cut 1 piece in half lengthwise to make 2 narrow panels. Join 1 narrow panel to each side of wider panel; press seam allowances toward narrow panels.
2. Layer backing, batting, and quilt top; baste. Quilt as desired. Quilt shown was quilted in the ditch around the stars, with original designs in the star centers and sashing, and feathers in the outer borders *(Quilting Diagram* on page 19*)*.
3. Join (2¼"-wide) dark blue batik strips into 1 continuous piece for straight-grain French-fold binding. Add binding to quilt.

Quilting Diagram

WEB EXTRA

To download the quilting designs Lynn used, visit our Web site at www.FonsandPorter.com/starsnightquilting

TRIED & TRUE

Make a patriotic quilt using reds and blues. Our version features fabrics from the Enduring Blooms collection by P&B Textiles.

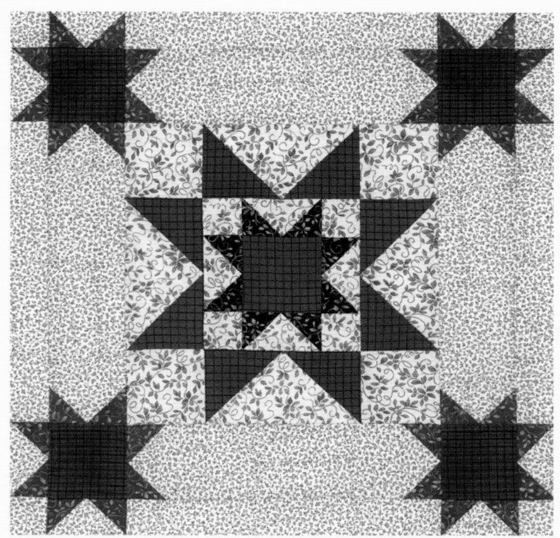

SIZE OPTIONS

	Crib (34½" × 47")	Throw (59½" × 72")	Queen/King (97" × 109½")
Blocks	6	20	56
Setting	2 × 3	4 × 5	7 × 8
Purple Batik	½ yard	1¼ yards	3⅛ yards
Dark Blue Batik	1⅝ yards	3¼ yards	7 yards
Light Blue Batik	1 yard	2¾ yards	7 yards
Backing Fabric	1½ yards	3¾ yards	8¾ yards
Batting	Crib-size	Twin-size	King-size

WEB EXTRA

Go to www.FonsandPorter.com/starsnightsizes to download *Quilt Top Assembly Diagrams* for these size options.

DESIGNER

Lynn Witzenburg has been quilting since 1979. She has a custom machine quilting business and also loves to lecture and teach machine quilting and dimensional hand appliqué. Look for Lynn's book, *Machine Quilting The Basics & Beyond,* published by Landauer Books. ⁂

TEENY TINY Stars

Try designer Sally Collins' helpful hints on page 21 for piecing miniatures and her oversize custom cut technique on page 22 to make these tiny blocks like a pro.

PROJECT RATING: INTERMEDIATE

Size: 9¾" × 9¾"

Blocks: 9 (1½") Ohio Star blocks

MATERIALS

9 (2" × 7") strips assorted light prints for block backgrounds

9 (5") squares assorted medium/dark prints for star point units

9 (1") squares assorted prints for block centers

1 (1" × 40") strip each of red and gold for strip set

1 (2" × 40") strip medium purple for sashing strips

¼ yard dark purple for inner border and binding

1 (1" × 40") strip multicolor stripe for middle border

⅜ yard blue print for outer border

12" square backing fabric

12" square quilt batting

Cutting

Measurements include ¼" seam allowances.

From each light print, cut:

- 1 (2") square. Cut square in half diagonally in both directions to make 4 quarter-square B triangles.
- 4 (1") A squares.

From each medium/dark print, cut:

- 2 (2") squares. Cut squares in half diagonally in both directions to make 8 quarter-square C triangles.
- 1 (2") square. Cut square in half diagonally in both directions to make 4 quarter-square D triangles.

From medium purple strip, cut:

- 24 (¾" × 2") sashing strips.

From dark purple, cut:

- 4 (⅞"-wide) **lengthwise** strips. From strips, cut 2 (⅞" × 6") side inner borders and 2 (⅞" × 6¾") top and bottom inner borders.
- 2 (2¼"-wide) strips for binding.

From multicolor stripe, cut:

- 2 (1" × 6¾") side middle borders.
- 2 (1" × 7") top and bottom middle borders.

From blue print, cut:

- 4 (2½"-wide) **lengthwise** strips for outer borders.

Block Assembly

1. Choose 1 matching set of 4 background A squares and 4 B triangles, 8 matching C star point triangles, 4 matching D center diamond triangles, and 1 E center square. Refer to *Sew Easy: Sally's Oversize Custom Cut Technique* on page 22 to make 4 star point units.
2. Lay out A squares, star point units, and E square as shown in *Block Assembly Diagram*. Join pieces into rows. Trim seams as you sew. Join rows to complete 1 Ohio Star block *(Block Diagram)*. Make 9 blocks.

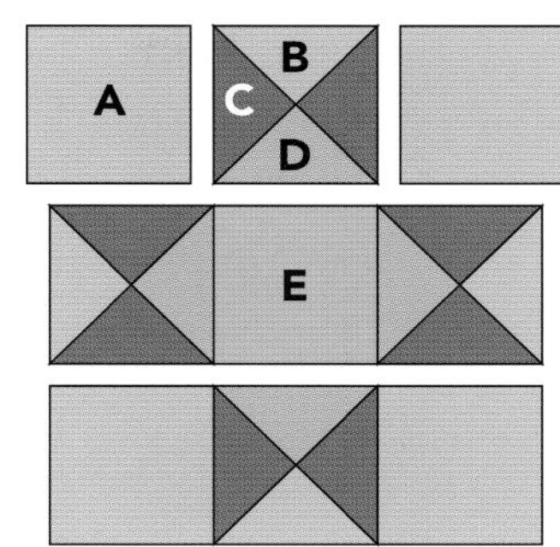

Block Assembly Diagram

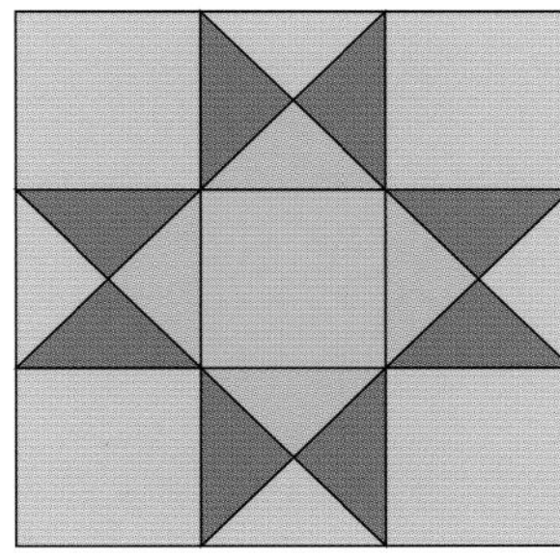
Block Diagram

Quilt Assembly

1. Refer to *Sew Easy: Sally's Oversize Custom Cut Technique* on page 22 to make 16 four patch units for sashing squares.
2. Lay out blocks, sashing strips and four patch sashing squares as shown in photo on page 20. Join into rows; join rows to complete quilt center.
3. Add dark purple side borders to quilt center. Add dark purple top and bottom borders to quilt.
4. Add multicolor print middle borders to sides of quilt. Trim seam allowance to exactly ⅛". Press seam toward middle border. In the same manner, add multicolor middle borders to top and bottom of quilt.
5. Add blue borders to quilt; mitering corners (See *Sew Easy: Mitered Borders* on page 23).

Finishing

1. Layer backing, batting, and quilt top; baste. Quilt as desired.
2. Join 2¼"-wide dark purple strips into 1 continuous piece for straight-grain French-fold binding. Add binding to quilt.

HINTS FOR PIECING MINIATURES

- Cut borders and strips on the lengthwise grain for stability.
- Sew with an **exact** ¼" seam allowance. Keep edges of fabric aligned perfectly to assure an accurate seam allowance.
- After sewing, trim ¼" seam allowances to a generous ⅛" to lessen bulk.
- Press with a hot, dry iron only.
- Press stitches to set seams before opening them for final pressing.
- Use a stiletto or similar tool to help guide small fabric pieces under the needle.
- Measure and monitor your work as you sew. Make sure your seams are straight and even.
- Measure completed blocks to be sure they are square and the correct size.

DESIGNER

Sally Collins is an award-winning quilter who has been making quilts since 1978. Although she is best known for her miniature quilts, Sally enjoys creating quilts of all sizes. When not traveling around the country teaching and lecturing for guilds and conferences, she enjoys spending time in California with her husband Joe. ✻

Sally's Oversize Custom Cut Technique

Achieve greater accuracy for your miniature patchwork blocks by cutting pieces larger than needed and then trimming after they are joined.

by Sally Collins

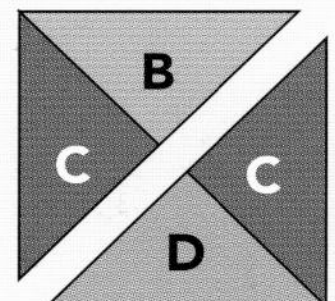

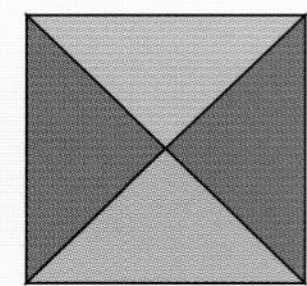

Star Point Assembly Diagrams

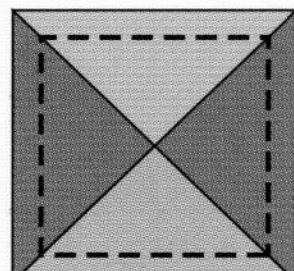

Star Point Unit Diagram

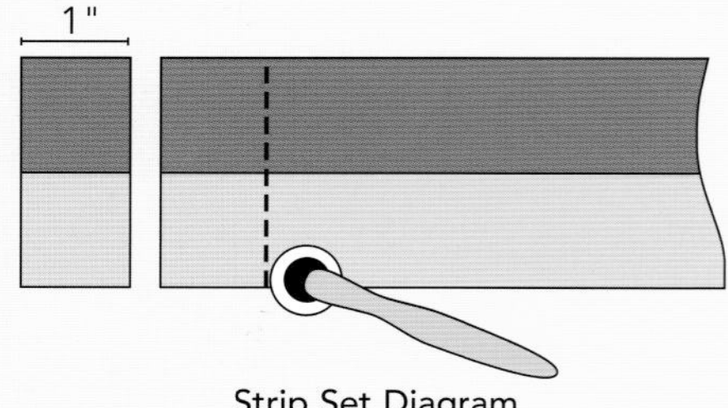

Strip Set Diagram

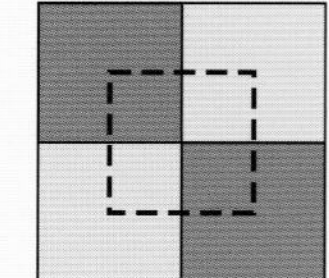

Four Patch Diagram

Star Point Unit

1. Lay out 1 B, 2 C, and 1 D triangle as shown in *Star Point Assembly Diagrams.*
2. Place 1 C triangle atop 1 B triangle, right sides facing. With the C triangle on top, sew from the corner to the point with a ¼" seam. Finger press seam allowances toward C. (Do not use the iron at this point.) Trim seam allowances to generous ⅛". In the same manner, join 1 C triangle to 1 D triangle.
3. Sew CB unit and CD unit together, matching and pinning center intersection exactly. Press seam open and trim seam allowances to generous ⅛". Make 4 star point units.
4. Refer to *Star Point Unit Diagram* to custom cut an exact 1" square from star point unit. Place the ½" intersection of your ruler over the center intersection of star point unit with lines on the ruler parallel to the outside edges of star point unit. Trim 2 edges. Rotate star point unit. Align the 1" lines of ruler with the 2 newly cut edges and cut the remaining 2 edges.

Four Patch Unit

1. Join 1 red strip to 1 gold strip, carefully aligning both edges exactly, to make strip set *(Strip Set Diagram).* Press seam open and trim seam allowances to generous ⅛". Cut 32 (1") segments from strip set as shown.
2. Referring to *Four Patch Diagram,* join 2 segments, matching and pinning the center intersection exactly, to make 1 four patch unit. Press seam open and trim seam allowances to generous ⅛".
3. Refer to *Four Patch Diagram* to custom cut an exact ¾" square from each oversized four patch unit. Place the ⅜" intersection of your ruler over the center intersection of four patch unit with a horizontal and vertical line on the ruler on the seams. Trim 2 edges. Rotate four patch unit. Align the ¾" lines of ruler with the 2 newly cut edges and cut the remaining 2 edges.

Mitered Borders

The subtle seam of a mitered corner creates the illusion of a continuous line around the quilt. Mitered corners are ideal for striped borders, pieced borders, or multiple plain borders.

1. Referring to *Measuring Quilt Center Diagram,* measure your quilt length through the middle of the quilt rather than along the edges. Then measure quilt width. Add to measurements twice the width of the border plus 2". Trim borders to these measurements.

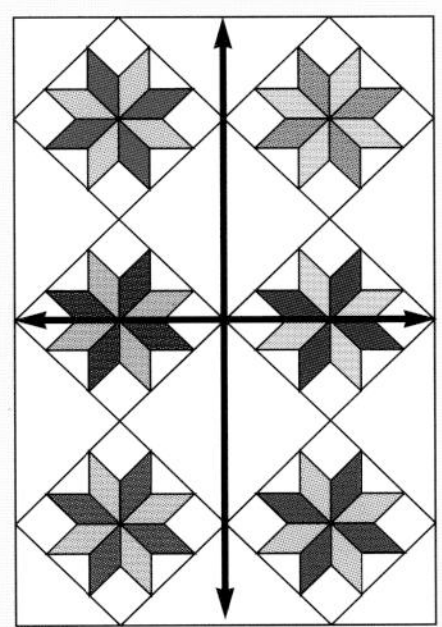

Measuring Quilt Center Diagram

2. On wrong side of quilt top, mark ¼" seam allowances at each corner.
3. Fold quilt top in half and place a pin at the center of the quilt side. Fold border in half and mark center with pin.
4. With right sides facing and raw edges aligned, match center pins on the border and the quilt. Working from the center out, pin the border to the quilt, right sides facing. The border will extend beyond the quilt edges. Do not trim the border.
5. Sew the border to the quilt. Start and stop stitching ¼" from the corner of the quilt top, backstitching at each end. Press the seam allowance toward the border. Add the remaining borders in the same manner.
6. With right sides facing, fold the quilt diagonally as shown in *Mitering Diagram 1,* aligning the raw edges of the adjacent borders. Pin securely.

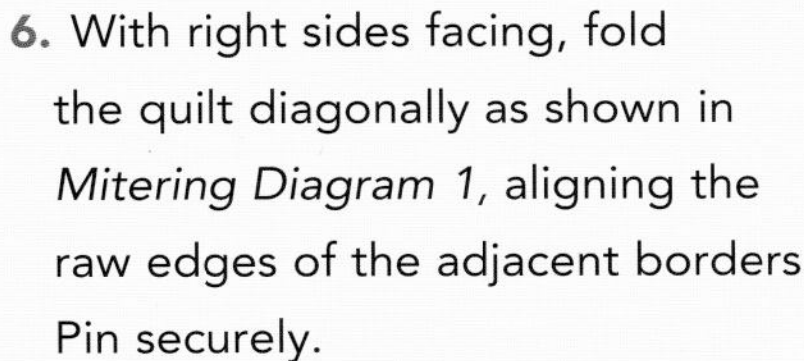

7. Align a ruler along the diagonal fold, as shown in *Mitering Diagram 2.* Holding the ruler firmly, mark a line from the end of the border seam to the raw edge.
8. Start machine-stitching at the beginning of the marked line, backstitch, and then stitch on the line out to the raw edge.
9. Unfold the quilt to be sure that the corner lies flat *(Mitered Borders Diagram).* Correct the stitching if necessary. Trim the seam allowance to ¼".
10. Miter the remaining corners. Press the corner seams open.

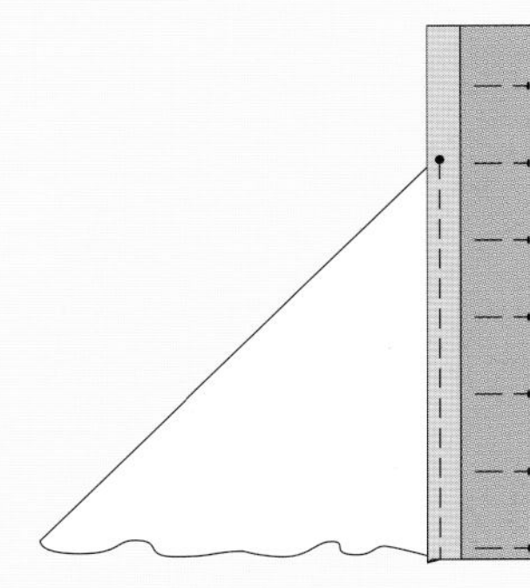

Mitering Diagram 1

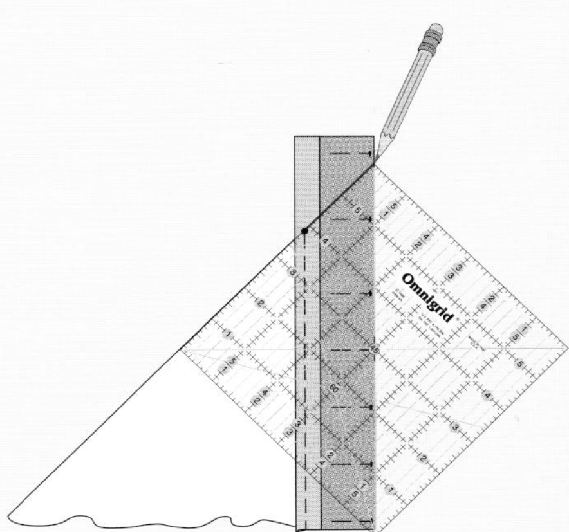

Mitering Diagram 2

Mitered Borders Diagram

BY **Lynn Witzenburg**

QUILTING THE Mini

Quilting a smaller quilt requires a special approach. Because I'm a professional machine quilter who loves miniatures, I've learned to make certain adjustments when working with these little quilts.

Mini quilts are wonderful. They decorate small spaces and allow us to try new patterns without a large investment of time and fabric. In fact, I can make several minis in the time it takes to make just one bed-size quilt.

Whether quilted by hand or by machine, minis are especially spectacular when you use quilting designs that replicate those used for full-size quilts.

Design Size

When I find a stencil design I like, I use the reduction feature on a photocopier to make the design a usable size. First, I draw the design onto tracing paper, connecting any broken lines. I then take the design to the copy machine and reduce it by 3%. Next, I reduce my copy by another 3%. I continue making these slight reductions, sometimes as many as 20 or 30, until I reach the smallest usable design. I have found that the simpler a design is in its larger form, the better miniature design it makes.

Design Library

Using these reduction methods expands the possibilities for smaller quilting designs beyond belief! I currently have a shelf full of binders with multiple quilting designs in multiple sizes three-hole punched and organized by style, ready to go. This allows me to choose the design that is the perfect size for each quilt.

From Design to Quilt

Once I have chosen my design, I quilt it through paper marked with the design.

To make multiple copies, I begin by choosing the width of quilting paper most appropriate for the size of my designs. (I use 12"-, 18"-, or 24"-wide rolls of Golden Threads paper.) I then rotary cut pieces of paper slightly larger than my designs—one for each space I will quilt.

Using a permanent marker, I trace my quilting design onto 1 piece of paper. I stack up to 15 layers of paper and place the marked paper on top. With my sewing machine unthreaded, I stitch the design along the marked lines through all layers. The needle of the machine perforates the design into all the papers at once.

To quilt, I center the design on the area to be quilted, and pin it in place on the layered quilt top using open safety pins. Then I quilt through the paper and tear it away when I am finished.

NOTE: Be sure to use a permanent marker when tracing onto quilting paper. Permanent ink ensures that the markings will stay on the paper and not transfer onto the thread.

Thread Size and Color

When planning quilting for a mini, I not only scale down my design, but also use finer thread for machine quilting. The quilting needs to complement, rather than overwhelm, the wonderful tiny patchwork or appliqué.

Thread is sized by numbers. The larger the number, the finer the thread. I recommend very fine cotton thread for minis. Some of my favorites are Aurifil 50 wt. and Mettler 50 wt. or 60 wt. Both of these brands are available in a variety of beautiful colors.

Scaling down to thinner threads for minis helps solve potential machine quilting tension problems when using thin batting.

To emphasize fancy quilting motifs, I often choose a thread color

Designs adapted from *Fine Feathers*

© Marianne Fons 1988.

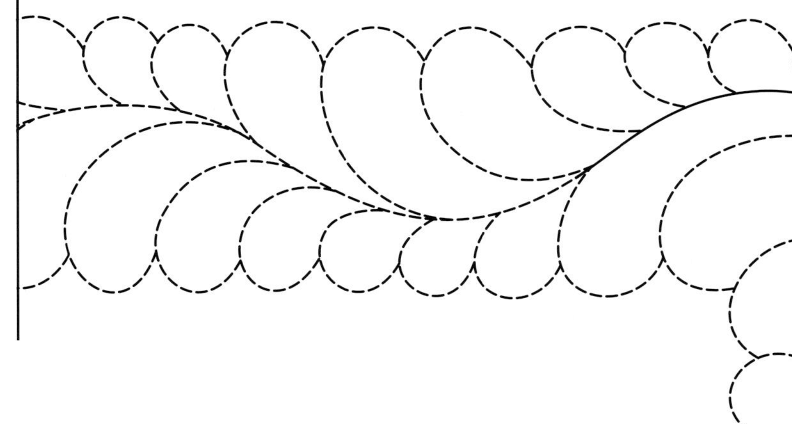

or shade that contrasts slightly with the fabrics. I have learned when I'm trying to decide between two shades of thread to go for the darker because it will be more subtle than the lighter color.

Choosing Batting for Minis

Scaling down the filler for miniature quilts is important as well. A batting which is too thick can ruin the special charm of a small quilt.

I put very low-loft cotton in my minis. Another good choice is a piece of cotton flannel. I use white or natural so there is no dye in the flannel that might come through on the top of the quilt.

Quilting and Finishing

I usually begin by stitching in the ditch along the edges of my blocks. For ditch quilting, I match the thread color to the background of the design to keep it understated. I then add fancy quilting in the setting blocks, sashing, and borders. Often, I don't add any quilting on the blocks themselves if the individual patchwork pieces are ¾" or smaller.

To finish my quilts, I often scale down my binding, cutting it 2" wide for French-fold, rather than the usual 2¼".

Side Border Design

Nancy's Fancy

Create this stunning woven-look scrap quilt designed by Nancy Martin. Although it looks challenging, it's constructed of simple squares and triangles, and goes together easily.

PROJECT RATING: INTERMEDIATE

Size: 62" × 62"

Blocks: 9 (16") Nancy's Fancy blocks

MATERIALS

8 fat quarters★ assorted cream prints

8 fat quarters★ assorted blue prints

6 fat quarters★ assorted pink prints

1¾ yards floral print for blocks and outer border

Fons & Porter Quarter Inch Seam Marker (optional)

⅞ yard blue print for inner border and binding

4 yards backing fabric

Twin-size quilt batting

★fat quarter = 18" × 20"

Cutting

Measurements include ¼" seam allowances. Border strips are exact length needed. You may want to make them longer to allow for piecing variations.

> **Sew Smart™**
> To make triangle-squares from squares, refer to ***Sew Easy: Quick Triangle Squares*** on page 74. Do not cut the 2⅞" squares in half if using this method.
> —Marianne

From each cream fat quarter, cut:

- 3 (2⅞"-wide) strips. From strips, cut 16 (2⅞") squares. Cut squares in half diagonally to make 32 half-square A triangles.
- 2 (2½"-wide) strips. From strips, cut 9 (2½") B squares.

From each blue fat quarter, cut:

- 3 (2⅞"-wide) strips. From strips, cut 16 (2⅞") squares. Cut squares in half diagonally to make 32 half-square A triangles.
- 1 (2½"-wide) strip. From strip, cut 5 (2½") B squares.

From each pink fat quarter, cut:

- 1 (2⅞"-wide) strip. From strip, cut 6 (2⅞") squares. Cut squares in half diagonally to make 12 half-square A triangles.
- 3 (2½"-wide) strips. From strips, cut 18 (2½") B squares.

From floral print, cut:

- 6 (6½"-wide) strips. Piece strips to make 2 (6½" × 62½") top and bottom outer borders and 2 (6½" × 50½") side outer borders.
- 3 (2⅞"-wide) strips. From strips, cut 36 (2⅞") squares. Cut squares in half diagonally to make 72 half-square A triangles.
- 3 (2½"-wide) strips. From strips, cut 36 (2½") B squares.

From blue print, cut:

- 7 (2¼"-wide) strips for binding.
- 6 (1½"-wide) strips. Piece strips to make 2 (1½" × 50½") top and bottom inner borders and 2 (1½" × 48½") side inner borders.

Block Assembly

1. Referring to *Triangle-Square Diagram*, join 1 blue A triangle and 1 pink A triangle to make a triangle-square. Make 8 pink and blue triangle-squares, 8 floral print and cream triangle-squares, and 20 blue and cream triangle-squares.

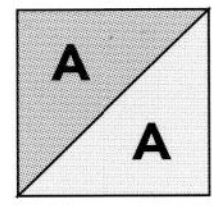

Triangle-Square Diagram

2. Referring to *Quadrant 1 Diagram* on page 28, lay out 7 blue and cream triangle-squares, 2 pink and blue triangle-squares, 3 pink B squares, 2 blue B squares, and 2 cream B squares as shown. Join into rows; join rows to complete Quadrant 1. Make 2 Quadrant 1.

3. Referring to *Quadrant 2 Diagram,* lay out 4 floral and cream triangle-squares, 3 blue and cream triangle-squares, 2 pink and blue triangle-squares, 3 pink B squares, 2 floral B squares, and 2 cream B squares as shown. Join into rows; join rows to complete Quadrant 2. Make 2 Quadrant 2.
4. Referring to *Block Assembly Diagram,* join quadrants into rows; join rows to complete block *(Block Diagram).* Make 9 blocks.

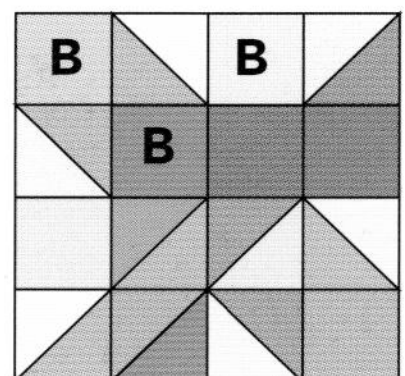

Quadrant 1 Diagram

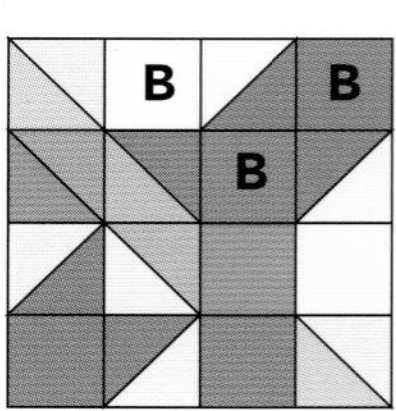

Quadrant 2 Diagram

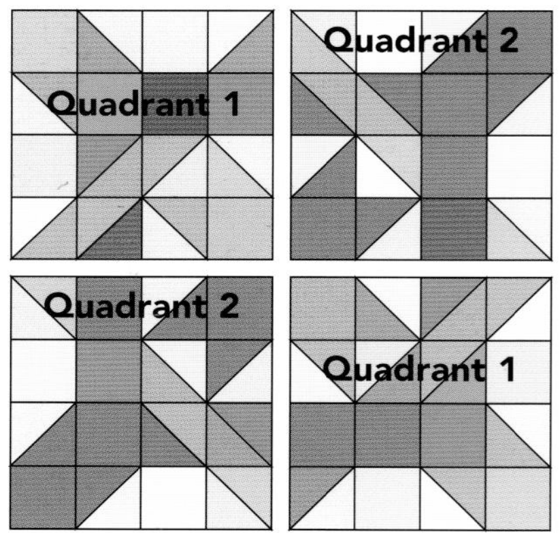

Block Assembly Diagram

Block Diagram

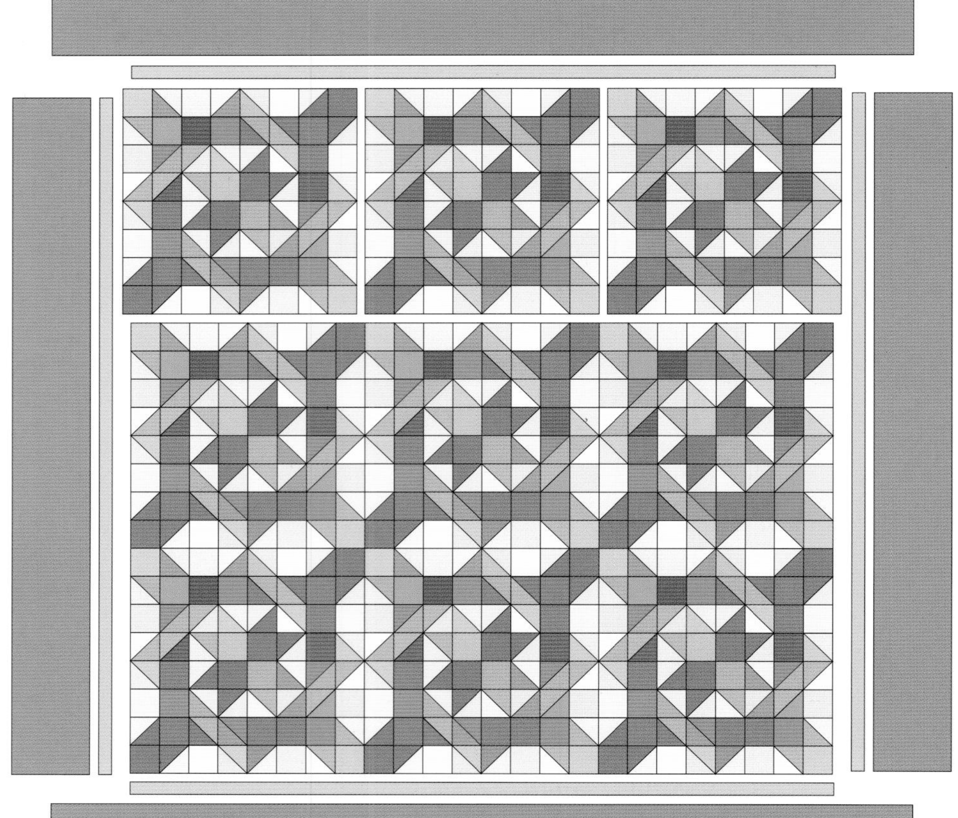
Quilt Top Assembly Diagram

Quilt Assembly

1. Lay out blocks as shown in *Quilt Top Assembly Diagram.* Join into rows; join rows to complete quilt center.
2. Add blue print side inner borders to quilt center. Add top and bottom inner borders to quilt.
3. Repeat for floral print outer borders.

Finishing

1. Divide backing fabric into 2 (2-yard) lengths. Cut 1 piece in half lengthwise to make 2 narrow panels. Join 1 narrow panel to each side of wider panel; press seam allowances toward narrow panels.
2. Layer backing, batting, and quilt top; baste. Quilt as desired. Quilt shown was quilted in the ditch in the blocks and with cable designs in the pink and blue rings and border *(Quilting Diagram).*
3. Join 2¼"-blue print strips into 1 continuous piece for straight-grain French-fold binding. Add binding to quilt.

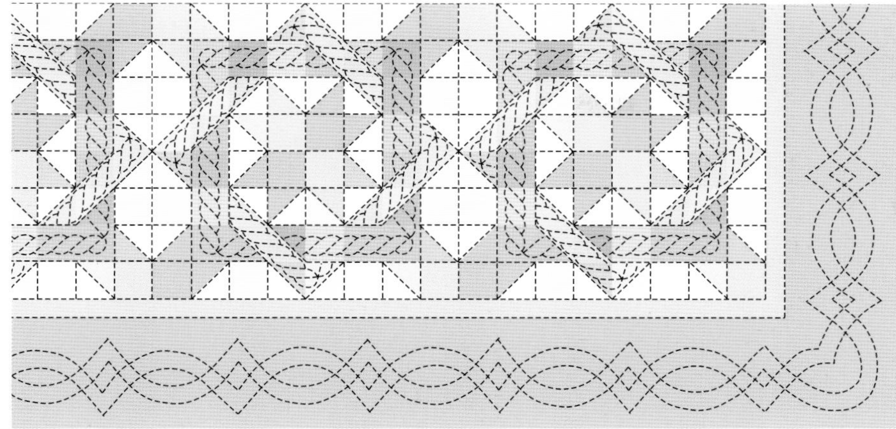
Quilting Diagram

TRIED & TRUE

Create a vintage look using reproduction prints such as the ones shown here from Windham Fabrics®.

WEB EXTRA

Go to FonsandPorter.com/nanfansizes to download a multiple size chart and assembly diagrams for this quilt.

DESIGNER

Nancy Martin, who began her quilting career over thirty years ago, was the recipient of the prestigious Silver Star Award at International Quilt Festival 2002. She is the founder of Martingale & Company, publisher for some of the most talented quilters worldwide. ✳

SMOKEY POINT Star

Designer Jayne Conwell started this beautiful quilt in a retreat led by Marianne and Liz in Smokey Point, Washington. See the chart on page 34 for more size options.

PROJECT RATING: INTERMEDIATE

Size: 77" × 95"

Blocks: 20 (16") Star blocks

MATERIALS

10 fat quarters★ assorted dark brown prints

12 fat quarters★ assorted dark orange and rust prints

10 fat quarters★ assorted beige prints

2⅝ yards multi-color print for background and outer border

⅜ yard black solid for border flange

1 yard dark brown print for inner border

⅝ yard rust print for binding

7⅛ yards backing fabric

Queen-size quilt batting

★fat quarter = 18" × 20"

Cutting

Measurements include ¼" seam allowances. Border strips are exact length needed. You may want to make them longer to allow for piecing variations.

From each dark brown print fat quarter, cut:

- 2 (3"-wide) strips. From strips, cut 8 (3") squares. Cut squares in half diagonally to make 16 half-square D triangles.

  NOTE: Label these triangles and set aside for border.

- 4 (2⅞"-wide) strips. From strips, cut 24 (2⅞") squares. Cut squares in half diagonally to make 48 half-square A triangles.

From each rust print fat quarter, cut:

- 1 (3"-wide) strip. From strip, cut 6 (3") squares. Cut squares in half diagonally to make 12 half-square D triangles.

  NOTE: Label these triangles and set aside for border.

- 3 (2⅞"-wide) strips. From strips, cut 14 (2⅞") squares. Cut squares in half diagonally to make 28 half-square A triangles.
- 2 (2½"-wide) strips. From strips, cut 14 (2½") B squares.

From each beige fat quarter, cut:

- 4 (2⅞"-wide) strips. From strips, cut 24 squares in half diagonally to make 48 half-square A triangles.
- 2 (2½"-wide) strips. From strips, cut 16 (2½") B squares.

From multi-color print, cut:

- 4 (7¼"-wide) strips. From strips, cut 19 (7¼") squares. Cut squares in half diagonally in both directions to make 76 quarter-square E triangles.
- 10 (4⅞"-wide) strips. From strips, cut 80 (4⅞") squares. Cut squares in half diagonally to make 160 half-square C triangles.
- 2 (4¼"-wide) strips. From strips, cut 17 (4¼") squares. Cut squares in half diagonally in both directions to make 68 quarter-square F triangles.

From black solid, cut:

- 8 (1½"-wide) strips for border flange.

From dark brown print, cut:

- 4 (3"-wide) strips. Piece strips to make 2 (3" × 80½") side inner borders.
- 4 (4"-wide) strips. Piece strips to make 2 (4" × 69½") top and bottom inner borders.

From rust print, cut:

- 9 (2¼"-wide) strips for binding.

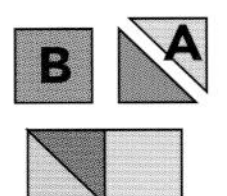

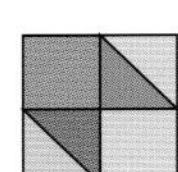

Unit 1 Diagrams

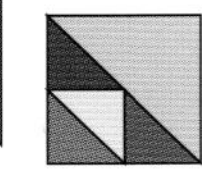

Unit 2 Diagrams

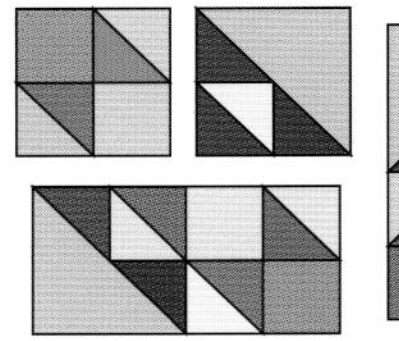

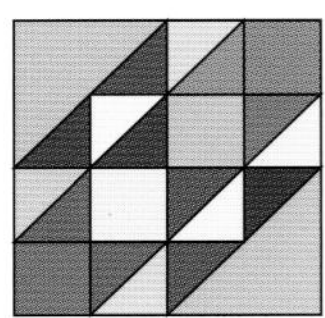
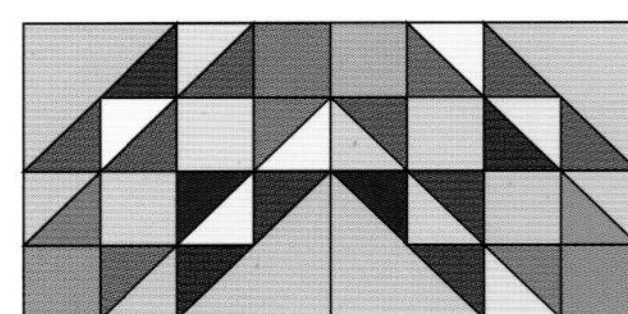

Block Assembly Diagram

Block Diagram

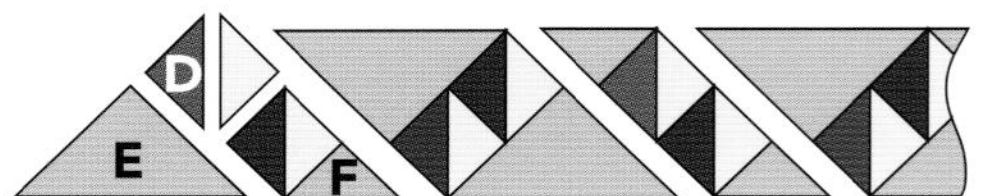

Border Assembly Diagram

Block Assembly

1. Referring to *Unit 1 Diagrams*, lay out 2 beige A triangles, 2 rust A triangles, 1 rust B square, and 1 beige B square as shown. Join to make 1 Unit 1. Make 8 Unit 1.
2. Referring to *Unit 2 Diagrams*, lay out 3 dark brown A triangles, 1 beige A triangle, and 1 multi-color print C triangle as shown. Join to make 1 Unit 2. Make 8 Unit 2.
3. Referring to *Block Assembly Diagram*, lay out 8 Unit 1 and 8 Unit 2 as shown. Join into quadrants; join quadrants to make one Star block *(Block Diagram)*. Make 20 blocks.

Quilt Assembly

1. Referring to *Quilt Top Assembly Diagram*, lay out blocks as shown. Join into horizontal rows; join rows to complete quilt center.
2. Join 1½"-wide black strips into one continuous strip. Press strip in half lengthwise, wrong sides facing. From strip, cut 2 (1½" × 80½") side flanges and 2 (1½" × 64½") top and bottom flanges.
3. Align raw edges of 1 side flange with one side of quilt; baste in place. Repeat for opposite side. In the same manner, baste top and bottom flanges in place.
4. Add side inner borders to quilt center. Add top and bottom inner borders to quilt.

Pieced Border Assembly

1. Join 1 dark brown print D triangle and 1 rust D triangle to make a triangle-square. Make 144 triangle-squares.
2. Referring to *Border Assembly Diagram*, lay out 40 triangle-squares, 19 multi-color print F triangles, and 21 E triangles. Join into diagonal units; join units to make 1 side border. Repeat for other side border. Add borders to quilt.
3. In the same manner, join 32 triangle-squares, 15 multi-color print F triangles, and 17 E triangles to make top border. Repeat for bottom border. Add borders to quilt.

Finishing

1. Divide backing into 3 (2⅜-yard) pieces. Join pieces lengthwise. Seams will run horizontally.
2. Layer backing, batting, and quilt top; baste. Quilt as desired. Quilt shown was quilted with a sunburst pattern, concentric triangles, and scrolls in the Star blocks, a scroll on inner border, and freehand arcs and angular meandering in the outer border *(Quilting Diagram* *on page 33)*.
3. Join 2¼"-wide rust print strips into 1 continuous piece for straight-grain French-fold binding. Add binding to quilt.

Quilt Top Assembly Diagram

DESIGNER

Fabric textures and colors attracted Jayne Conwell to quilting. She loves to share the art with anyone who is interested in quilting. In her spare time, Jayne enjoys riding her bike or hiking in the Rocky Mountains, taking in the beauty of the area while imagining ways to capture it in her quilting. ✻

Quilting Diagram

WEB EXTRA

To download *Quilt Top Assembly Diagrams* for these size options, go to www.FonsandPorter.com/smokysizes.

MORE SIZE OPTIONS

	Wallhanging (41" × 41")	Throw (59" × 71")	Queen (95" × 95")
Blocks	4	12	25
Setting	2 × 2 blocks	3 × 4 blocks	5 × 5 blocks
Materials			
Dark Browns	6 fat quarters	8 fat quarters	12 fat quarters
Dark Oranges	6 fat quarters	8 fat quarters	12 fat quarters
Med. Oranges	3 fat quarters	4 fat quarters	5 fat quarters
Beige Prints	6 fat quarters	8 fat quarters	12 fat quarters
Multi Print Fabric	¾ yard	2 yards	3¼ yards
Dark Brown for Inner Border	⅛ yard	½ yard	1⅛ yards
Black for Flange	—	⅜ yard	½ yard
Rust Binding	⅜ yard	½ yard	⅝ yard
Backing Fabric	3 yards	5 yards	8 yards
Batting	Crib-size	Twin-size	Queen-size
Cutting for Borders			
Black	—	6 (1½"-wide) strips for flange	9 (1½"-wide) strips for flange
Dark Brown	4 (1"-wide) strips for inner border **NOTE:** Inner border is narrower and there is no flange.	3 (3"-wide) strips for top and bottom inner borders 4 (2"-wide) strips for side inner borders	9 (4"-wide) strips for inner border

TRIED & TRUE

Try making *Smokey Point Star* in stunning black-and-white. We made our sample block using prints from Timeless Treasures.

QUILT DESIGNED BY **Bonnie Sullivan**. PIECED BY **Margie Bergen**.

FOLK ART Fancy Stars

Folk art motifs in the centers of Sawtooth Star blocks give this flannel quilt its historical character. Designer Bonnie Sullivan got the idea for this quilt from an antique throw rug. "Look at the world with an open mind," Bonnie says. "Inspiration is all around you."

PROJECT RATING: EASY

Size: 45½" × 55½"

Blocks: 20 (10") Star blocks

MATERIALS

NOTE: Fabrics are from the "Folk Art Fancies," "Woolies," and "2 Cats in the Yard" collections from Maywood Studio.

20 fat quarters★ assorted flannels for blocks and binding

1 yard Folk Art Fancies fabric with 5" motifs or enough theme or novelty fabric to cut 20 (5½") squares

½ yard black stripe flannel for border

3½ yards backing fabric

Twin-size quilt batting

★fat quarter = 18" × 20"

Cutting

Measurements include ¼" seam allowances. Border strips are exact length needed. You may want to make them longer to allow for piecing variations.

From each fat quarter, cut:

- 4 (3"-wide) strips. From strips, cut 4 (3" × 5½") A rectangles and 12 (3") B squares.
- 1 (2½" × 20") strip for binding.

From motif fabric, cut:

- 20 (5½") squares for block centers.

From black stripe fabric, cut:

- 5 (3"-wide) strips. Join strips to make 2 (3" × 50½") side borders and 2 (3" × 45½") top and bottom borders.

Block Assembly

1. Choose 1 set of 4 matching A rectangles and 4 B squares for background and 8 contrasting B squares for star points. Referring to *Star Point Unit Diagrams* on page 38, place 1 B square atop 1 A rectangle, right sides facing. Stitch diagonally from corner to corner. Trim ¼" beyond stitching. Press open to reveal triangle. Repeat on opposite corner to complete 1 Star Point Unit. Make 4 Star Point Units.

OUR HOME

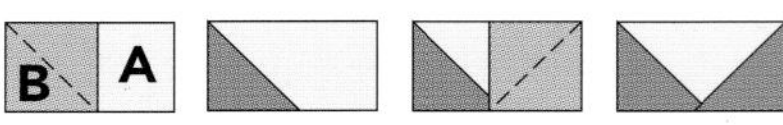

Star Point Unit Diagrams

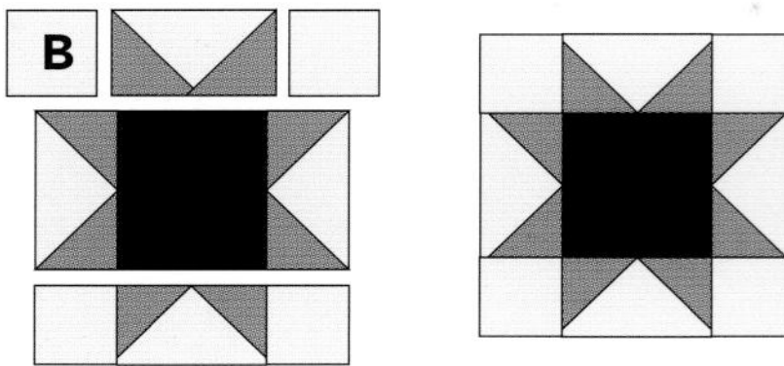

Block Assembly Diagram   Block Diagram

2. Lay out 4 Star Point Units, 4 B squares, and 1 center square as shown in *Block Assembly Diagram.* Join into rows; join rows to complete 1 Star block *(Block Diagram).* Make 20 Star blocks.

Quilt Assembly

1. Referring to photo on page 39, lay out blocks as shown. Join blocks into rows; join rows to complete quilt center.
2. Add side borders to quilt center. Add top and bottom borders to quilt.

Finishing

1. Divide backing fabric into 2 (1½-yard) pieces. Cut 1 piece in half lengthwise. Sew 1 narrow panel to 1 side of wider panel. Press seam allowances toward narrow panel. Seam will run horizontally. Remaining panel is extra and may be used to make a hanging sleeve.

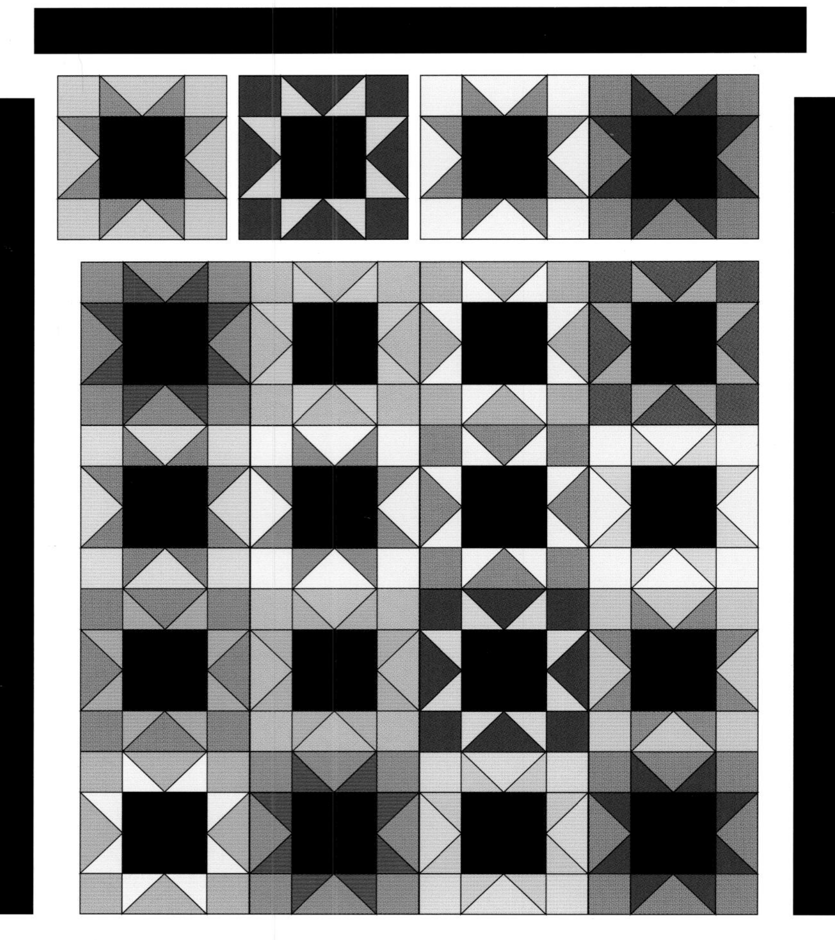

Quilt Top Assembly Diagram

2. Layer backing, batting, and quilt top; baste. Quilt as desired. Quilt shown was quilted in the ditch around all pieces.
3. Join 2½"-wide binding strips into 1 continuous piece for straight-grain French-fold binding. Add binding to quilt.

DESIGNER

A quilter for more than twenty years, Bonnie Sullivan has designed more than 60 patterns for quilts and wool projects. She has written several books and also has designed many fabric lines for Maywood Studios. ⁂

SUSAN McCORD'S QUILTS
A FARMWIFE'S LEGACY
Johnson
Mississippi Quilts
2
RED WING
UNION STONEWARE
CO.
RED WING MINN.

FRIENDS ARE Daytime Stars

The variety and placement of the different size blocks add interest and sparkle to this quilt.

PROJECT RATING: INTERMEDIATE

Size: 48" × 72"

Blocks: 22 (3"), 13 (6"), 5 (9"), and 5 (12") Star Rays blocks

MATERIALS

14 fat eighths* assorted blue prints for blocks

3 yards beige print fabric for block background and inner border

1⅜ yards navy print for border and binding

Tri-Recs™ tools

3 yards backing

Twin-size batting

*fat eighth = 9" × 20"

Sew Smart™

We recommend using the Tri-Recs™ tools to cut the "Peaky and Spike" triangles for the Star Point units. See *Sew Easy: Using Tri-Recs™ Tools* on page 45 for tips on using these tools. If you prefer to use templates to cut these pieces, patterns are on page 44. —Marianne

Cutting

Measurements include ¼" seam allowances. Border strips are exact length needed. You may want to make them longer to allow for piecing variations.

From each of 5 blue fat eighths, cut:

- 1 (4½" × 20") strip. From strip, cut:
  - 1 (4½") A12 square.
  - 4 P12 ("Peaky") triangles and 4 P12 reverse triangles, using Recs tool or P12 template.

From each of 5 blue fat eighths, cut:

- 1 (3½" × 20") strip. From strip, cut:
  - 1 (3½") A9 square.
  - 4 P9 triangles and 4 P9 reverse triangles, using Recs tool or P9 template.

From each of 13 blue fat eighths, cut:

- 1 (2½" × 20") strip. From strip, cut:
  - 1 (2½") A6 square.
  - 4 P6 triangles and 4 P6 reverse triangles, using Recs tool or P6 template.

From each of 14 blue fat eighths, cut:

- 1 or 2 (1½" × 20") strips. You will need a total of 22 strips. From each strip, cut:
  - 1 (1½") A3 square.
  - 4 P3 triangles and 4 P3 reverse triangles, using Recs tool or P3 template.

From beige background print, cut:

- 5 (4½"-wide) strips. From strips, cut:
  - 20 (4½") A12 squares.
  - 20 S12 triangles, using Tri tool.
- 9 (3½"-wide) strips. From strips, cut:
  - 20 (3½") A9 squares.
  - 13 (3½") B squares.
  - 20 S9 triangles, using Tri tool.
  - 14 (3½" × 6½") E rectangles.
  - 12 (2½"-wide) strips. Piece strips to make 2 (2½" × 40½") top and bottom inner borders and 2 (2½" × 60½") side inner borders. From remaining strips, cut:
    - 52 (2½") A6 squares.
    - 52 S6 triangles, using Tri tool.

- 7 (1½"-wide) strips. From strips, cut:
  - 88 (1½") A3 squares.
  - 88 S3 triangles, using Tri tool.

From navy print for borders, cut:

- 6 (4½"-wide) strips. Piece strips to make 2 (4½" × 48½") top and bottom borders and 2 (4½" × 64½") side borders.
- 7 (2¼"-wide) strips for binding.

Block Assembly

1. To make 1 (12") block, choose 1 matching blue set of 4 P12, 4 P12 reverse, and 1 A12 square, 4 beige A12 squares, and 4 beige S12 triangles.

2. Referring to *Star Point ("Peaky and Spike") Assembly Diagram,* join 1 P12 and 1 P12 reverse triangle to sides of beige S12 triangle to make star point unit. Make 4 star point units. (Refer to *Sew Easy: Using Tri-Recs™ Tools* on page 45 for instructions on assembling "Peaky and Spike" units.)

Star Point ("Peaky and Spike") Assembly Diagram

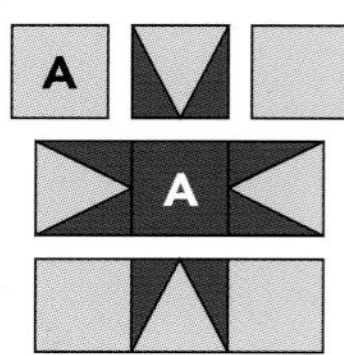

Block Assembly Diagram

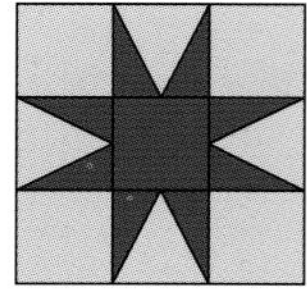

Block Diagram

Quilt Top Assembly Diagram

3. Lay out 4 star point units, 4 beige A12 squares, and 1 blue A12 square as shown in *Block Assembly Diagram.* Join into rows; join rows to complete 1 (12") block *(Block Diagram).* Make 5 (12") Star Rays blocks.

4. To make 1 (9") block, choose 1 matching blue set of 1 A9 square, 4 P9, and 4 P9 reverse triangles. You will also need 4 beige A9 squares and 4 beige S9 triangles. Repeat steps 2 and 3 to make 1 (9") Star Rays block. Make 5 (9") blocks.

5. To make 1 (6") block, choose 1 matching blue set of 1 A6 square, 4 P6, and 4 P6 reverse triangles. You will also need 4 beige A6 squares and 4 beige S6 triangles. Repeat steps 2 and 3 to make 1 (6") Star Rays block. Make 13 (6") blocks.

6. To make 1 (3") block, choose 1 matching blue set of 1 A3 square, 4

P3, and 4 P3 reverse triangles. You will also need 4 beige A3 squares and 4 beige S3 triangles. Repeat steps 2 and 3 to make 1 (3") Star Rays block. Make 22 (3") blocks.

Quilt Assembly

1. Lay out blocks as shown in *Quilt Top Assembly Diagram*. Refer to the color key for the diagram to place blocks according to block size.
2. Fill in the spaces with beige B squares and E rectangles.
3. Join groups of blocks and beige background pieces into 13 (12"-square) units. Heavy lines on *Quilt Top Assembly Diagram* denote 12" units.
4. Join 5 (12") units to make right row of blocks. Join 5 (12") units to make middle row of blocks.
5. To make left row of blocks, begin by assembling remaining blocks and background units into 1 (12" × 24") unit. Join 12" units and 12" × 24" unit into block row.
6. Join rows of blocks to complete inner quilt.
7. Add beige side inner borders to sides of quilt. Add beige top and bottom borders to quilt.
8. Add navy side outer borders to sides of quilt. Add navy top and bottom borders to quilt.

Finishing

1. Divide backing fabric into 2 (1½-yard) lengths. Join panels lengthwise. Seam will run horizontally.
2. Layer backing, batting, and quilt top; baste. Quilt as desired. Quilt shown was machine quilted with stars and meander quilting. Outer border was quilted with continuous spirals.
3. Join 2¼"-wide navy strips into 1 continuous piece for straight-grain French-fold binding. Add binding to quilt.

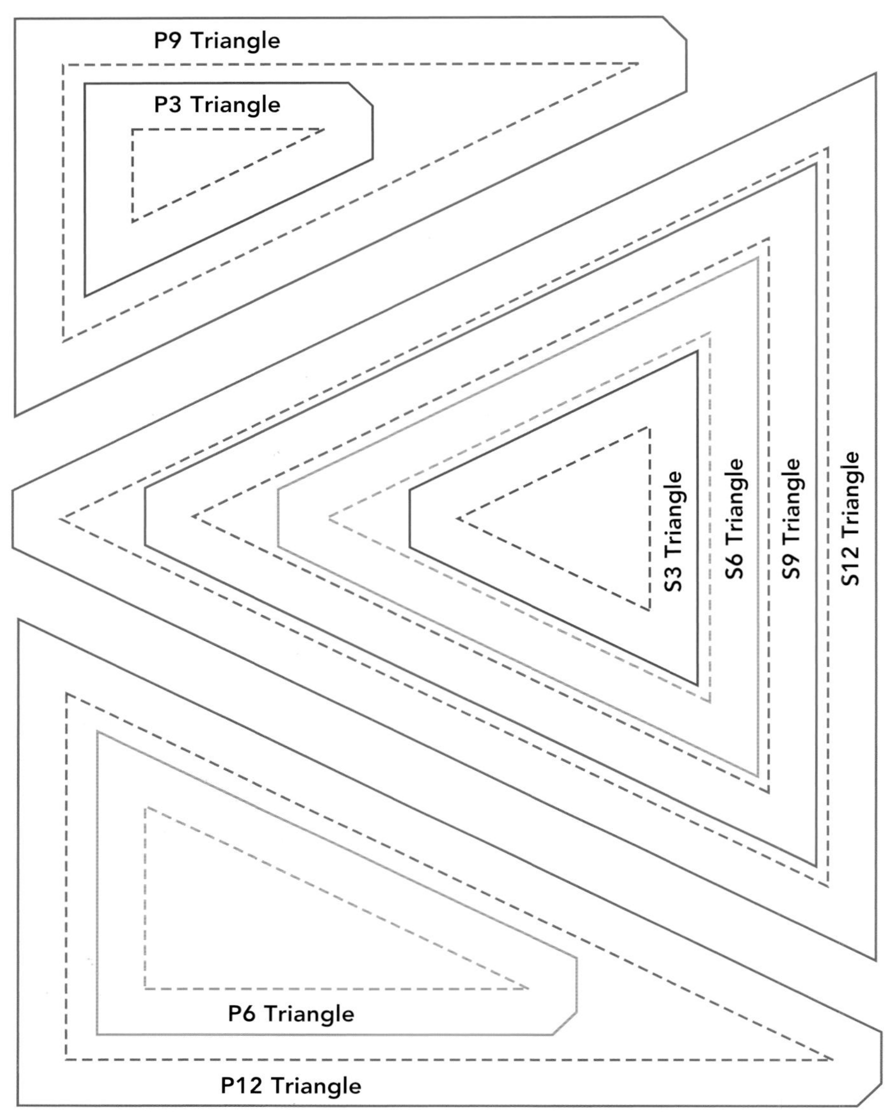

TRIED & TRUE

Fabrics from the Folk Art Christmas III collection by Robyn Pandolph for Moda™ fabrics give the Star Rays blocks a country Christmas feel.

DESIGNER

Cathy Busch enjoys working with design, fabric, and color. Together with some terrific hand and machine quilters, she has created several ribbon-winning quilts. Cathy and her husband David live in Waverly, Iowa.

Sew *Easy*™ Using Tri-Recs™ Tools

A

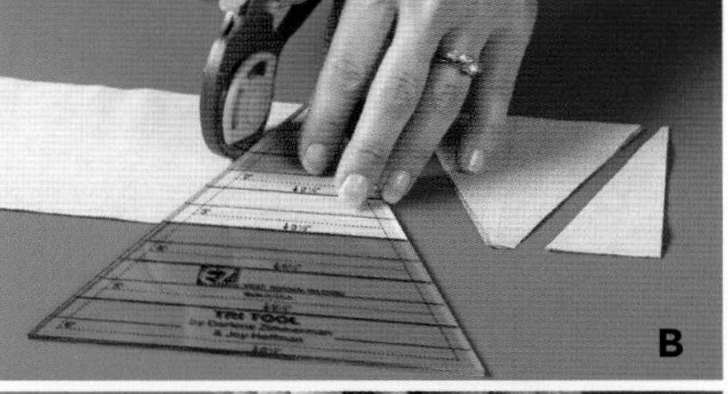

B

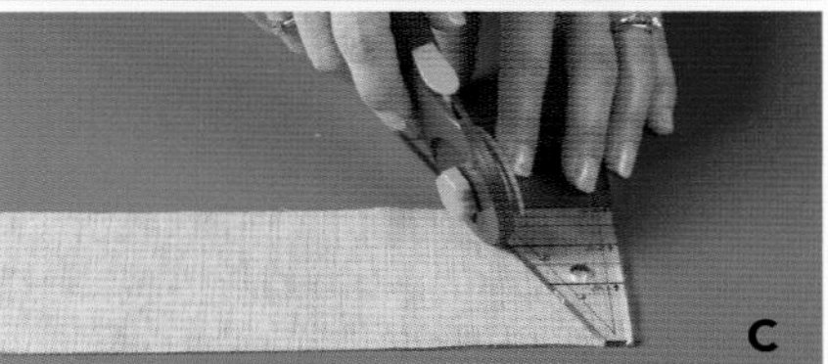
C

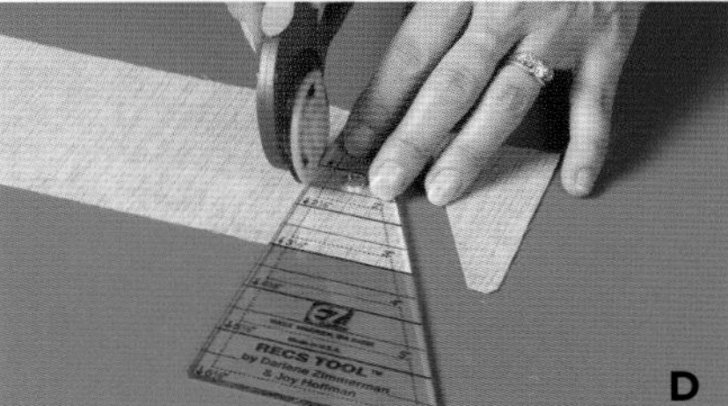

D

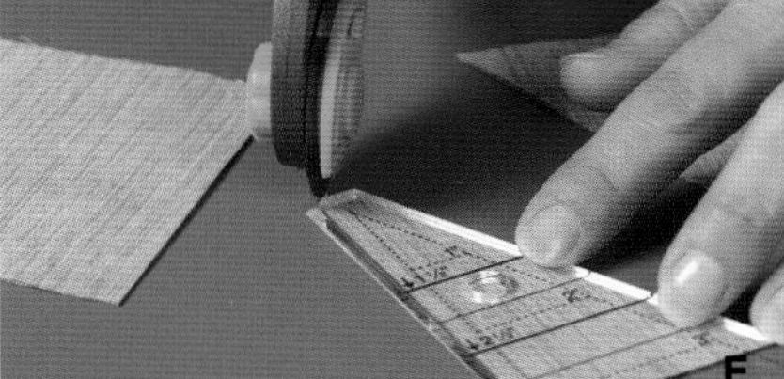
E

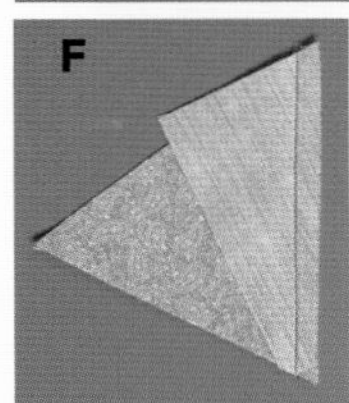
F

G

H

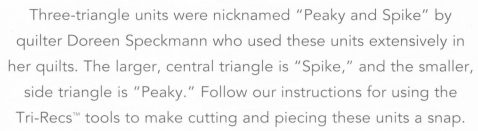

Three-triangle units were nicknamed "Peaky and Spike" by quilter Doreen Speckmann who used these units extensively in her quilts. The larger, central triangle is "Spike," and the smaller, side triangle is "Peaky." Follow our instructions for using the Tri-Recs™ tools to make cutting and piecing these units a snap.

Cutting "Peaky and Spike" Triangles

1. Begin by cutting 1 fabric strip from each of the colors you wish to combine in a "Peaky and Spike" unit. To determine the strip size, add ½" to the desired finished size of the unit. For example, for a 3" finished size unit, cut strips 3½" wide.
2. Working with the strip for the center "Spike" triangle, position the Tri tool atop the strip, aligning the mark corresponding to your strip width along bottom edge of strip. Cut along both angled sides of Tri tool *(Photo A).*
3. Reposition Tri tool with strip width line along top edge of strip and side along previously cut edge. Cut another "Spike" triangle *(Photo B).* Continue in this manner to cut desired number of "Spike" triangles.
4. Fold the strip for the side "Peaky" triangles in half with right sides together so you will be cutting two mirror image pieces at one time. Position the Recs tool atop the strip, aligning the mark corresponding to your strip width along bottom edge of strip. Cut on both sides of Recs tool to cut 2 "Peaky" triangles—1 right and 1 left *(Photo C).*
5. Reposition Recs tool with strip width line along top edge of strip. Cut 2 more side "Peaky" triangles *(Photo D).* Continue in this manner to cut desired number of pairs of "Peaky" triangles.
6. As you cut "Peaky" triangles, be sure to trim along the short angled line at the top of the Recs tool. This angled cut makes it easier to align pieces for sewing *(Photo E).*

Assembling "Peaky and Spike" Units

1. Position right "Peaky" triangle along right side of "Spike" triangle, making sure the angle aligns with the side of the "Spike" triangle. Join pieces *(Photo F).* Open out "Peaky" triangle; press seam allowances toward "Peaky" triangle.
2. Add left "Peaky" triangle to adjacent side as shown *(Photo G).*
3. Open out "Peaky" triangle; press seam allowances toward "Peaky" triangle *(Photo H).*
4. Trim excess seam allowances even with sides of "Peaky and Spike" unit *(Photo I).*

I

STAR OF Bethlehem

Make an exact replica of this antique quilt using reproduction prints from Andover Fabrics. The fabrics are identical to those in the original quilt.

PROJECT RATING: CHALLENGING

Size: 92⅞" × 92⅞"

MATERIALS

NOTE: Fabrics in the quilt shown are from the Keystone collection by Andover Fabrics.

1¼ yards each of 7 assorted indigo and cheddar prints
7¾ yards cream print
Paper-backed fusible web (optional)
8¼ yards backing fabric
King-size quilt batting

Cutting

Measurements include ¼" seam allowances. Patterns for appliqué pieces and Border Triangles are on pages 50–53. Follow manufacturer's instructions if using fusible web.

From assorted indigo prints, cut:

- 6 (7¼"-wide) strips. From strips, cut 108 Border Triangles *(Triangle Cutting Diagram).*

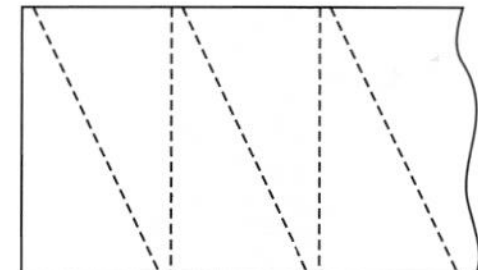

Triangle Cutting Diagram

- 32 (2¼"-wide) strips for strip sets.
- 4 Border Corner Triangles reversed.
- 8 A.
- 24 B.
- 24 C.
- 28 D.
- 1 Star.

From cream solid, cut:

- 1 (33⅛"-wide) strip. From strip, cut 1 (33⅛") square. Cut square in half diagonally in both directions to make 4 quarter-square setting triangles.
- 4 (24"-wide) strips. From strips, cut 4 (24") squares.
- 6 (7¼"-wide) strips. From strips, cut 104 Border Triangles and 4 Border Triangles reversed.
- 4 Border Corner Triangles.
- 42 (2¼"-wide) strips. You will use 31 for strip sets and 11 for binding.

Star Assembly

1. Refer to *Sew Easy: Pieced Diamonds* on page 51 for instructions. Join 5 assorted indigo print strips and 4 cream print strips, offsetting strips by 1¾" as shown in *Strip Set #1 Diagrams.* Make 4 Strip Set #1. Trim left end of each strip set at a 45° angle. From strip sets, cut 40 (2¼"-wide) #1 segments.

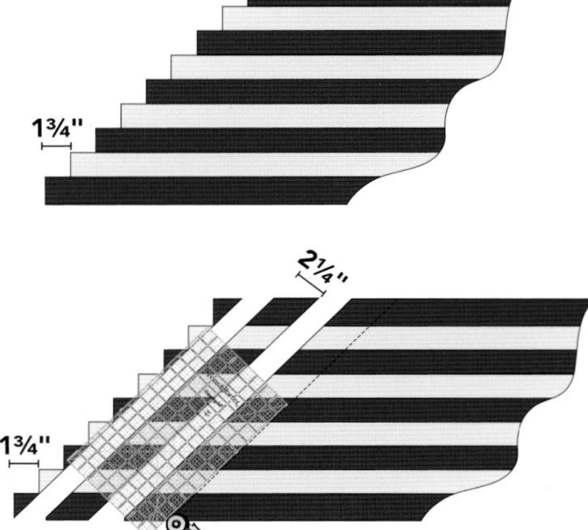

Strip Set #1 Diagrams

2. In the same manner, join 5 cream print strips and 4 assorted indigo print strips as shown in *Strip Set #2 Diagram.* Make 3 Strip Set #2. Trim left end of each strip set at 45° angle. From strip sets, cut 32 (2¼"-wide) #2 segments.

Strip Set #2 Diagram

3. Join 5 #1 segments and 4 #2 segments to make 1 Large Pieced Diamond as shown in *Star Assembly Diagram* on page 48. Make 8 Large Pieced Diamonds.

QUILT FROM THE COLLECTION OF **International Quilt Study Center & Museum 1997-007-0660**.

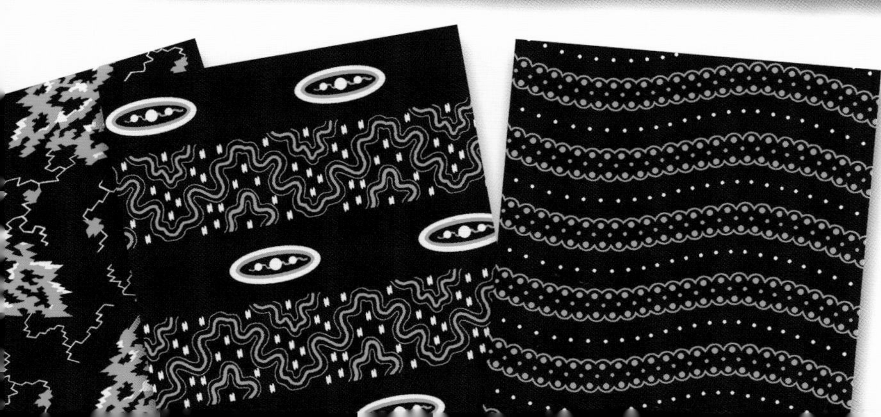

4. Join Large Pieced Diamonds to make Star as shown in *Star Assembly Diagram*.

Appliqué

1. Position 1A, 4B, 4C, and 4D on 1 cream print square as shown in *Corner Block Diagram*. Appliqué pieces in place to complete 1 corner block. Make 4 corner blocks. Trim blocks to 23" square.

Corner Block Diagram

2. Position 1A, 2B, 2C, and 3D on 1 cream print quarter-square setting triangle; appliqué in place as shown in *Setting Triangle Diagram*. Trim appliqué pieces even with edge of triangle. Make 4 setting triangles.

Setting Triangle Diagram

Star Assembly Diagram

Border Assembly

1. Join 1 indigo print border triangle and 1 cream print border triangle as shown in *Border Unit Diagrams*. Make 104 Border Units.

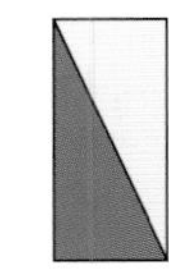

Border Unit Diagrams

2. Join 26 Border Units to make a border as shown in *Quilt Top Assembly Diagram*. Make 4 borders.
3. Join 1 indigo print border triangle, 1 cream print border triangle reversed, 1 indigo print corner triangle reversed, and 1 cream print corner triangle to make 1 Border Corner block *(Border Corner Diagrams)*. Make 4 Border Corner blocks.

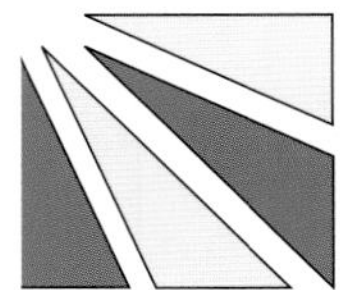
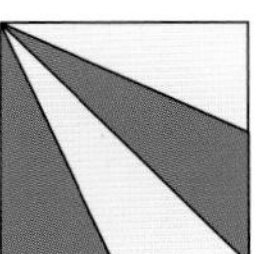

Border Corner Diagrams

Quilt Assembly

1. Add Corner blocks and setting triangles to pieced star to complete quilt center.

Quilt Top Assembly Diagram

Sew Smart™
Refer to *Sew Easy: Set-In Seams* on page 73. —Liz

2. Add borders to opposite sides of quilt center.
3. Add 1 Border Corner block to each end of remaining borders. Add borders to quilt.
4. Appliqué star atop center of quilt top. If desired, trim excess fabric behind appliquéd star.

Finishing

1. Divide backing into 3 (2¾-yard) lengths. Join panels lengthwise.
2. Layer backing, batting, and quilt top; baste. Quilt as desired.
3. Join 2¼"-wide cream print strips into 1 continuous piece for straight-grain French-fold binding. Add binding to quilt.

Suggested Quilting Diagram

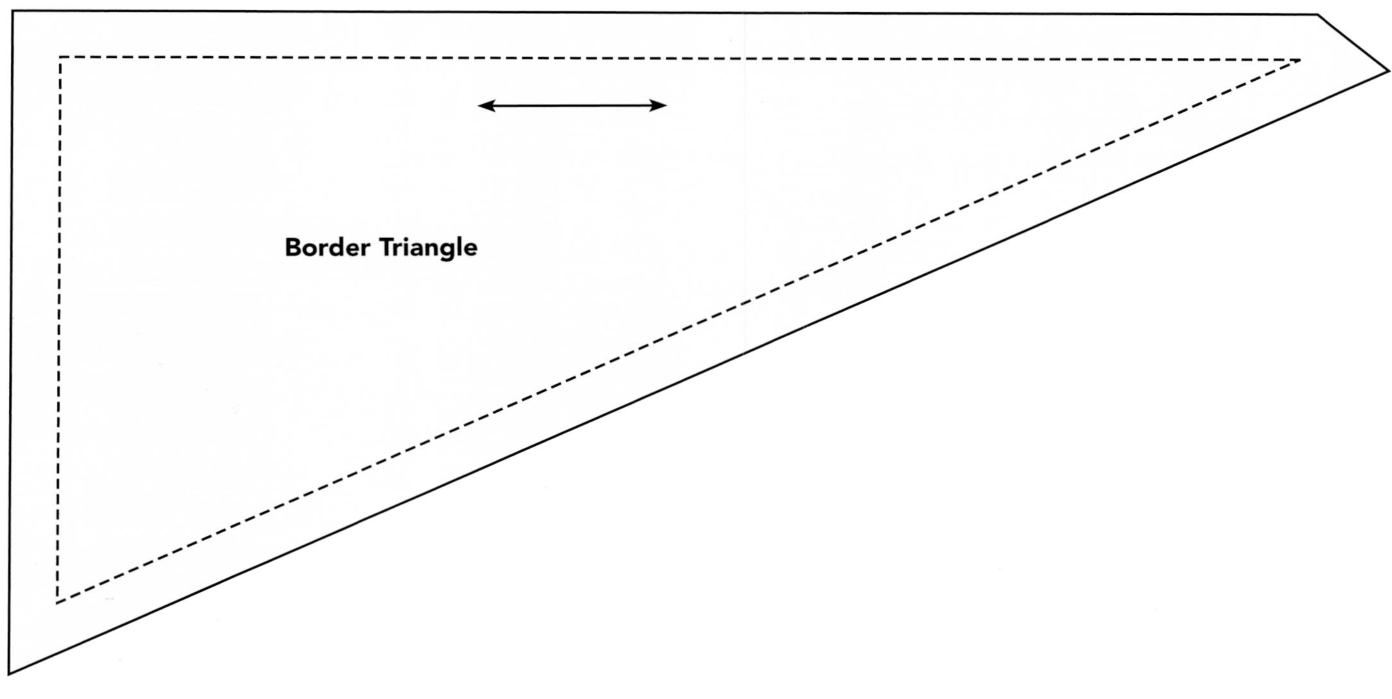

From the Curator

An unknown quilter from Eastern Pennsylvania hand pieced and hand appliquéd this vibrant *Star of Bethlehem* quilt circa 1845. Square and triangular Oak Leaf setting blocks between the points of the star enhance the square shape of the top. An unusual elongated sawtooth border repeats the prints used in the center star.

The quilt was pieced with a variety of small-scale cheddar patterns printed on deep blue indigo backgrounds. The pattern of the quilt appears to advance and recede before one's eyes due to the quiltmaker's choice to cut diagonally across the striped fabrics. This gives complexity to the overall design.

Stable and durable blue indigo dye was derived from the leaves of the indigo plant. India, China, and Japan produced indigo-dyed fabric for thousands of years, and it remained a rare commodity in Europe until the seventeenth century. By the mid-nineteenth century, indigo became an important commercial dye crop in the United States, and much of it was exported from Southern ports such as Charleston. Indigo and cheddar patterns, like those in this quilt, were found in printed fabric in America from the 1830s through the 1920s.

About the Collection: This quilt is owned by the International Quilt Study Center & Museum at the University of Nebraska-Lincoln. The Center has the largest publicly held quilt collection in the world. See other gorgeous quilts from the collection and enjoy interactive Web features at www.quiltstudy.org under Quilt Explorer. ⁂

Sew *Easy*™ Pieced Diamonds

Follow these strip piecing instructions to make pieced diamonds for *Star of Bethlehem* on page 46.

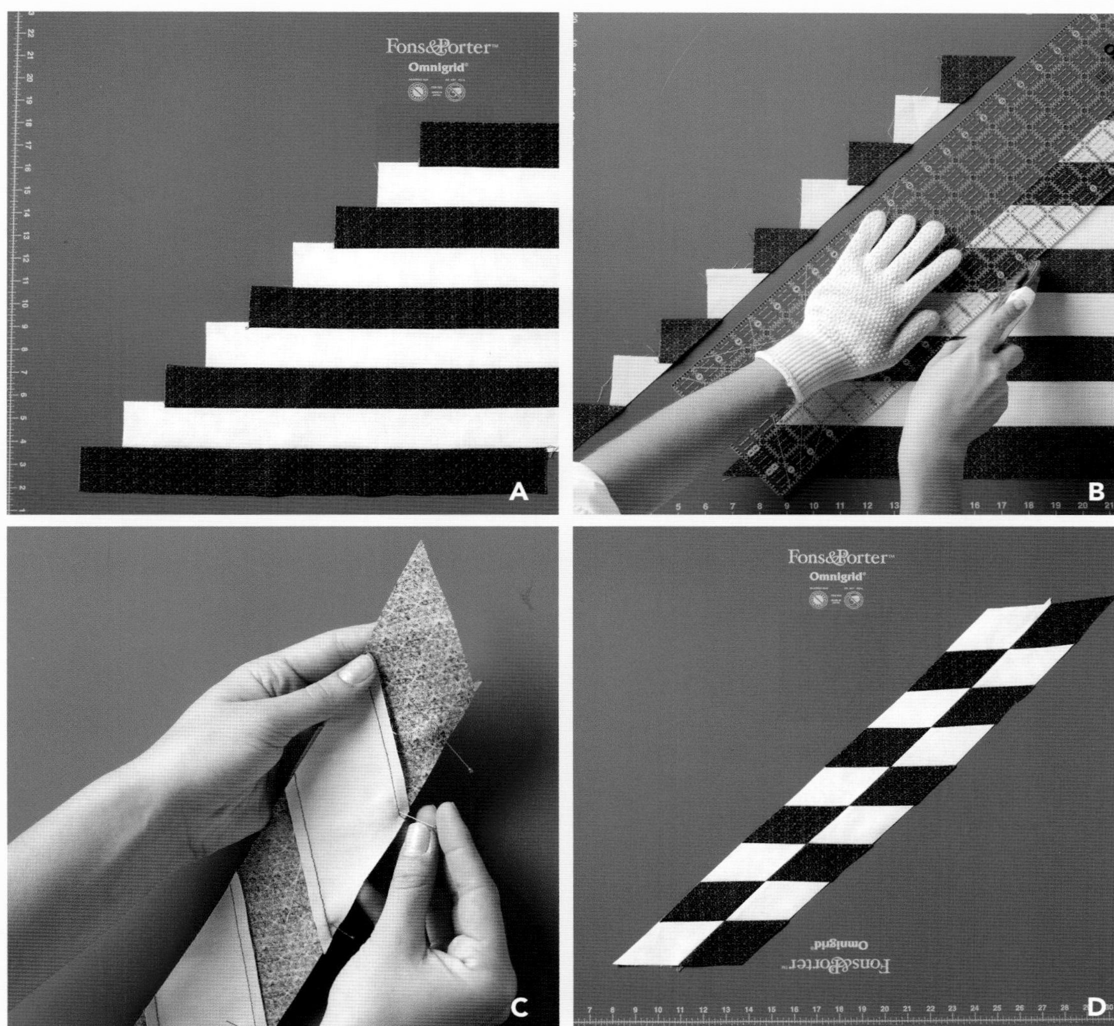

1. Join strips, offsetting them at left end, as shown *(Photo A)*.
2. Trim left end of strip set at 45-degree angle. Place 2¼" line of ruler on angled edge of strip set; cut 1 segment *(Photo B)*.
3. Layer 1 Strip Set #1 segment and 1 Strip Set #2 segment right sides facing. Place pin at each seam allowance *(Photo C)*.

> Sew **Smart**™
> **Stick pin straight into seam ¼" from edge of top piece. Pin should exit seam of bottom piece ¼" from edge. —Liz**

4. Join strip set segments *(Photo D)*.

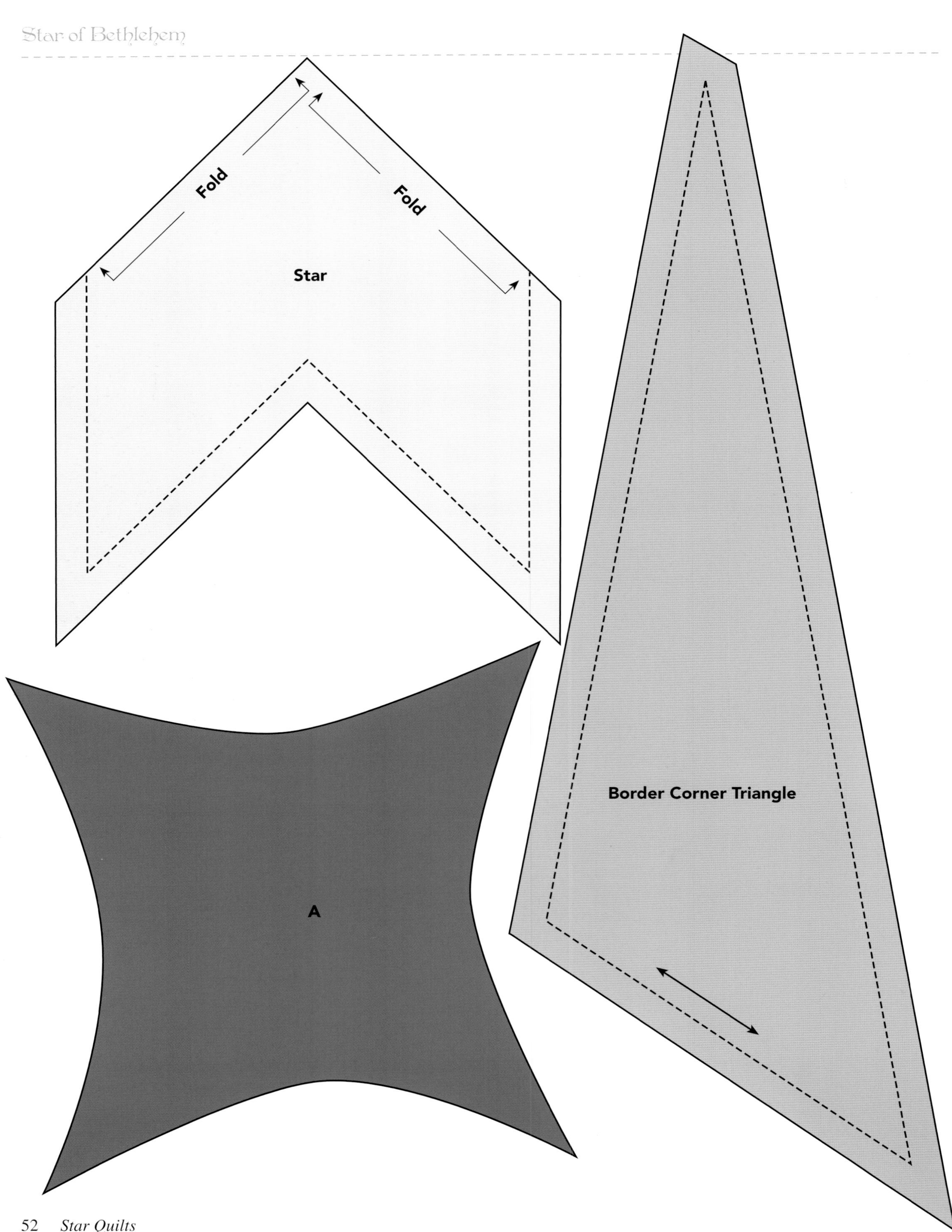
Fold
Fold
Star
A
Border Corner Triangle

Patterns are shown full size and are reversed for use with fusible web. Add 3⁄16" seam allowance for hand appliqué.

Radiant Blue

The Feathered Star block variation Marsha McCloskey used for her stunning quilt is also known as Chestnut Burr or Radiant Star.

PROJECT RATING: CHALLENGING

Size: 51" × 51"

Blocks: 4 (15") Feathered Star blocks

MATERIALS

1⅞ yards light blue print for borders

8 fat eighths★ assorted medium blue prints

9 fat quarters★★ assorted white prints

1 yard blue-and-white print

¾ yard dark blue print

3¼ yards backing fabric

Twin-size quilt batting

Template material

★fat eighth = 9" × 20"

★★fat quarter = 18" × 20"

Cutting

Patterns for templates are on page 60. Measurements include ¼" seam allowances. Border strips are exact length needed. You may want to make them longer to allow for piecing variations.

> Sew **Smart**™
>
> **Two methods are given for cutting the pieces for the triangle-squares in this quilt. Marsha's quick method is explained in *Sew Easy: Bias-Strip Piecing* on page 61. If you prefer, you may use traditional cutting methods. Read through all instructions before cutting.**

From light blue print, cut:

- 5 (5½"-wide) strips. Piece strips to make 2 (5½" × 51½") top and bottom outer borders and 2 (5½" × 41½") side outer borders.
- 6 (2¼"-wide) strips for binding.
- 12 (1½"-wide) strips for strip sets.

From medium blue fat eighths, cut a total of:

- 8 (1½" × 20") strips for strip sets.
- 32 Kites.
- 4 Octagons.
- 32 Diamonds.

From assorted white print fat quarters, cut a total of:

- 2 (7½"-wide) strips. From strips, cut 4 (7½") squares. Cut squares in half diagonally in both directions to make 16 quarter-square B triangles.
- 4 (4⅞"-wide) strips. From strips, cut 16 (4⅞") D squares.
- 2 (2⅛"-wide) strips. From strips, cut 16 (2⅛") squares. Cut squares in half diagonally to make 32 half-square C triangles.
- 2 (12"-wide) strips. From strips, cut 4 (12") squares to make 160 triangle-squares using Bias-Strip Piecing method.
- 4 (1⅞"-wide) strips. From strips, cut 32 (1⅞") squares. Cut squares in half diagonally to make 64 half-square triangles **OR for traditional piecing, cut:**

  12 (1⅞"-wide) strips. From strips, cut 112 (1⅞") squares. Cut squares in half diagonally to make 224 half-square A triangles (for 160 triangle-squares and 64 single A triangles).

From blue-and-white print, cut:

- 20 (1½"-wide) strips. From strips, cut 8 (1½" × 15½") border strips and 4 (1½") H squares. Remaining strips will be used for strip sets.

From dark blue print, cut:

- 2 (12"-wide) strips. From strips, cut 4 (12") squares to make 160 triangle-squares using Bias-Strip Piecing method **OR for**

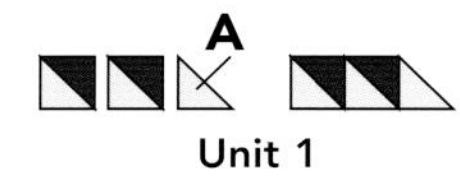

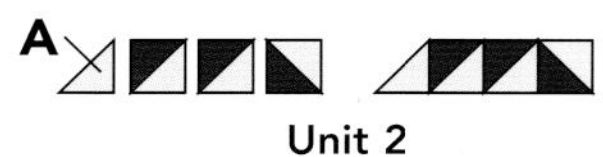

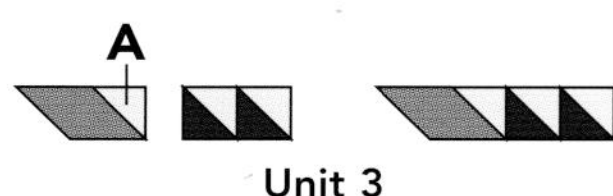

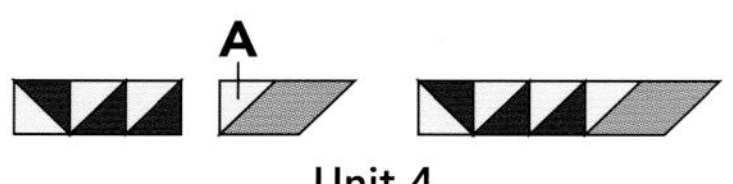

Feather Unit Diagrams

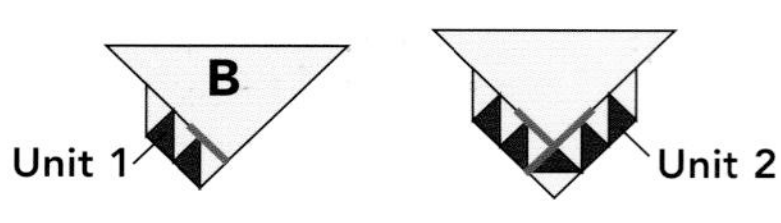

Partial Seams Diagrams

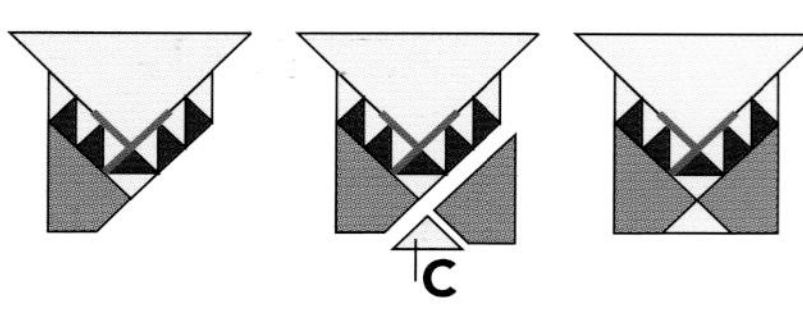

Side Unit Diagrams

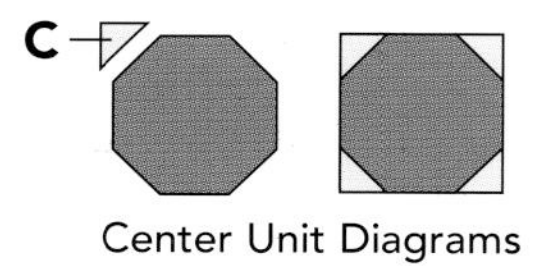

Center Unit Diagrams

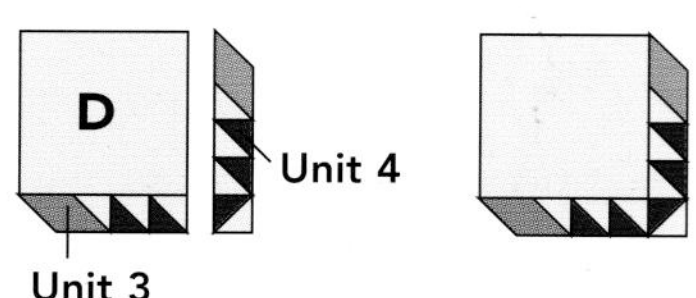

Corner Unit Diagrams

traditional piecing, cut:
4 (1⅞"-wide) strips. From strips, cut 80 (1⅞") squares. Cut squares in half diagonally to make 160 half-square A triangles.

Block Assembly

1. Referring to *Sew Easy: Bias-Strip Piecing* on page 61, make 160 (1½") triangle-squares (1" finished size) from (12") dark blue print squares and (12") white print squares **OR for traditional piecing,** join 1 white print A triangle and 1 dark blue print A triangle to make 1 triangle-square. Make 160 triangle-squares.
2. Join 2 triangle-squares and 1 white print A triangle as shown in *Feather Unit Diagrams* to complete 1 Unit 1. Make 16 Unit 1.
3. In the same manner, join 3 triangle-squares and 1 white print A triangle to make Unit 2. Make 16 Unit 2.

> ### Sew **Smart**™
> **Press seams open in Feather rows. Press the rest of the seams to one side (the direction they tend to go). —Marianne**

4. Referring to *Partial Seams Diagrams,* add 1 white print B triangle to 1 Unit 1, using a partial seam as indicated by red line. Add 1 Unit 2, using a partial seam.
5. Add 1 medium blue kite piece as shown in *Side Unit Diagrams.* Join 1 white print C triangle to 1 medium blue kite piece. Add this segment as shown to complete 1 Side Unit. Make 16 Side Units.
6. Choose 4 white print C triangles and 1 medium blue print octagon. Join 1 white print C triangle to each bias edge of octagon to make 1 Center Unit *(Center Unit Diagrams).* Make 4 Center Units.

> ### Sew **Smart**™
> **Use the pink Fons & Porter Triangle Trimmer to trim points of C triangles so they are easier to match up and stitch to the octagons. Complete instructions for using the Fons & Porter Triangle Trimmers are at: <u>www.FonsandPorter.com/trimming points</u> —Liz**

7. Referring to *Unit 3* in *Feather Unit Diagrams,* join 1 medium blue diamond to 1 white print A triangle. Add 2 triangle-squares to complete Unit 3. Make 16 Unit 3.
8. Referring to *Unit 4* in *Feather Unit Diagrams,* join 1 medium blue diamond to 1 white print A triangle. Add 3 triangle-squares to complete Unit 4. Make 16 Unit 4.
9. Add 1 Unit 3 to bottom of 1 white print D square. Add 1 Unit 4 to right side of square to complete 1 Corner Unit. Make 16 Corner Units.
10. Referring to *Block Assembly Diagrams* on page 57, lay out 4 Corner Units, 4 Side Units, and 1 Center Unit as shown in *Step 1 Diagram.* Join units into rows; complete partial seams (indicated by red lines) as shown in *Step 2*

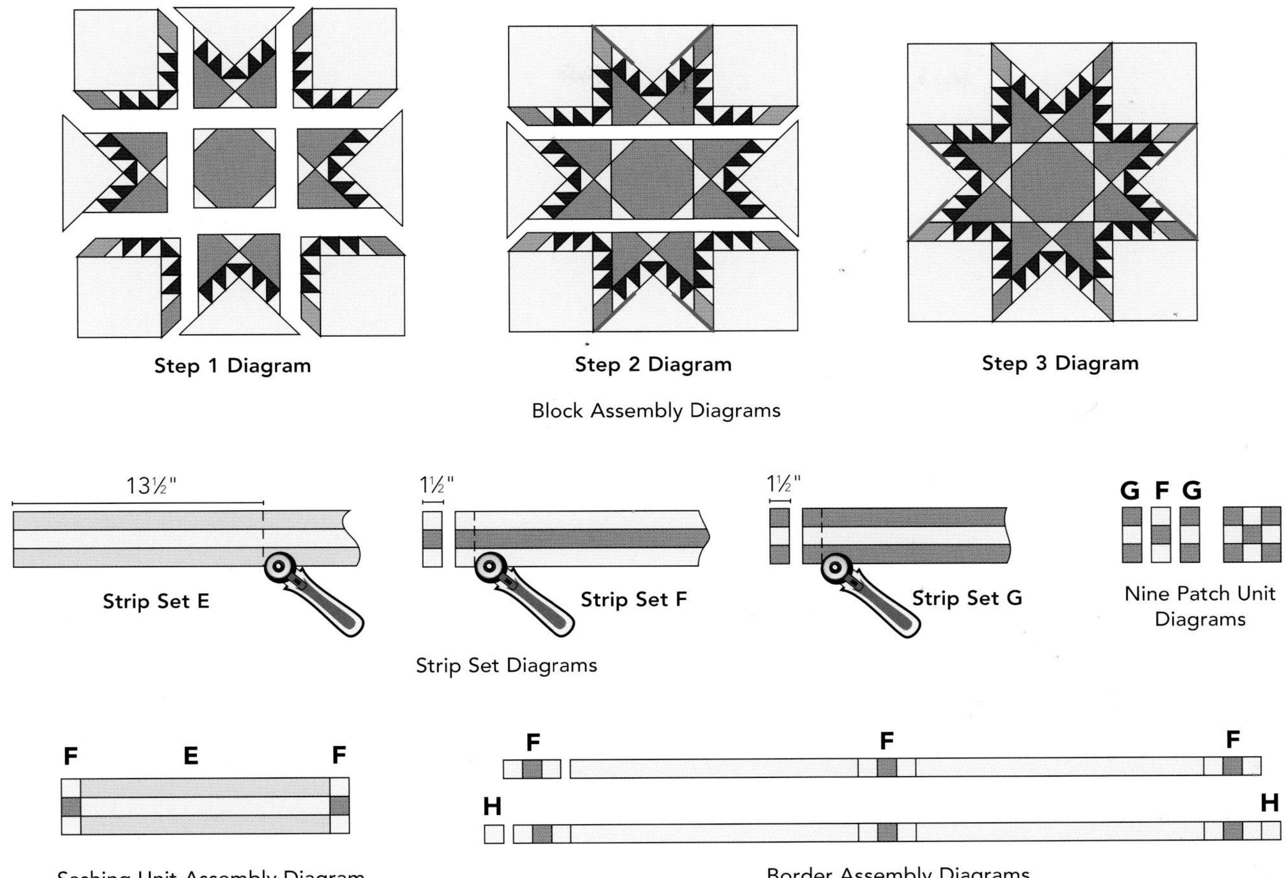

Diagram. Join rows; complete partial seams (indicated by red lines) as shown in *Step 3 Diagram* to complete 1 Feathered Star block. Make 4 Feathered Star blocks.

Sashing Assembly

1. Referring to *Strip Set Diagrams,* join 1 (1½"-wide) blue-and-white print strip and 2 (1½"-wide) light blue print strips to make 1 Strip Set E. Make 6 Strip Set E. From strip sets, cut 12 (13½"-wide) E segments.
2. Join 1 (1½" × 20") medium blue print strip and 2 (1½" × 20") blue-and-white print strips to make 1 Strip Set F. Make 4 Strip Set F. From strip sets, cut 45 (1½"-wide) F segments.
3. Join 1 (1½" × 20") blue-and-white print strip and 2 (1½" × 20") medium blue print strips to make 1 Strip Set G. Make 2 Strip Set G. From strip sets, cut 18 (1½"-wide) G segments.
4. Referring to *Nine Patch Unit Diagrams,* join 1 F segment and 2 G segments to make 1 Nine Patch Unit. Make 9 Nine Patch Units.
5. Referring to *Sashing Unit Assembly Diagram,* join 1 F segment to each end of 1 E segment to make 1 Sashing Unit. Make 12 Sashing Units.

Pieced Border Assembly

1. Join 3 F segments and 2 (1½" × 15½") blue-and-white print border strips to make 1 inner border. Make 4 inner borders *(Border Assembly Diagrams).*
2. Join 1 blue-and-white print H square to each end of 2 borders for top and bottom inner borders.

Quilt Assembly

1. Lay out blocks, Sashing Units, and Nine Patch Units as shown in *Quilt Top Assembly Diagram* on page 58. Join into rows; join rows to complete quilt center.
2. Add side inner borders to quilt center. Add top and bottom inner borders to quilt. Repeat for light blue print outer borders.

Finishing

1. Divide backing fabric into 2 (1⅝-yard) pieces. Cut 1 piece in half lengthwise to make 2 narrow panels. Join 1 narrow panel to wider panel; press seam allowances toward narrow panel. Remaining panel is extra and may be used to make a hanging sleeve.
2. Layer backing, batting, and quilt top; baste. Quilt as desired. Quilt shown was quilted in the ditch around feathered stars and has a star in each block center and a feather design in outer border *(Quilting Diagram).*
3. Join 2¼"-wide light blue print strips into 1 continuous piece for straight-grain French-fold binding. Add binding to quilt.

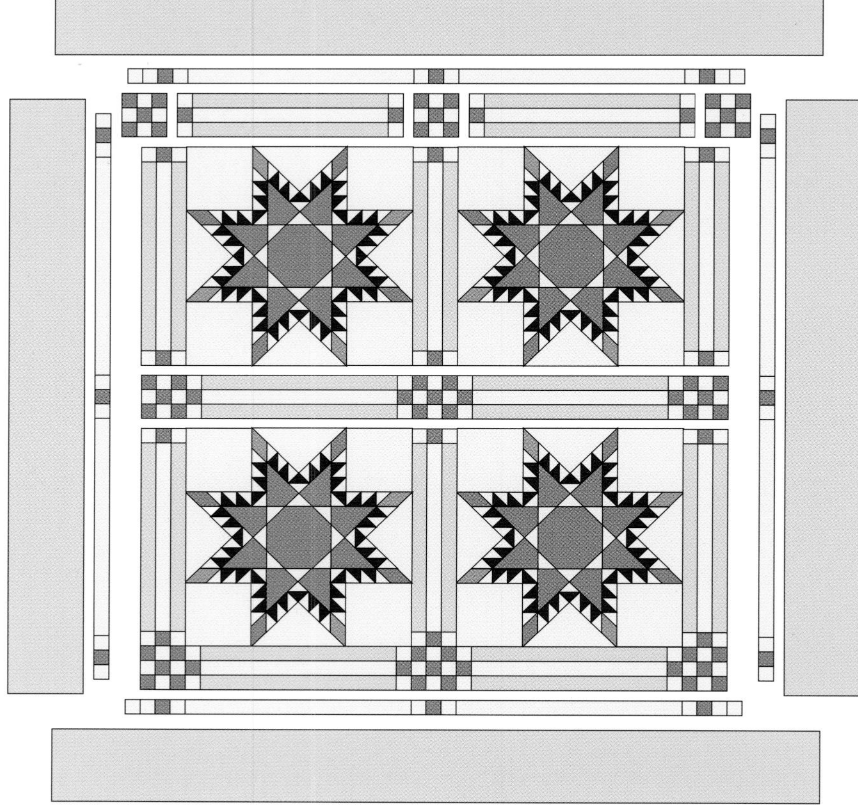

Quilt Top Assembly Diagram

For a cool wintry look, make a light star with a dark background. We used a navy snowflake print fabric by Moda.

Quilting Diagram

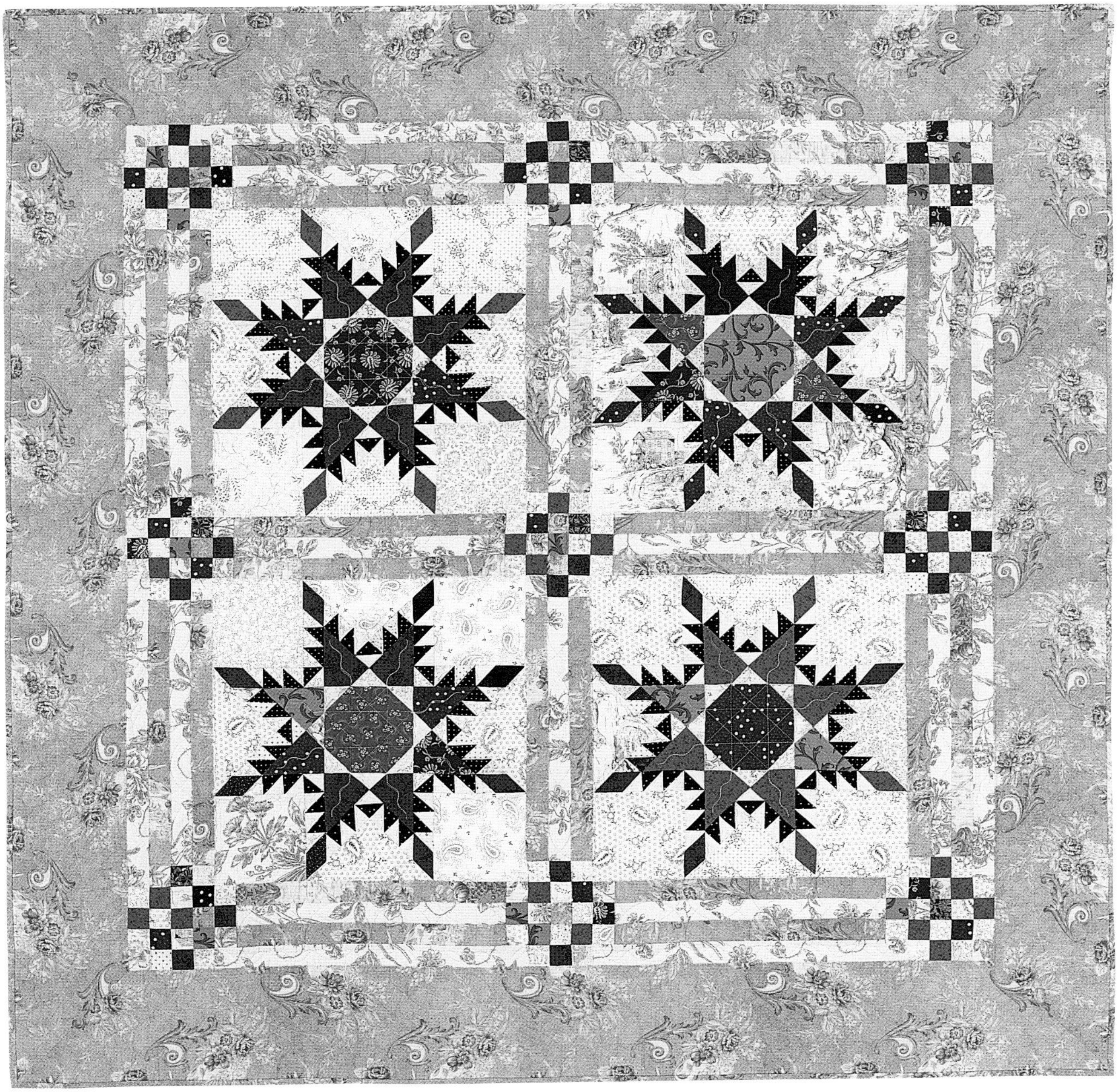

DESIGNER

Marsha McCloskey has written or co-authored over twenty-nine books on quiltmaking and has taught classes throughout the United States and abroad. She has her own publishing company, Feathered Star Productions, Inc., and has been designing fabrics for quilters since 1996. ⁎

WEB EXTRA

To download *Quilt Top Assembly Diagrams* for these size options, go to www.FonsandPorter.com/rbluesizes.

MORE SIZE OPTIONS

	Wallhanging **(33" × 33")**	Throw **(51" × 69")**
Blocks	1	6
Setting	—	2 × 3 blocks
Materials		
Light Blue Print	1 yard	2¼ yards
White Print	½ yard or 4 fat eighths	3 yards or 12 fat quarters
Medium Blue Prints	1 fat quarter or scraps	10 fat eighths
Dark Blue Print	⅜ yard	1⅛ yards
Backing Fabric	1⅛ yards	3¼ yards
Batting	18" × 21"	Twin-size

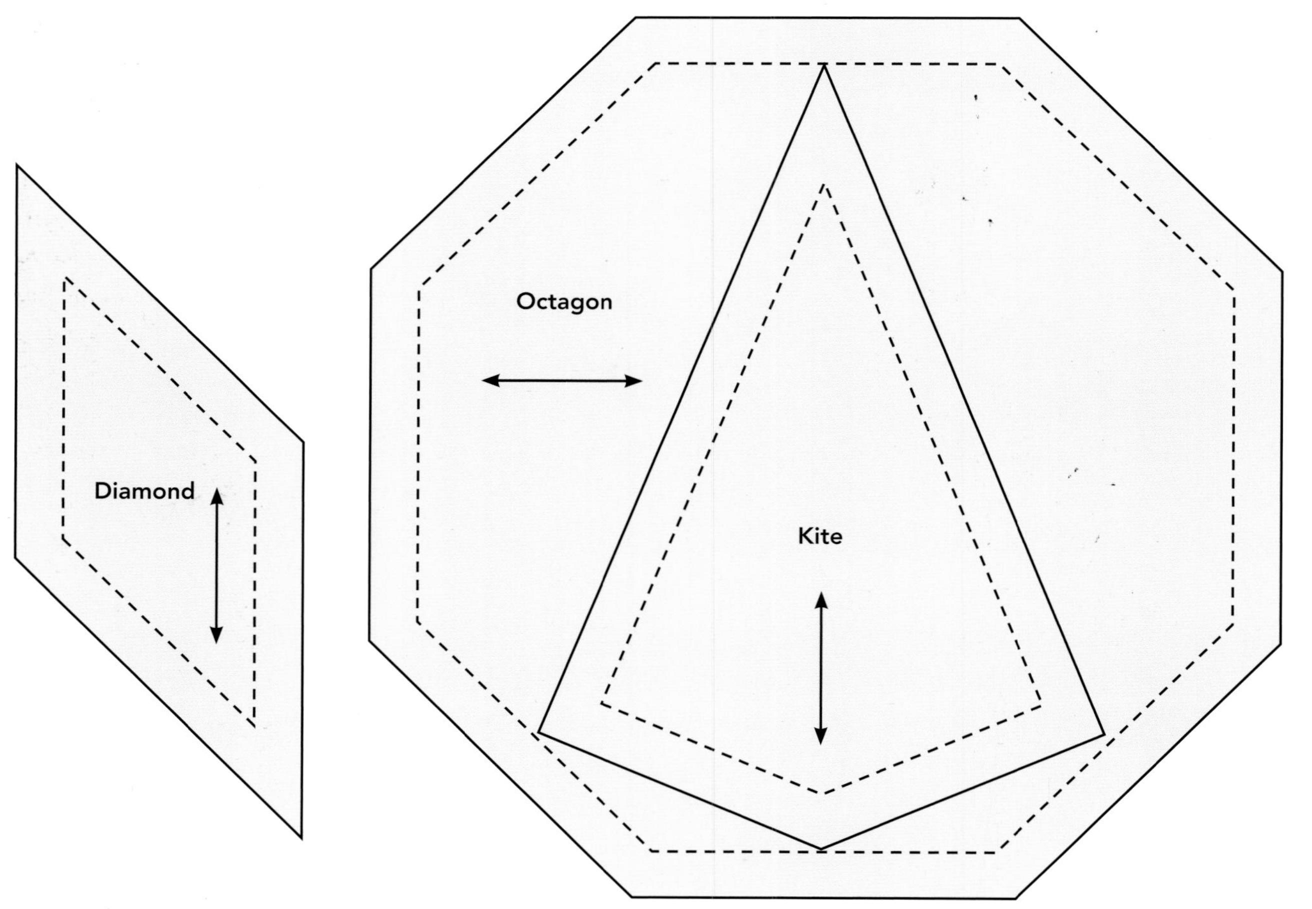

Sew *Easy*™ Bias-Strip Piecing

Make multiple 1"-finished triangle-squares quickly using this easy method. For instructions to make triangle-squares in other sizes, see Marsha McCloskey's book *Feathered Star Quilt Blocks I*.

1. Place 1 (12") light square atop 1 (12") dark square, right sides facing. Cut squares in half diagonally to make 2 triangles.
2. Measuring from the long side, cut 3 (2"-wide) strips from each pair of triangles *(Photo A)*. You will have 6 bias-strip pairs and 2 corner triangle pairs.
3. Join bias-strip pairs and corner triangle pairs as shown in *Photo B*; press seam allowances open.
4. Join the bias-strip pairs, alternating light and dark *(Photo C)*.
5. Using a Bias Square® ruler or other square ruler, cut 6 triangle-squares from the bottom of the pieced unit. Place the diagonal line of the ruler on the seam line and cut a square that is slightly larger (a few threads) than desired size. Cut along the top edges of the ruler *(Photo D)*.
6. Continue cutting from the bottom edge *(Photo E)* until entire piece is cut into triangle-squares. You should get enough triangle-squares for 1 star block from each pair of 12" squares.
7. Turn the squares and trim opposite sides to desired size *(Photo F)*.

Sew **Smart**™ To make cutting easier, use the Bias Square® Ruler, available at www.MarshaMcCloskey.com.

QUILT BY **Julie M. Lynch**.

Aspen

FEATHERED STAR

Make this beautiful wallhanging in a weekend! Partial seams and large pieces make this feathered star easy to assemble.

PROJECT RATING: INTERMEDIATE

Size: 50" × 50"

MATERIALS

NOTE: Fabrics are from the Aspen collection by Marianne Elizabeth for Benartex.

1¼ yards black floral print
¾ yard red print
⅜ yard red floral print
⅜ yard orange print
⅞ yard yellow print
¾ yard yellow/red print
1 fat quarter* green floral print
1 fat quarter* dark green print
1 fat quarter* light green print
3¼ yards backing fabric
Twin-size quilt batting
*fat quarter = 18" × 20"

Cutting

Measurements include ¼" seam allowances. Border strips are exact length needed. You may want to make them longer to allow for piecing variations.

From black floral print, cut:

- 1 (13¾"-wide) strip. From strip, cut 1 (13¾") center square.
- 5 (4¾"-wide) strips. Piece strips to make 4 (4¾" × 42") outer borders.

From red print, cut:

- 1 (6⅛"-wide) strip. From strip, cut 4 (6⅛") squares. Cut squares in half diagonally to make 8 half-square C triangles.
- 6 (2¼"-wide) strips for binding.

From red floral print, cut:

- 2 (2⅞"-wide) strips. From strips, cut 16 (2⅞") squares. Cut squares in half diagonally to make 32 half-square A triangles.
- 2 (2¾"-wide) strips. From strips, cut 20 (2¾") squares. Cut squares in half diagonally to make 40 half-square B triangles.

From orange print, cut:

- 1 (2⅞"-wide) strip. From strip, cut 12 (2⅞") squares. Cut squares in half diagonally to make 24 half-square A triangles.
- 2 (2¾"-wide) strips. From strips, cut 18 (2¾") squares. Cut squares in half diagonally to make 36 half-square B triangles.
- 1 (2½"-wide) strip. From strip, cut 4 (2½") D squares.

From yellow print, cut:

- 1 (18½"-wide) strip. From strip, cut 1 (18½") square. Cut square in half diagonally in both directions to make 4 quarter-square F triangles.
- 1 (8½"-wide) strip. From strip, cut 4 (8½") E squares.

From yellow/red print, cut:

- 1 (9½"-wide) strip. From strip, cut 3 (9½") squares. Cut squares in half diagonally in both directions to make 12 quarter-square G triangles.
- 1 (9⅛"-wide) strip. From strip, cut 2 (9⅛") squares. Cut squares in half diagonally to make 4 half-square H triangles.

From green floral print, cut:

- 1 (9½"-wide) strip. From strip, cut 2 (9½") squares. Cut squares in half diagonally in both directions to make 8 quarter-square G triangles.

From dark green print, cut:

- 1 (9½") square. Cut square in half diagonally in both directions to make 4 quarter-square G triangles.
- 1 (4¾"-wide) strip. From strip, cut 4 (4¾") corner squares.

From light green print, cut:

- 1 (9½") square. Cut square in half diagonally in both directions to make 4 quarter-square G triangles.

Center Assembly

1. Join 1 orange print A triangle and 1 red floral A triangle to make 1 A triangle-square *(Triangle-Square Diagrams)*. Make 24 A triangle-squares.

Triangle-Square Diagrams

2. Referring to *Corner Unit Assembly Diagram*, lay out 6 A triangle-squares, 2 red floral A triangles, 1 orange print D square, and 1 yellow print E square as shown. Join to complete 1 Corner Unit *(Corner Unit Diagram)*. Make 4 Corner Units.

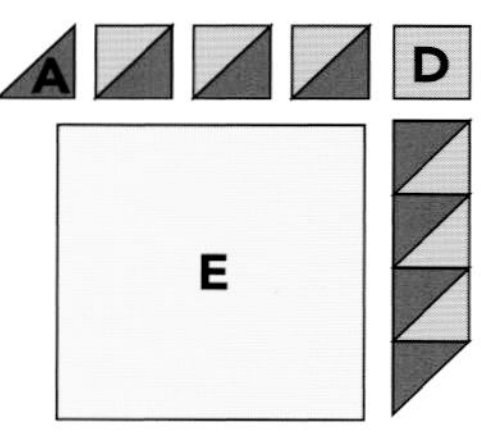

Corner Unit Assembly Diagram

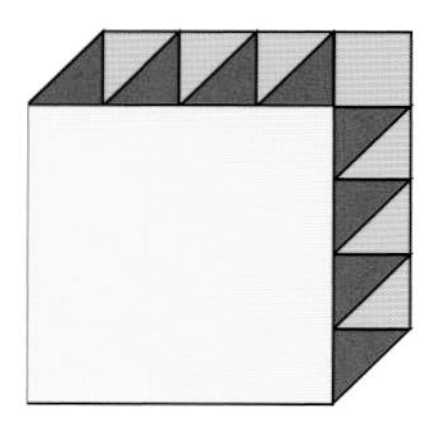

Corner Unit Diagram

3. Join 1 orange print B triangle and 1 red floral B triangle to make 1 B triangle-square. Make 32 B triangle-squares.
4. Referring to *Left Side Unit Assembly Diagram*, lay out 4 B triangle-squares, 1 red floral B triangle, 1 orange print B triangle, and 1 red print C triangle as shown. Join to make 1 Left Side Unit *(Left Side Unit Diagram)*. Make 4 Left Side Units.

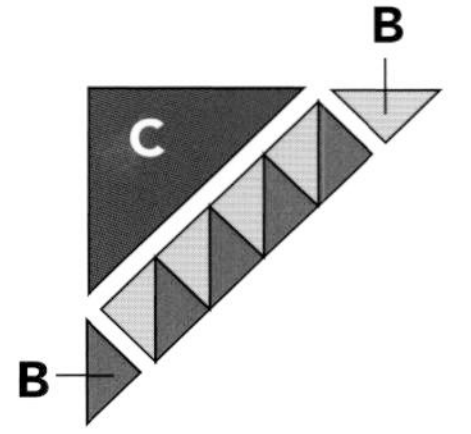

Left Side Unit Assembly Diagram

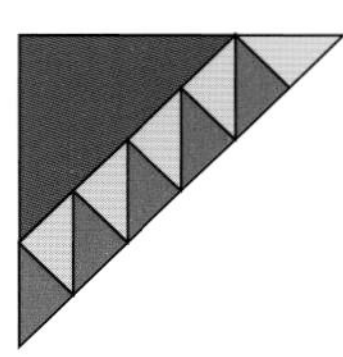
Left Side Unit Diagram

5. Referring to *Right Side Unit Assembly Diagram*, lay out 4 B triangle-squares, 1 red floral B triangle, and 1 red print C triangle as shown. Join to make 1 Right Side Unit *(Right Side Unit Diagram)*. Make 4 Right Side Units.

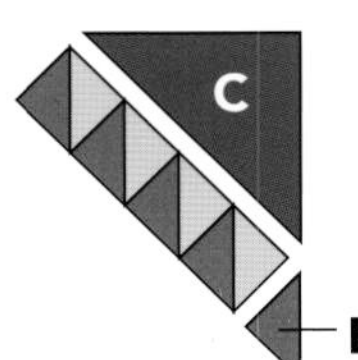

Right Side Unit Assembly Diagram

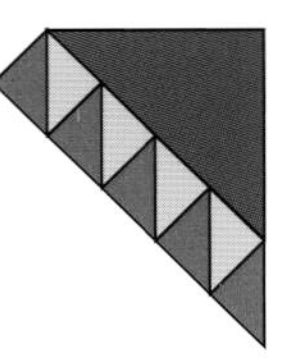
Right Side Unit Diagram

6. Referring to *Side Unit Assembly Diagram*, join 1 Right Side Unit to yellow print F triangle with a partial seam, stopping at edge of last triangle-square. Join Left Side Unit to remaining short side of F triangle with a partial seam, stopping at edge of last triangle-square *(Side Unit Diagram)*. Make 4 Side Units.

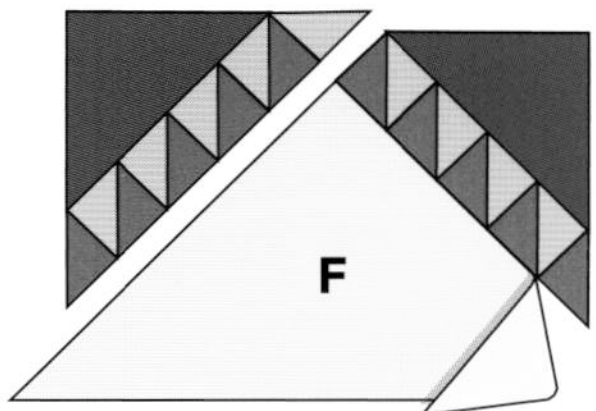

Side Unit Assembly Diagram

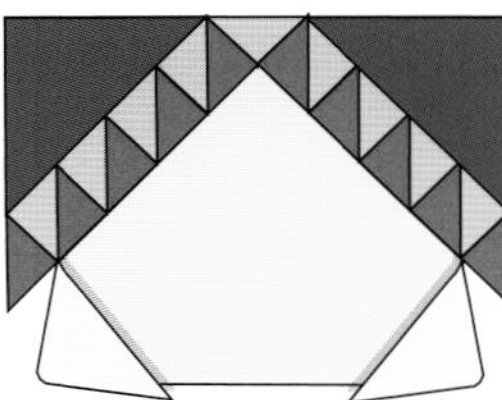
Side Unit Diagram

7. Referring to *Quilt Top Assembly Diagram*, lay out black floral center square, Side Units, and Corner Units as shown. Join Side Units to sides of center square to make center section. Join Corner Units to remaining Side Units with partial seams to make top and bottom sections. Join top and bottom sections to center section with partial seams.
8. Finish sewing partial seams to complete quilt center.

Quilt Assembly

1. Referring to *Quilt Top Assembly Diagram* on page 66, join 2 green floral G triangles, 1 light green print G triangle, 1 dark green print G triangle, and 3 yellow/red G triangles to make 1 pieced inner border. Make 4 pieced inner borders.
2. Add pieced inner borders to quilt center. Add yellow/red H triangles to corners of quilt.
3. Add black floral outer borders to sides of quilt. Add dark green print corner squares to ends of remaining 2 outer borders. Add borders to top and bottom of quilt.

Finishing

1. Divide backing fabric into 2 (1⅝-yard) lengths. Cut 1 piece in half lengthwise to make 2 narrow panels. Join 1 narrow panel to wider panel. Remaining panel is extra and can be used to make a hanging sleeve.
2. Layer backing, batting, and quilt top; baste. Quilt as desired. Quilt shown was quilted with allover designs *(Quilting Diagram)*.
3. Join 2¼"-wide red print strips into 1 continuous piece for straight-grain French-fold binding. Add binding to quilt.

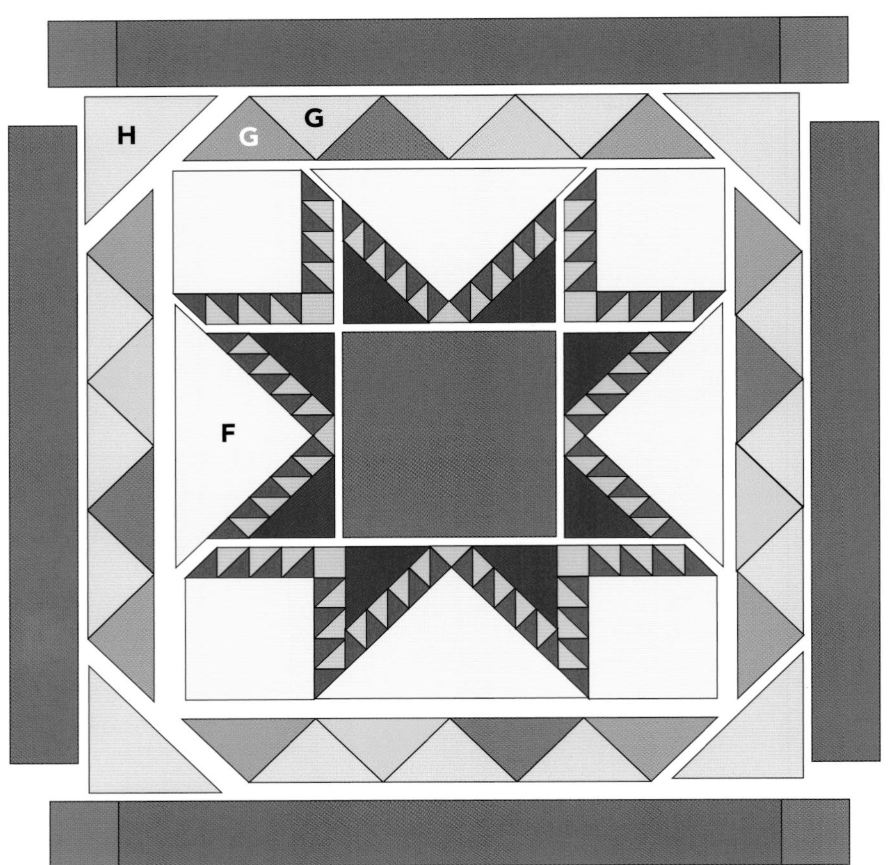

Quilt Top Assembly Diagram

Quilting Diagram

DESIGNER

Julie Lynch holds degrees in Art and Education, and has dabbled in most art media. When she began working at The Quilting Bee in Spokane, Washington, she became hopelessly hooked on the colors, textures, and designs of the quilts and fabrics. Julie says, "From the looks of my stash, I'll be exploring new challenges for a long, long time." ✻

European FEATHERED STAR

Designer Bev Getschel used fabrics with subtle value variations to create this dynamic quilt. Use the large background areas to show off your best quilting.

PROJECT RATING: INTERMEDIATE

Size: 54" × 60"

Blocks: 38 (6") Variable Star blocks

MATERIALS

NOTE: Fabrics in the quilt shown are from the European Taupe IV collection by Kinkame for Clothworks.

1⅝ yards rose print for center background

½ yard teal print for center border

1¼ yards light teal print for center star and blocks

1⅜ yards teal plaid for inner border and binding

¼ yard beige print for center star

1¼ yards light beige print for blocks

¾ yard taupe print for center star

½ yard brown print for blocks

3½ yards backing fabric

Twin-size quilt batting

Cutting

Measurements include ¼" seam allowances.

NOTE: Refer to *Diamond Cutting Diagrams* on page 70 to cut diamonds. Cut left end of each strip at 45° angle. From strips cut small diamonds by placing 2⅛" line on ruler along angled cut edge. Cut large diamonds by placing 5⅛" line on ruler along angled cut edge.

From rose print, cut:

- 1 (13⅝"-wide) strip. From strip, cut 1 (13⅝") square. Cut square in half diagonally in both directions to make 4 quarter-square I triangles.
- 2 (3⅞"-wide) strips. From strips, cut 12 (3⅞") squares. Cut squares in half diagonally to make 24 half-square E triangles.
- 4 (3½"-wide) strips. From strips, cut 2 (3½" × 36½") top and bottom inner borders and 2 (3½" × 30½") side inner borders.
- 2 (3¼"-wide) strips. From strips, cut 4 (3¼" × 9¼") G rectangles and 4 (3¼" × 6½") F rectangles.
- 2 (2½"-wide) strips. From strips, cut 32 (2½") squares. Cut squares in half diagonally to make 64 half-square H triangles.
- 3 (2"-wide) strips. From strips, cut 16 (2" × 3½") C rectangles and 16 (2") B squares.

From teal print, cut:

- 2 (3⅞"-wide) strips. From strips, cut 12 (3⅞") squares. Cut squares in half diagonally to make 24 half-square E triangles.
- 2 (2"-wide) strips. From strips, cut 32 (2") B squares.

From light teal print, cut:

- 2 (2½"-wide) strips. From strips, cut 32 (2½") squares. Cut squares in half diagonally to make 64 half-square H triangles.
- 1 (2⅛"-wide) strip. From strip, cut 8 small diamonds.
- 14 (2"-wide) strips. From strips, cut 272 (2") B squares.

From teal plaid, cut:

- 5 (3½"-wide) strips. Piece strips to make 4 (3½" × 42½") middle borders.
- 240" of 2¼"-wide bias strips. Join strips to make bias binding.

From beige print, cut:

- 1 (5⅛"-wide) strip. From strip, cut 4 large diamonds.

From light beige print, cut:

- 5 (2⅜"-wide) strips. From strips, cut 68 (2⅜") squares. Cut squares in half diagonally to make 136 half-square D triangles.

- 13 (2"-wide) strips. From strips, cut 136 (2" × 3½") C rectangles.

From taupe print, cut:

- 1 (5⅛"-wide) strip. From strip, cut 4 large diamonds.
- 4 (3½"-wide) strips. From strips, cut 38 (3½") A squares.

From brown print, cut:

- 5 (2⅜"-wide) strips. From strips, cut 68 (2⅜") squares. Cut squares in half diagonally to make 136 half-square D triangles.

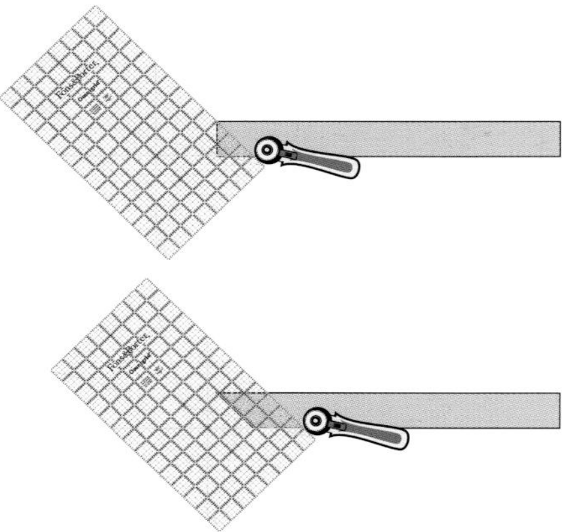

Diamond Cutting Diagrams

Variable Star Block Assembly

1. Join 1 brown print D triangle and 1 light beige print D triangle as shown in *Triangle-Square Diagrams.* Make 136 brown triangle-squares.

Triangle-Square Diagrams

2. Referring to *Star Point Unit Diagrams*, place 1 light teal print B square atop 1 light beige print C rectangle, right sides facing. Stitch diagonally from corner to corner as shown. Trim ¼" beyond stitching. Press open to reveal triangle. Repeat for opposite end of rectangle to complete 1 Star Point Unit. Make 136 beige Star Point Units.

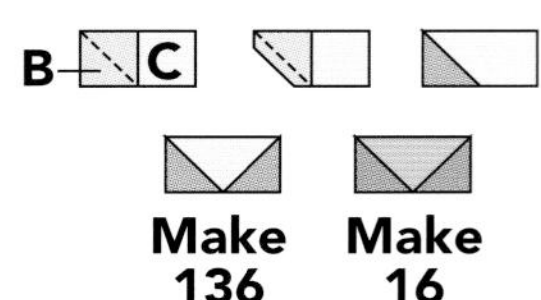

Star point Unit Diagrams

3. In the same manner, make 16 rose Star Point Units using 2 teal print B squares and 1 rose print C rectangle in each.
4. Lay out 4 beige Star Point Units, 4 brown triangle-squares, and 1 taupe print A square as shown in *Variable Star Block Assembly Diagram.* Join into rows; join rows to complete 1 Variable Star block *(Variable Star Block Diagrams).* Make 34 Variable Star blocks.

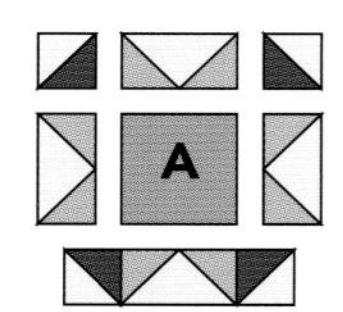

Variable Star Block Assembly Diagram

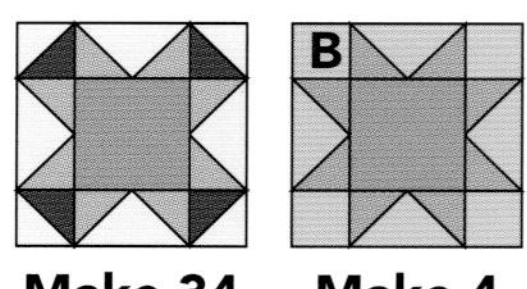

Variable Star Block Diagrams

5. In the same manner, make 4 rose Variable Star blocks using 4 rose Star Point Units, 4 rose print B squares, and 1 taupe print A square in each.

Center Assembly

1. Join 1 light teal print H triangle and 1 rose print H triangle as shown in *Triangle-Square Diagrams.* Make 48 teal small triangle-squares.

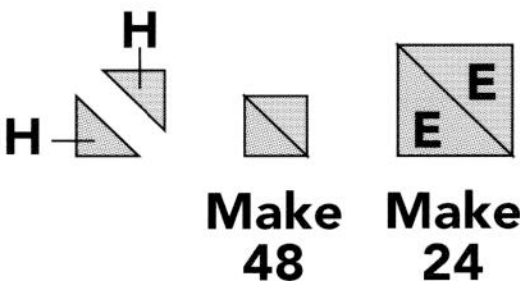

Triangle-Square Diagrams

2. In the same manner, make 24 large triangle-squares using teal print and rose print E triangles.
3. Referring to *Feather Unit 1 Diagrams,* join 3 small triangle-squares, 1 light teal print H triangle, and 1 rose print H triangle as shown to complete 1 Feather Unit 1. Make 8 Feather Unit 1.

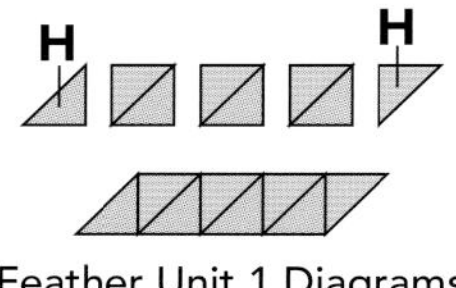

Feather Unit 1 Diagrams

4. In a similar manner, make 8 Feather Unit 2 using 3 small triangle-squares, 1 light teal print H triangle, 1 rose print H triangle, and 1 light teal small diamond in each *(Feather Unit 2 Diagrams).*

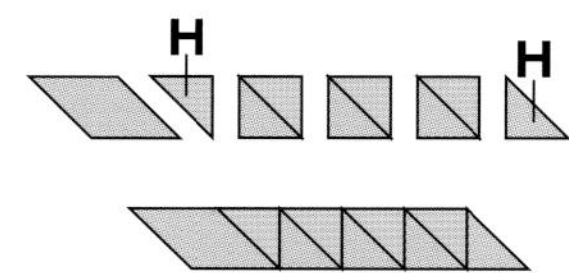

Feather Unit 2 Diagrams

5. Join 1 rose Variable Star block, 1 rose print F rectangle, and 1 rose print G rectangle as shown in *Corner Unit Diagrams.* Make 4 Corner Units.

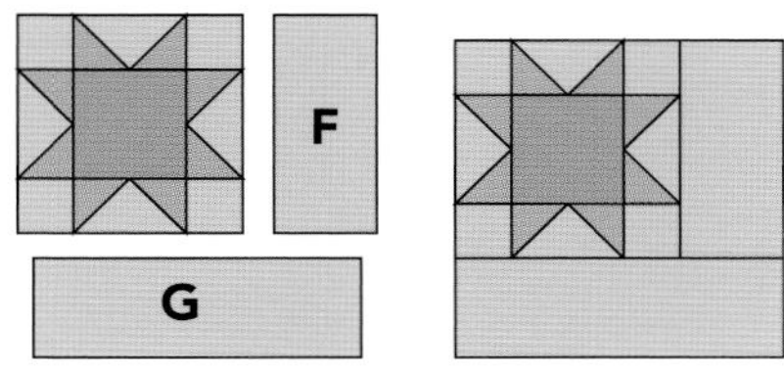

Corner Unit Diagrams

6. Join 1 beige print large diamond, 1 Feather Unit 1, and 1 Feather Unit 2 as shown in *Feathered Star Unit Diagrams*. Make 4 Feathered Star Units with beige print diamonds and 4 Feathered Star Units with taupe print diamonds.

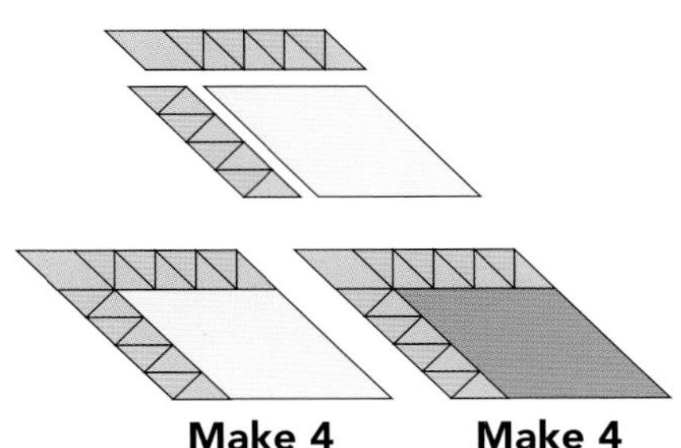

Feathered Star Unit Diagrams

7. Lay out Feathered Star Units, Corner Units, and rose print I triangles as shown in *Center Diagrams*. Join into sections, join sections to complete quilt center.

NOTE: See *Sew Easy: Set-in Seams* on page 73.

Border Assembly

1. Referring to *Quilt Top Assembly Diagram* on page 72, join 12 large triangle-squares and 1 rose print top inner border as shown to make pieced top inner border. Repeat for pieced bottom inner border.

2. Join 8 beige Variable Star blocks to make 1 pieced side outer border. Make 2 pieced side outer borders.

3. In the same manner, make pieced top outer border using 9 beige Variable Star blocks. Repeat for pieced bottom outer border.

Quilt Assembly

1. Add rose print side inner borders to quilt center. Add pieced top and bottom inner borders to quilt.

2. Repeat for teal plaid middle borders and pieced outer borders.

Finishing

1. Divide backing into 2 (1¾-yard) lengths. Join panels lengthwise. Seam will run horizontally.

2. Layer backing, batting, and quilt top; baste. Quilt as desired. Quilt shown was quilted with feather designs *(Quilting Diagram)*.

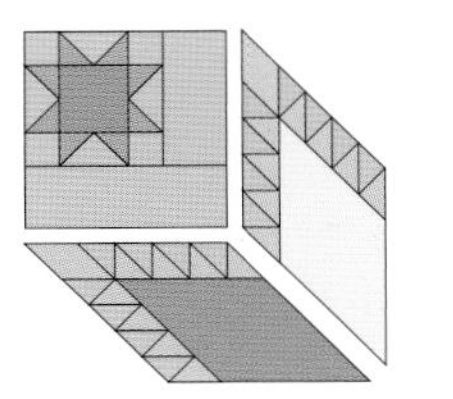
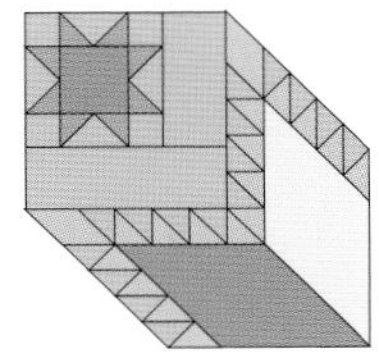
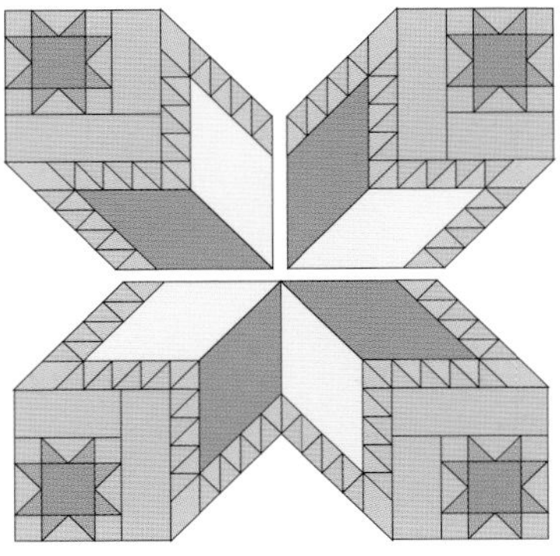
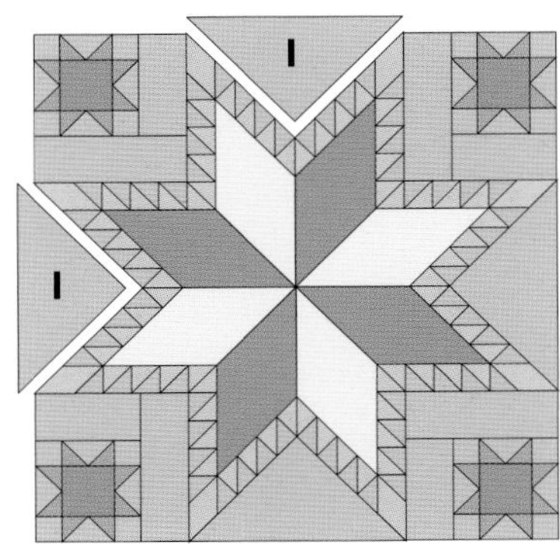

Center Diagrams

Quilt Top Assembly Diagram

Quilting Diagram

Sew *Easy*™ Set-In Seams

Use these tips and techniques for set-in seams as you stitch *European Feathered Star* on page 68 and *Star of Bethlehem* on page 46.

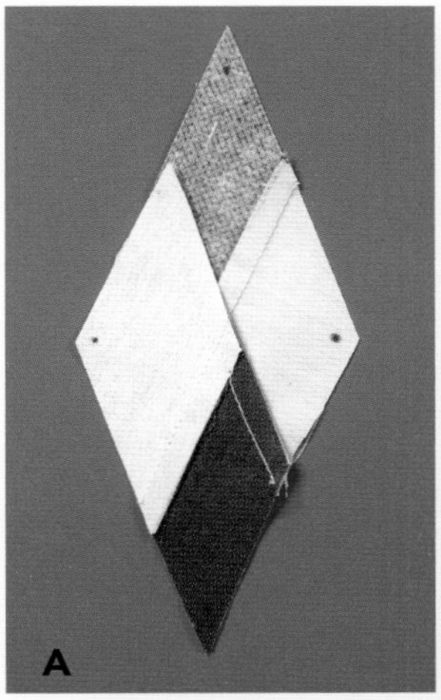

A

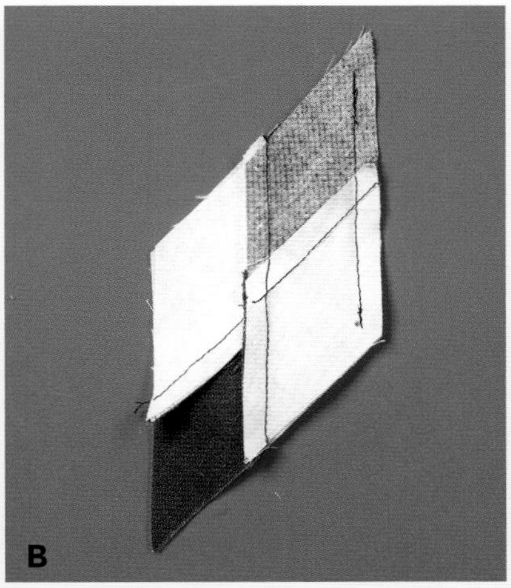

B

C

D

E

F

1. Mark a dot on wrong side of each pieced diamond, corner square, and side triangle at intersection of ¼" seam allowances as shown in *Photo A*. **2.** Join 2 pieced diamonds, stitching from center point to dot; backstitch at dot *(Photo B)*. **3.** Pin triangle to diamond unit, aligning outer points. Stitch from outer edge to dot; backstitch *(Photo C)*. **4.** Stitch triangle to adjoining diamond unit to make a side unit *(Photo D)*. **5.** Join side units *(Photo E)*. **6.** Set in squares in the same manner as triangles to complete Star block *(Photo F)*.

Sew *Easy*™ Quick Triangle-Squares

Use this technique to make the triangle-squares for *Nancy's Fancy* on page 26. The Fons & Porter Quarter Inch Seam Marker offers a neat way to mark accurate sewing lines for this method.

1. From each of 2 fabrics, cut 1 square ⅞" larger than the desired finished size of the triangle-square. For example, to make a triangle-square that will finish 2" as in the *Nancy's Fancy*, cut 2⅞" squares.
2. On wrong side of lighter square, place the Quarter Inch Seam Marker diagonally across the square, with the yellow center line positioned exactly at opposite corners. Mark stitching lines along both sides of the Quarter Inch Seam Marker *(Photo A).*
3. Place light square atop darker square, right sides facing; stitch along both marked sewing lines.
4. Cut between rows of stitching to make 2 triangle-squares *(Photo B).*

DESIGNER

Bev Getschel fell in love with quilting in 2003, after having sewn all her life. She is the winner of several awards, and is regularly published in quilting magazines. ※

Little Wren

Little Wren is a smaller version of Kathy and Geri's award-winning quilt, Feathered Friends. Instead of binding, the quilt is finished with a unique scalloped border.

PROJECT RATING: CHALLENGING

Size: 45½" × 45½"

Blocks: 1 (22⅝") large Feathered Star and 4 (8") small Feathered Star

MATERIALS

⅜ yard light purple print
1½ yards medium purple print
1 yard dark purple print
1 fat quarter* lavender print
1¼ yards white solid
⅝ yard light green print
½ yard dark green print
Green, lavender, and brown print scraps for appliqué
Paper-backed fusible web
Fabric paint, colored pencils (optional)
Paper for foundation piecing
Lightweight interfacing
2¾ yards backing fabric
Crib-size quilt batting
*fat quarter = 18" × 20"

Cutting

Measurements include ¼" seam allowances. Border strips are exact length needed. You may want to make them longer to allow for piecing variations. Patterns for appliqué shapes, foundations, and scallops are on pages 82–83. See page 135 for instructions on paper foundation piecing. **NOTE**: Pieces for foundation piecing are cut over-size. Follow manufacturer's instructions if using fusible web.

From light purple print, cut:

- 2 (2⅜"-wide) strips. From strips, cut 20 (2⅜") squares. Cut squares in half diagonally to make 40 half-square A triangles.
- 16 I.

From medium purple print, cut:

- 2 (11¼"-wide) strips. From strips, cut 4 (11¼") squares. Cut squares in half diagonally to make 8 half-square H triangles.
- 4 (2¼"-wide) strips. From strips, cut 2 (2¼" × 40½") top and bottom outer borders and 2 (2¼" × 37") side outer borders.
- 1 (4½"-wide) strip. From strip, cut 4 (4½") squares. Cut squares in half diagonally in both directions to make 16 quarter-square K triangles.
- 2 (2⅞"-wide) strips. From strips, cut 16 (2⅞") J squares.

From dark purple print, cut:

- 4 (1⅛"-wide) strips. From strips, cut 2 (1⅜" × 26⅛") center top and bottom border #2 and 2 (1⅜" × 24⅜") center side border #2.
- 8 (1⅛"-wide) strips. From strips, cut 4 (1⅛" × 42") facing strips.
- 8 D.
- 8 E.
- 72 Small Scallops.

From lavender print fat quarter, cut:

- 1 B.

From white solid, cut:

- 1 (2¾"-wide) strip. From strip, cut 4 (2¾") squares. Cut squares in half diagonally to make 8 half-square C triangles.
- 2 (2⅜"-wide) strips. From strips, cut 28 (2⅜") squares. Cut squares in half diagonally to make 56 half-square A triangles.
- 16 I.
- 5 (1½"-wide) strips. From strips, cut 112 (1½") squares. Cut squares in half diagonally to make 224 half-square triangles for foundation piecing.
- 80 Large Scallops.

From light green print, cut:

- 1 (10⅝"-wide) strip. From strip, cut 1 (10⅝") square. Cut square in half diagonally in both directions to make 4 quarter-square F triangles.
- 1 (7⅛"-wide) strips. From strips, cut 4 (7⅛") G squares.

From dark green print, cut:

- 2 (2"-wide) strips. From strips, cut 32 (2") squares for foundation piecing (diamond shape).
- 4 (1½"-wide) strips. From strips, cut 80 (1½") squares. Cut squares in half diagonally to make 160 half-square triangles for foundation piecing (triangle shape).
- 4 (1⅛"-wide) strips. From strips, cut 2 (1⅛" × 24⅜") center top and bottom border #1 and 2 (1⅛" × 23⅛") center side border #1.

From lavender scraps, cut:

- 1 Body.
- 1 Head.
- 1 Small Wing.

From brown scraps, cut:

- 1 Large Wing.
- 1 Tail.
- 1 Beak.
- 1 Eye.
- 1 Leg.

From interfacing, cut:

- 40 Large Scallops.
- 36 Small Scallops.

Large Feathered Star Assembly

1. Join 1 white A triangle and 1 light purple A triangle as shown in *Triangle-Square Diagrams.* Make 40 triangle-squares.

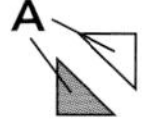

Triangle-Square Diagrams

2. Lay out 1 light green print G square, 2 dark purple print E diamonds, 2 white A triangles, and 5 triangle-squares as shown in *Corner Unit Diagrams.* Join into sections; join sections to complete 1 Corner Unit. Make 4 Corner Units.

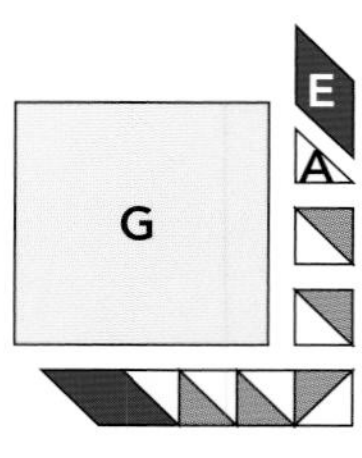

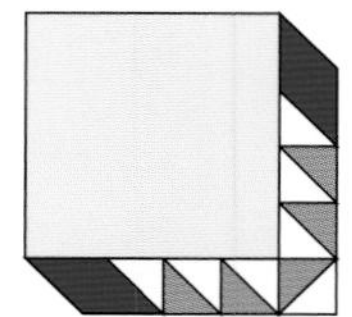

Corner Unit Diagrams

3. Join out 2 dark purple print D shapes, 1 white C triangle, 2 white A triangles, and 5 triangle-squares as shown in *Side Unit Diagrams.* Add 1 light green print F triangle, using partial seams to complete 1 Side Unit. Make 4 Side Units.

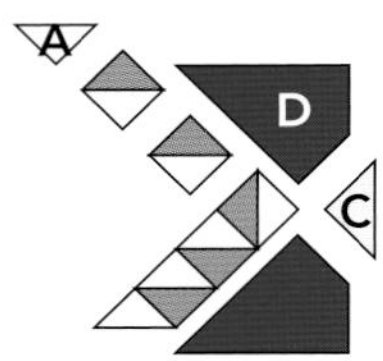

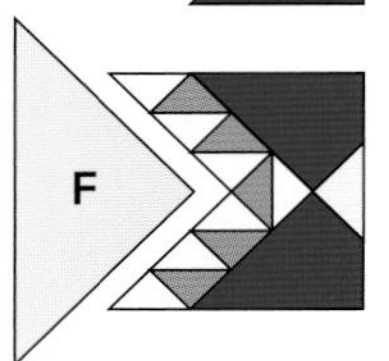

Partial Seam

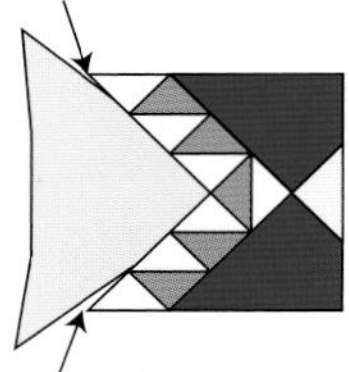

Partial Seam

Side Unit Diagrams

4. Add 4 white C triangles to lavender print B octagon as shown in *Center Unit Diagrams.*

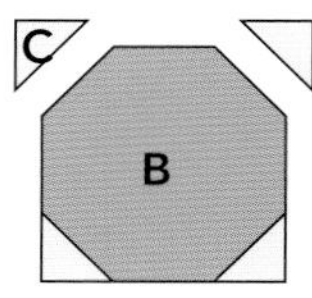

Center Unit Diagrams

5. Position appliqué pieces atop Center Unit; appliqué in place. **NOTE**: Kathy used fabric paint and pencils to make bird eye and beak. She applied printed leaves and flowers broderie perse style.

6. Lay out Center Unit, Side Units, and Corner Units as shown in *Feathered Star Assembly Diagram.* Join into rows; join rows. Complete partial seams to complete Feathered Star *(Feathered Star Diagram).*

Feathered Star Assembly Diagram

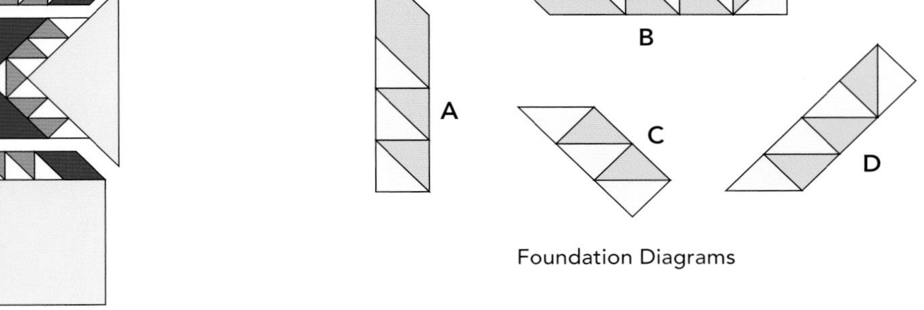

Foundation Diagrams

Feathered Star Diagram

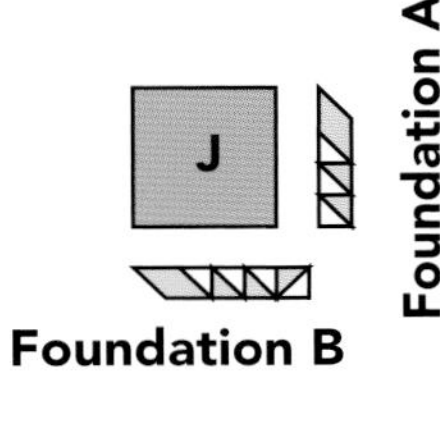

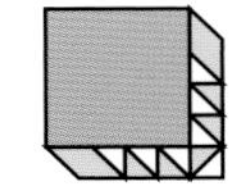

Corner Unit Diagrams

Small Feathered Star Block Assembly

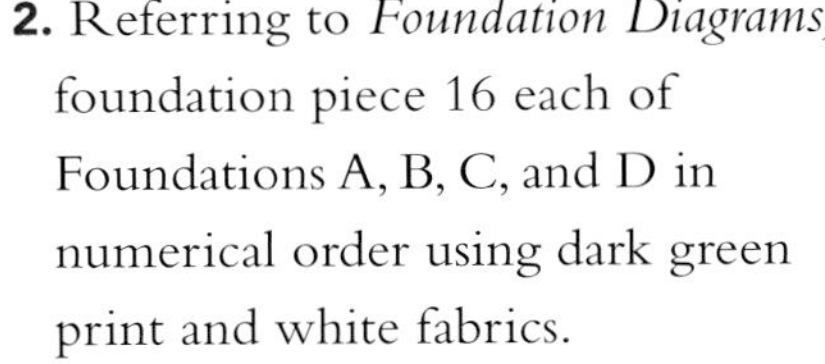

1. Trace or photocopy 16 each of Foundation A, B, C, and D.

2. Referring to *Foundation Diagrams,* foundation piece 16 each of Foundations A, B, C, and D in numerical order using dark green print and white fabrics.

3. Join 1 medium purple print J square, 1 Foundation A, and 1 Foundation B as shown in *Corner Unit Diagrams.* Make 16 corner Units.

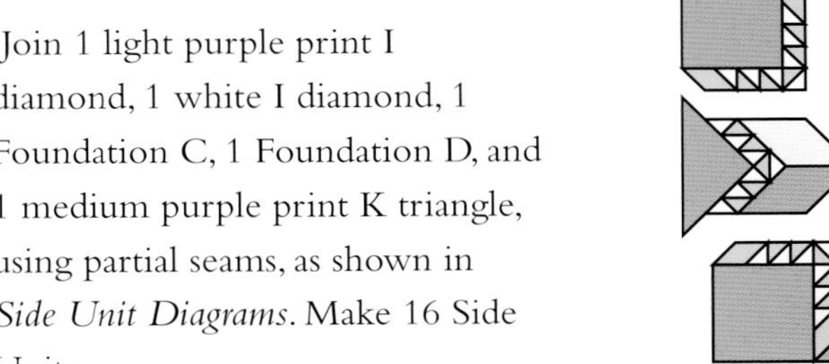

4. Join 1 light purple print I diamond, 1 white I diamond, 1 Foundation C, 1 Foundation D, and 1 medium purple print K triangle, using partial seams, as shown in *Side Unit Diagrams.* Make 16 Side Units.

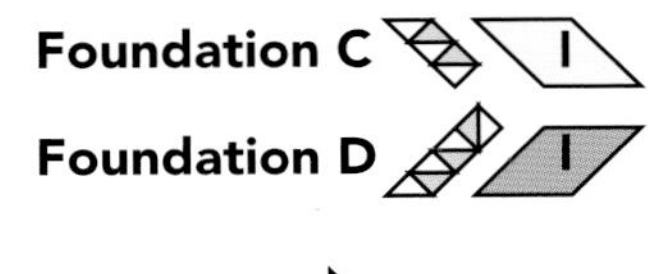

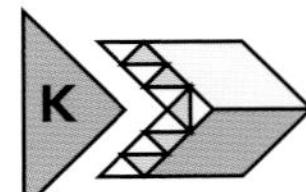

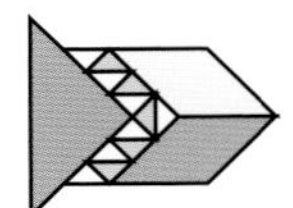

Side Unit Diagrams

5. Lay out 4 Side Units and 4 Corner Units as shown in *Small Feathered Star Assembly Diagram.* Join units; complete partial seams to complete 1 small Feathered Star block *(Small Feathered Star Diagram).* Make 4 Small Feathered Star Blocks.

Small Feathered Star Assembly Diagram

Small Feathered Star Diagram

Scallop Border Assembly

1. Layer 2 large white scallops, right sides facing, and 1 large interfacing scallop. Stitch along curved edge, using ¼" seam allowance as shown in *Scallop Diagrams*. Clip curves; turn right side out; press. Make 40 large scallops.

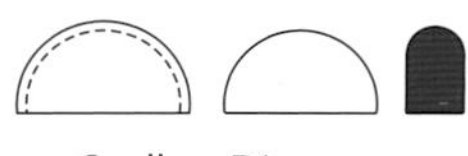

Scallop Diagrams

2. In the same manner, make 36 small dark purple scallops using 2 small dark purple scallops and 1 small interfacing scallop in each.

3. Add decorative machine stitching to curved edge of each white scallop using contrasting thread, if desired.

Quilt Top Assembly Diagram

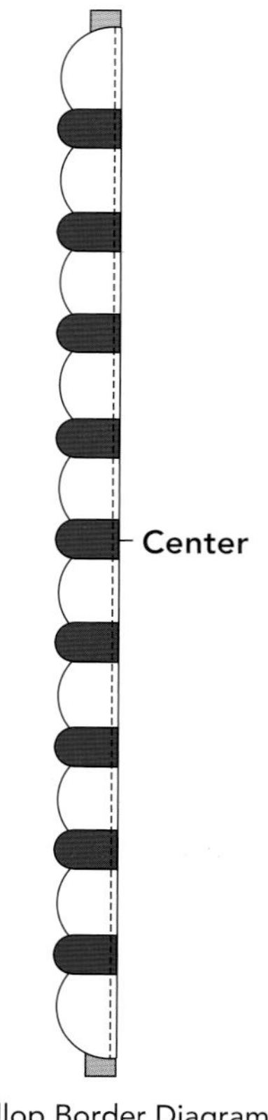

Scallop Border Diagram

4. Mark center of each facing strip. Pin 10 large white scallops and 9 small dark purple scallops, right sides facing, to one long edge of 1 facing strip, using center mark as a guide for placement as shown in *Scallop Border Diagram*. Stitch scallops to facing strip. Press seam allowance toward facing strip. Make 4 Scallop borders.

Quilt Assembly

1. Referring to *Quilt Top Assembly Diagram*, add dark green print side border #1 to Large Feathered Star. Add dark green print top and bottom border #1. Repeat for dark purple print center border #2.

2. Add 2 medium purple print H triangles to 1 Small Feathered Star Block as shown to complete 1 Corner Unit. Make 4 Corner Units.

3. Add Corner Units to bordered Feathered Star as shown.

4. Add medium purple print side outer borders to quilt center. Add medium purple print top and bottom outer borders to quilt.

Finishing

1. Divide backing into 2 (1⅜-yard) lengths. Cut 1 piece in half lengthwise to make 2 narrow panels. Join 1 narrow panel to wider panel. Remaining panel is extra and can be used to make a hanging sleeve.

2. Layer backing, batting, and quilt top; baste. Quilt as desired. Quilt shown was quilted in the ditch, with hummingbird designs in the large feathered star corners, and with feather designs in the purple background areas *(Quilting Diagram)*.

3. After quilting is complete, block and trim the quilt square.
4. Center and baste facing strips to sides of quilt on wrong side.
5. Place 1 Scallop Border atop quilt, right sides facing. Pin in place. Stitch border to quilt through all layers. Press border and back facing away from quilt. Trim ends of border and back facing even with edge of quilt.
6. Turn ¼" seam allowance on back facing strip toward wrong side; hand stitch facing to quilt, covering stitching line.
7. Sew 2 remaining borders and facing strips to top and bottom of quilt in the same manner. Trim ends of borders and back facings ¼" beyond edge of quilt. Turn ends of border and back facing, and long side of back facing toward wrong sides. Hand stitch facing to quilt.

Quilting Diagram

DESIGNER

Geri Parker and Kathy McNeil collaborate on one quilt a year. They take it layer by layer, designing from the center out. Geri does the traditional piecing and Kathy does the design and appliqué work. They love continuing the tradition of quilting with a dear friend. It is a crazy adventure every time. ✻

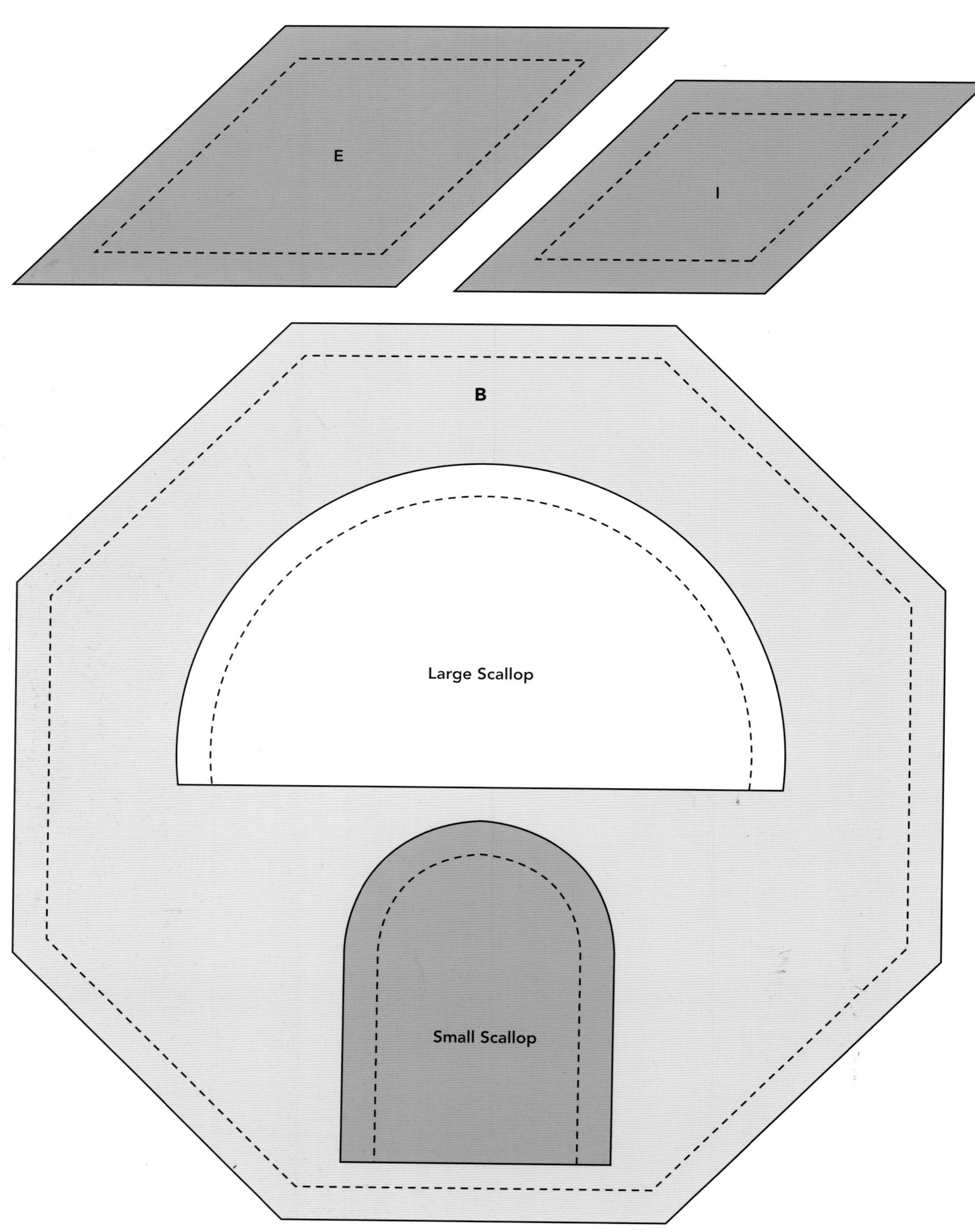
E
I
B
Large Scallop
Small Scallop

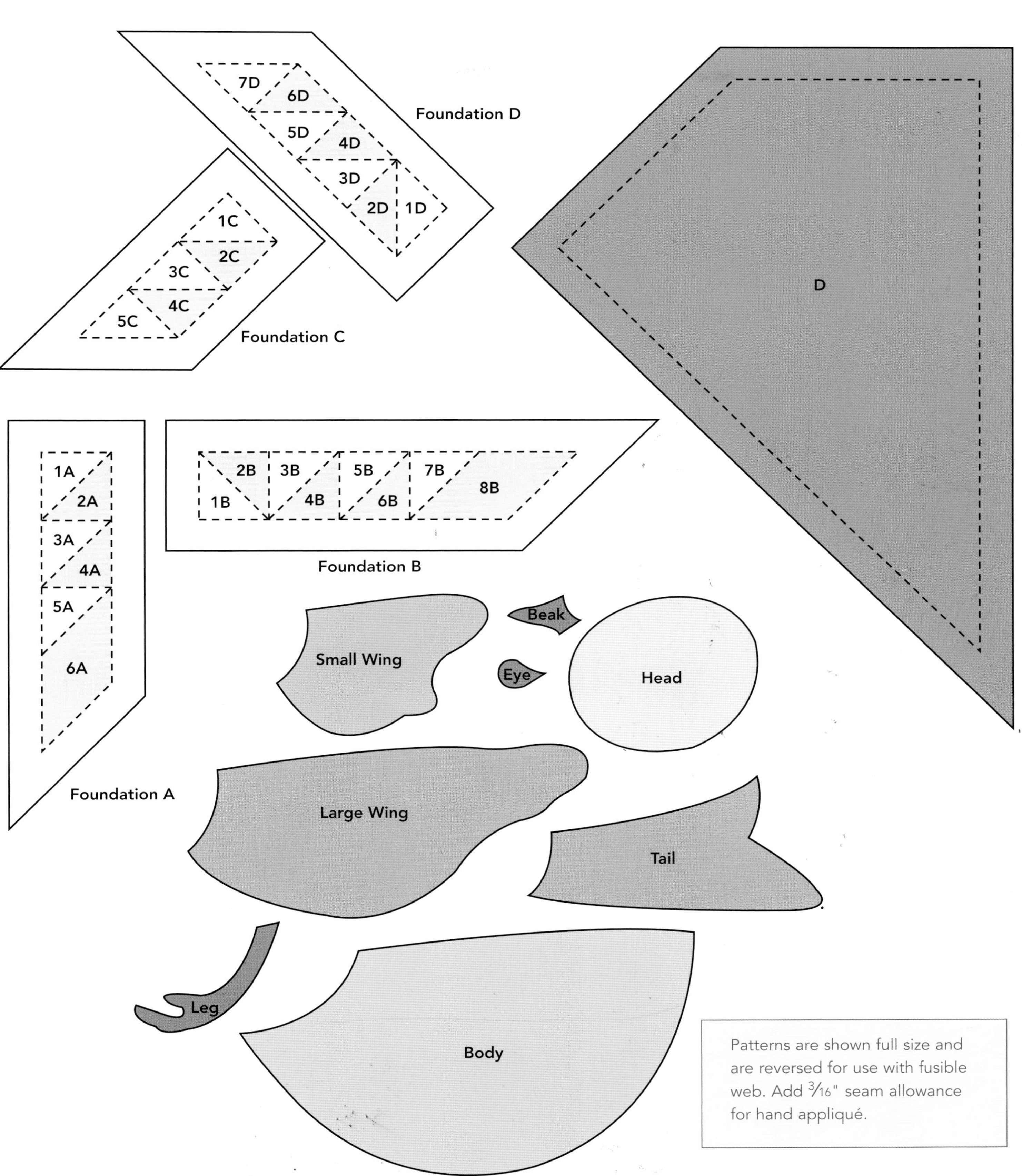

Patterns are shown full size and are reversed for use with fusible web. Add 3⁄16" seam allowance for hand appliqué.

Conestoga Star

Jewel-tone triangles really pop against a soft gold background in this contemporary quilt with a traditional flavor. Marion Watchinski joined tapered rows of flying geese to form her original star pattern. She quilted it by hand using light blue thread.

PROJECT RATING: CHALLENGING

Size: 88" × 100"

Blocks: 30 (12") blocks

MATERIALS

8¼ yards gold print for background and borders

30 fat quarters★ assorted jewel-tone prints for blocks and border

Paper for foundation piecing

Tri-Recs™ tools or template plastic

¾ yard blue print for binding

7⅞ yards backing fabric

Queen-size quilt batting

★fat quarter = 18" × 20"

NOTE: Refer to *Sew Easy: Using Tri-Recs™ Tools* on page 45.

Cutting

Paper piecing pattern for star points is on page 87. Measurements include ¼" seam allowances. Border strips are exact length needed. You may want to make them longer to allow for piecing variations. **NOTE:** If you are not using Tri-Recs™ tools, make templates for the A and C triangles from patterns on page 88.

From each fat quarter, cut:

- 1 (3⅞"-wide) strip. From strip, cut 2 (3⅞") squares. Cut squares in half diagonally to make 4 half-square B triangles. (You will have a few extra.)
- 1 (2⅞"-wide) strip. From strip, cut 3 (2⅞") squares. Cut squares in half diagonally to make 6 half-square E triangles. (You will have a few extra.)

From gold print, cut:

- 18 (6½"-wide) strips. From strips, cut 142 A triangles and 26 pairs of C triangles. (Fold the strip in half with right sides together so you will be cutting two mirror image pieces at one time.) If you are using Tri-Recs™ tools, cut around outside of triangles to cut A and C pieces.
- 5 (3⅞"-wide) strips. From strips, cut 42 (3⅞") squares. Cut squares in half diagonally to make 84 half-square B triangles.
- 7 (2⅞"-wide) strips. From strips, cut 86 (2⅞") squares. Cut squares in half diagonally to make 172 half-square E triangles.
- 29 (2½"-wide) strips. Piece strips to make 2 (2½" × 76½") top and bottom inner borders, 2 (2½" × 84½") side inner borders, 2 (2½" × 88½") top and bottom outer borders, and 2 (2½" × 96½") side outer borders. From remaining strips, cut 172 (2½") D squares.

From dark blue print, cut:

- 10 (2¼"-wide) strips for binding.

Block Assembly

1. Trace Star Point Unit paper piecing pattern on page 87. Referring to *Sew Easy: Paper Foundation Piecing* on page 135, paper piece unit in numerical order. Pieces #2, #5, and #8 are gold and remaining pieces are assorted jewel tones. Make 168 Star Point Units.
2. Referring to *Block Assembly Diagram* on page 86, lay out 4 Star Point Units, 4 tan A triangles, 2 gold B triangles, and 2 jewel-tone B triangles. Join pieces as shown to make 1 block *(Block Diagram)*. Make 30 blocks.

ABOUT FACE

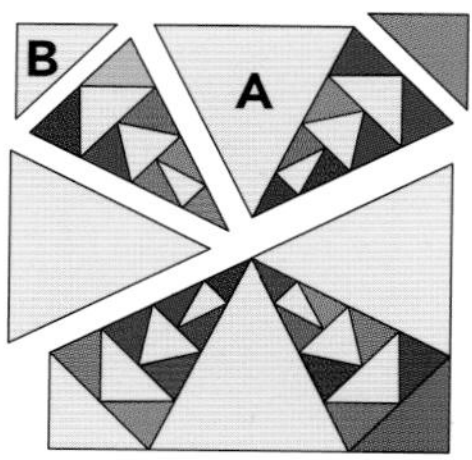

Block Assembly Diagram

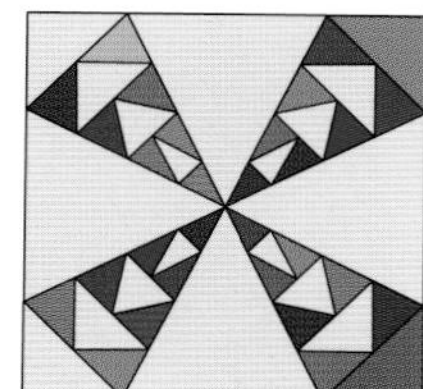
Block Diagram

Unit Assembly

1. Referring to *Unit 1 Diagram,* lay out 2 Star Point Units, 1 gold A triangle, 1 gold B triangle, 1 pair of gold C triangles, and one jewel-tone B triangle. Join to complete Unit 1. Make 10 Unit 1.

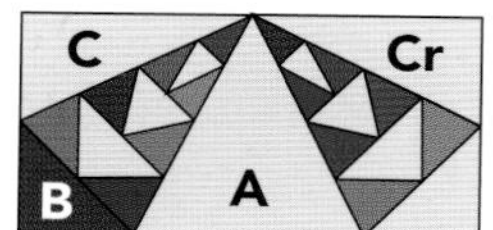

Unit 1 Diagram

Quilt Top Assembly Diagram

Unit 2 Diagram

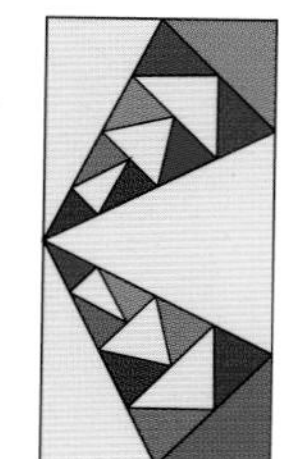
Unit 3 Diagram

Unit 4 Diagram

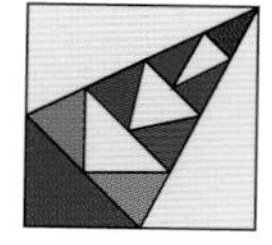
Unit 5 Diagram

2. In a similar manner, join pieces as shown to make 6 Unit 2, 6 Unit 3, 2 Unit 4, and 2 Unit 5 *(Unit 2–Unit 5 Diagrams).*

Quilt Assembly

1. Lay out blocks and Units 1–5 as shown in *Quilt Top Assembly Diagram.* Join into horizontal rows; join rows to complete quilt center.

2. Add side inner borders to quilt center. Add top and bottom inner borders to quilt.

3. Referring to *Border Unit Diagram,* lay out 2 gold D squares, 2 gold E triangles, and 2 jewel-tone E triangles as shown. Join pieces to complete 1 Border Unit. Make 86 Border Units.

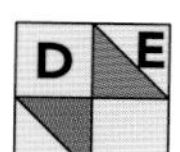

Border Unit Diagram

4. Join 22 Border Units to make 1 side border. Add to side of quilt. Repeat for other side.

5. Join 21 Border Units to make top border. Add to quilt. Repeat for bottom of quilt.
6. Add side outer borders to quilt center. Add top and bottom outer borders to quilt.

Finishing

1. Layer backing, batting, and quilt top; baste. Quilt as desired. Quilt shown is quilted in the ditch around stars, with feather motifs in the setting triangles, and diagonal lines in the borders.
2. Join 2¼"-wide blue print strips into 1 continuous piece for straight-grain French-fold binding. Add binding to quilt.

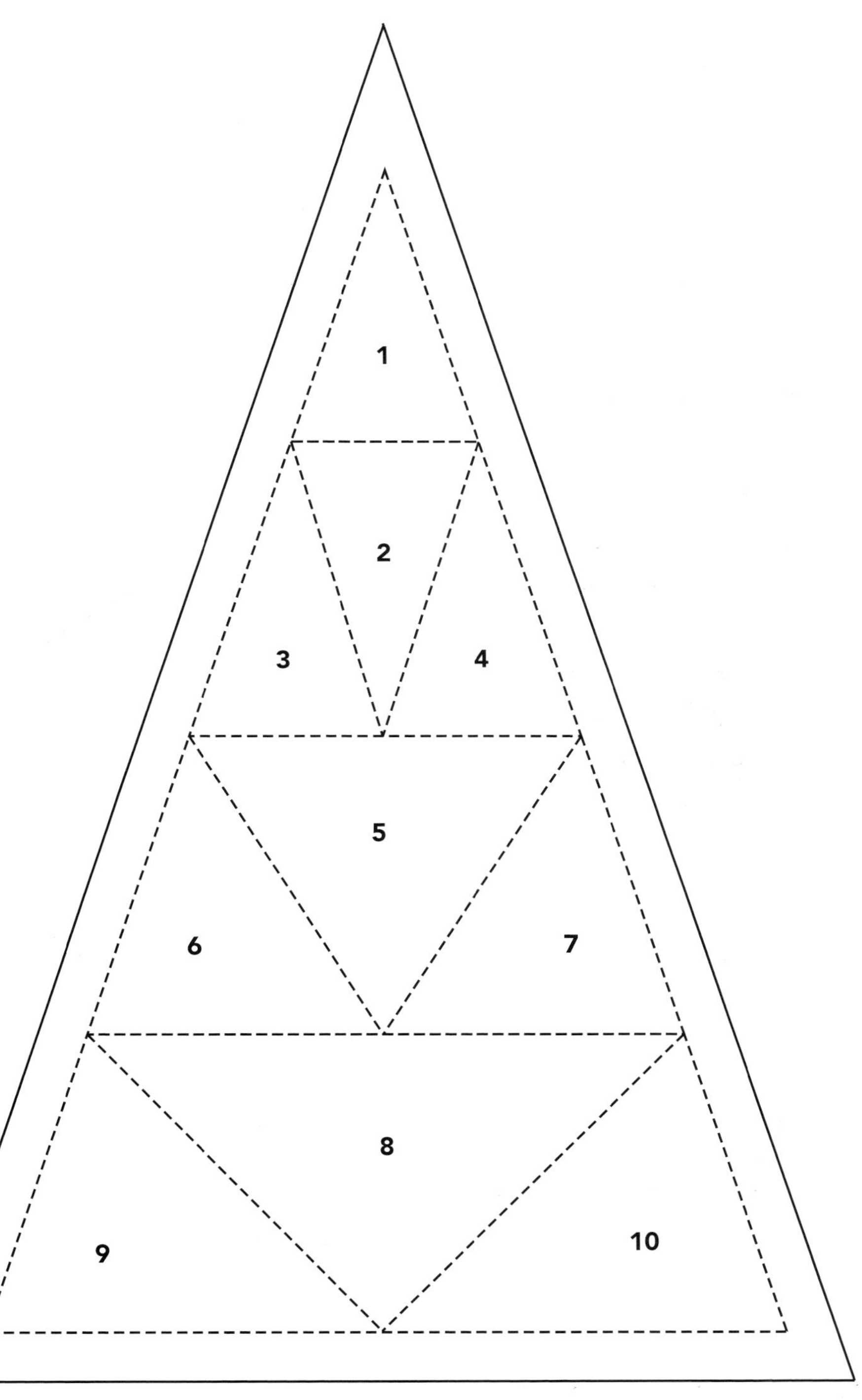

Star Point Unit Paper Piecing Pattern

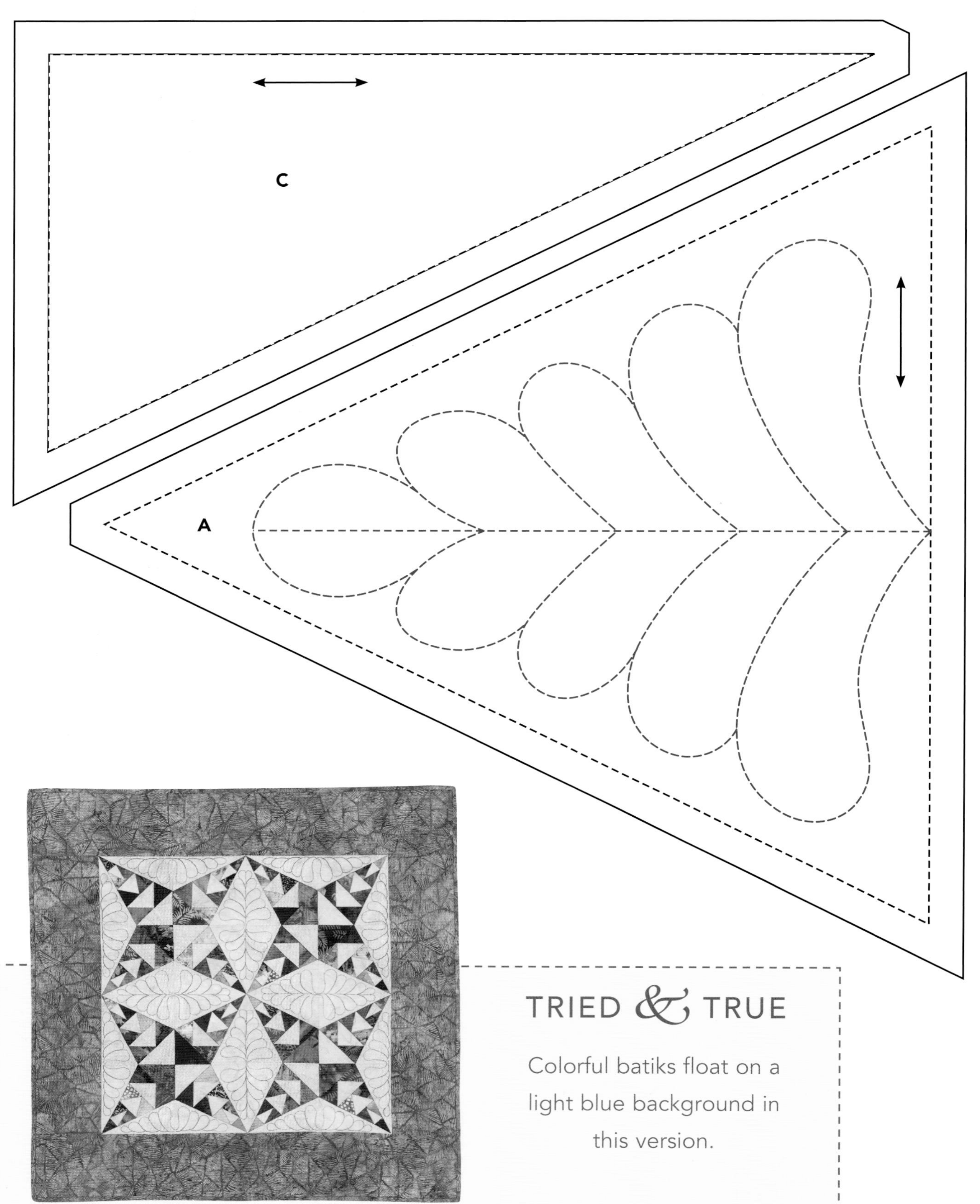

TRIED & TRUE

Colorful batiks float on a light blue background in this version.

DESIGNER

Marion Watchinski of Overland Park, Kansas, has made more than 100 quilts, from miniature to queen-size. Most of them are scrap quilts made with traditional blocks and are machine-pieced and hand-quilted. ⋇

Hunter Star

The basic block designer Mary Beth Hayes used for this quilt is a tessellation using equal parts of light and dark. The stars emerge when you put the blocks together. See Mary Beth's favorite method for making triangle-squares at www.FonsandPorter.com/thangles.

PROJECT RATING: EASY

Size: 49" × 63"

Blocks: 12 (14") Hunter Star blocks

MATERIALS

12 fat quarters★ assorted dark batiks for blocks

2⅛ yards light batik for background

1¾" Thangles™ triangle papers (optional)

½ yard dark batik for binding

3 yards backing fabric

Twin-size quilt batting

★fat quarter = 18" × 20"

Cutting

Measurements include ¼" seam allowances.

If you are using triangle papers to make the triangle-squares, cut strips 2¼" wide and do not cut into squares. Follow instructions in *Sew Easy™: Using Thangles™ Triangle Papers* at www.FonsandPorter.com/thangles.

From each fat quarter, cut:

- 2 (4"-wide) strips. From strips, cut 7 (4") A squares.
- 3 (2⅝"-wide) strips. From strips, cut 16 (2⅝") squares. Cut squares in half diagonally to make 32 half-square B triangles.

From light batik, cut:

- 8 (4"-wide) strips. From strips, cut 78 (4") A squares.
- 13 (2⅝"-wide) strips. From strips, cut 192 (2⅝") squares. Cut squares in half diagonally to make 384 half-square B triangles.

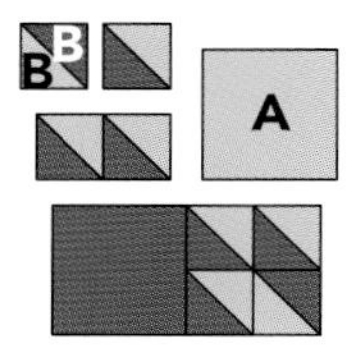

Quadrant Assembly Diagram

Block Diagram

Block Assembly

1. Choose 8 matching dark B triangles and 1 A square, 8 light B triangles, and 1 light A square. Join each dark B triangle to 1 light B triangle to make a triangle-square.
2. Lay out 8 triangle-squares, 1 dark A square and 1 light A square as shown in *Quadrant Assembly Diagram.* Join pieces to complete 1 quadrant. Make 4 quadrants, using assorted dark batiks.
3. Join 4 quadrants to complete 1 Hunter Star block *(Block Diagram).* Make 12 blocks.

Quilt Assembly

1. Lay out blocks in 4 rows with 3 blocks in each row.
2. Join blocks into rows; join rows to complete quilt center.
3. Referring to *Quilt Top Assembly Diagram* on page 92, join 8 light A squares and 8 dark A squares to make 1 side border. Add to quilt. Repeat for other side.
4. Join 7 light A squares and 7 dark A squares to make top border. Add to quilt. Repeat for bottom border.

Finishing

1. Divide backing fabric into 2 (1½-yard) pieces. Join panels lengthwise. Seam will run horizontally.
2. Layer backing, batting, and quilt top; baste. Quilt as desired. Quilt shown was quilted with allover swirling motifs.
3. Join 2¼"-wide dark batik strips into 1 continuous piece for straight-grain French-fold binding. Add binding to quilt.

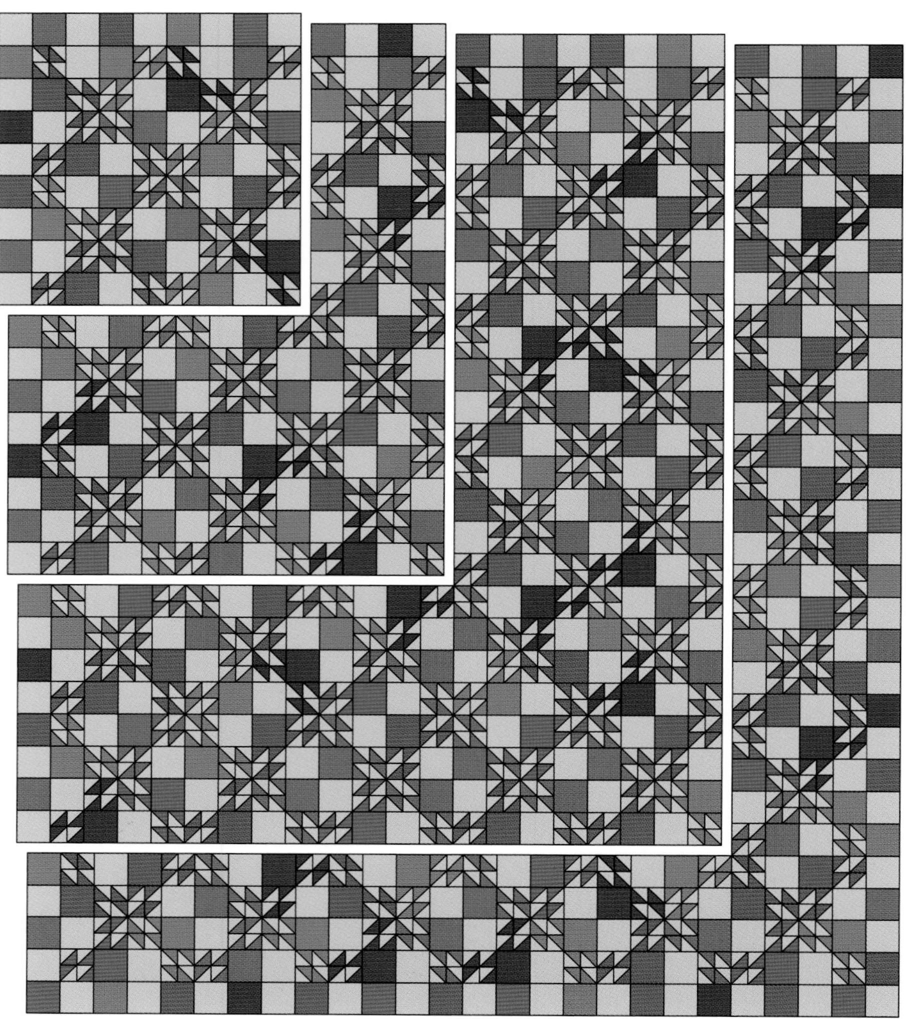

Quilt Top Assembly Diagram (Multiple Sizes Shown)

ALTERNATE SIZE CHART			
	Wallhanging	**Twin**	**Queen**
Size	35" × 35"	77" × 91"	91" × 105"
Blocks	4	30	42
Settings	2 × 2 blocks	5 × 6 blocks	6 × 7 blocks
Materials	4 dark fat quarters	30 dark fat quarters	42 dark fat quarters
	1 yard background fabric	4¾ yards background fabric	6⅛ yards background fabric
	1⅛ yards backing fabric	5½ yards backing fabric	8¼ yards backing fabric
	⅜ yard binding fabric	¾ yard binding fabric	⅞ yard binding fabric
	Crib-size quilt batting	Full-size quilt batting	King-size quilt batting
Border squares	18 light and 18 dark	46 light and 46 dark	54 light and 54 dark

TRIED & TRUE

Use a dramatic large-scale floral combined with a marbled green for a delightful two-fabric quilt.

DESIGNER

A machine quilter since the 1980s, Mary Beth Hayes developed Thangles™ while preparing to teach a science unit on inventions. Since 1996, she has worked full-time designing quilts that contain half-square triangles. ✲

Sowing Seeds

Polish your diamond cutting skills as you strip piece this beautiful star quilt. The pieced diamond border is a perfect finish for this stunning quilt.

PROJECT RATING: CHALLENGING

Size: 81⅝" × 81⅝"

Blocks: 25 (9⅝") Star blocks

MATERIALS

¼ yard each of 11 light shirting prints

¼ yard each of 11 medium and dark prints

2½ yards red solid for block background

2¾ yards cream print #1 for sashing

1¾ yards cream print #2 for outer border

⅜ yard gold print

¾ yard red print for binding

7½ yards backing fabric

Queen-size quilt batting

Cutting

Measurements include ¼" seam allowances. Border strips are exact length needed. You may want to make them longer to allow for piecing variations. Patterns for templates are on page 98.

From each light shirting print, cut:

- 3 (1½"-wide) strips for strip sets.

From each medium/dark print, cut:

- 3 (1½"-wide) strips for strip sets.

From remainders of medium/dark prints, cut:

- 4 (1½"-wide) strips. Referring to *Diamond Cutting Diagrams,* cut left end of each strip at 45° angle. From each strip, cut 8 (1½"-wide) C diamonds by placing 1½" line on ruler along angled cut edge.

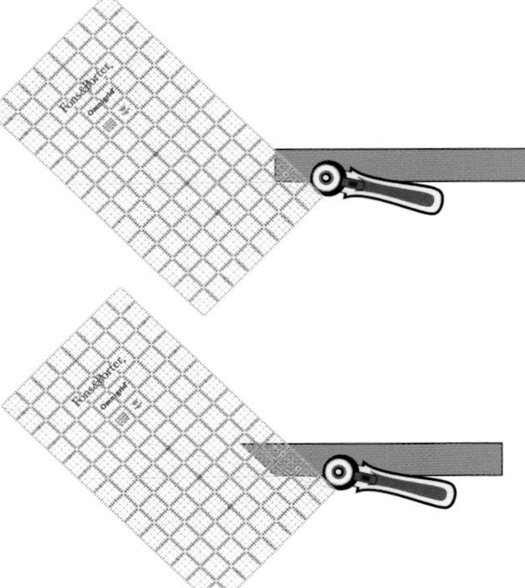

Diamond Cutting Diagrams

From red solid, cut:

- 4 (5¼"-wide) strips. From strips, cut 25 (5¼") squares. Cut squares in half diagonally in both directions to make 100 quarter-square B triangles.
- 10 (3⅜"-wide) strips. From strips, cut 100 (3⅜") A squares.
- 1 (3¼"-wide) strip. From strip, cut 4 (3¼") squares. Cut squares in half diagonally in both directions to make 16 quarter-square E triangles.
- 4 (2½"-wide) strips. Referring to *Diamond Cutting Diagrams,* cut left end of each strip at 45° angle. From strips, cut 32 (2½") H diamonds by placing 2½" line on ruler along angled cut edge of strip.
- 1 (2"-wide) strip. From strip, cut 16 (2") D squares.
- 3 (1⅝"-wide) strips. From strips, cut 8 (1⅝" × 7⅝") G rectangles and 8 (1⅝" × 5⅜") F rectangles.

From cream print #1, cut:

- 1 (76"-long) piece. From piece, cut 8 (3¾"-wide) **lengthwise** strips. From strips, cut 2 (3¾" × 68⅛") top and bottom inner borders, 2 (3¾" × 61⅝") side inner borders, and 4 (3¾" × 61⅝") horizontal sashing strips.

• 2 (10⅛"-wide) strips. From strips, cut 20 (3¾" × 10⅛") vertical sashing strips.

From cream print #2, cut:

• 7 (2¼"-wide) strips. Piece strips to make 4 (2¼" × 68⅛") strips for pieced outer border.

• 11 (3½"-wide) strips. From strips, cut 240 I triangles, 8 J triangles, and 8 J triangles reversed.

From gold print, cut:

• 4 (2½") strips. From strips, cut 32 (2½") H diamonds by placing 2½" line on ruler along angled cut edge of strip.

From red print, cut:

• 9 (2¼"-wide) strips for binding.

Block Assembly

1. Referring to *Strip Set Diagrams*, join 1 (1½"-wide) light shirting print strip and 1 (1½"-wide) medium or dark print strip to make a strip set. Make 33 strip sets. Cut left end of each strip set at 45° angle as shown. From each strip set, cut 16 (1½"-wide) segments by placing 1½" line on ruler along angled cut edge of strip.

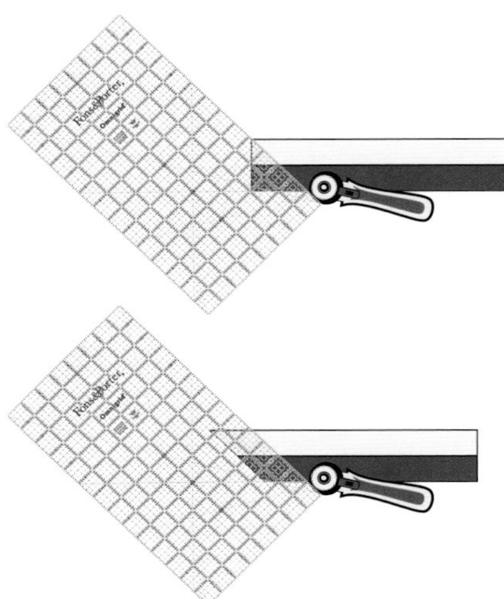

Strip Set Diagrams

2. Choose 1 set of 8 matching segments (label these A) and 2 sets of 4 matching segments (label these B and C). Join 1 segment A and 1 segment B to make 1 pieced diamond *(Pieced Diamond Diagrams)*. Make 4 matching pieced diamonds. Repeat to make 4 pieced diamonds using segments A and C.

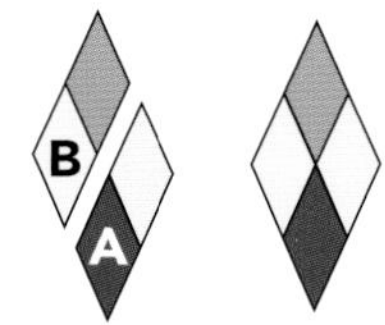

Pieced Diamond Diagrams

3. Referring to *Sew Easy: Set-In Seams* on page 73, make 1 Star Block using 8 Pieced Diamonds, 4 red A squares, and 4 red B triangles. Make 25 Star blocks.

Corner Star Assembly

1. Using set-in seams method, make 1 Corner Star using 2 sets of 4 C diamonds, 4 red D squares, and 4 red E triangles.

2. Add red F rectangles to sides of Corner Star. Add red G rectangles to top and bottom of block *(Corner Star Block Diagrams)*. Trim block to 7½" square. Make 4 Corner Star blocks.

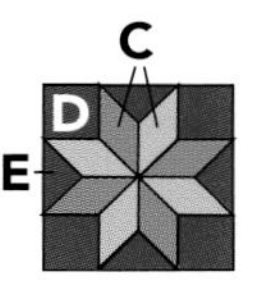

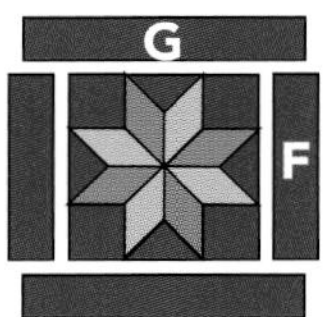

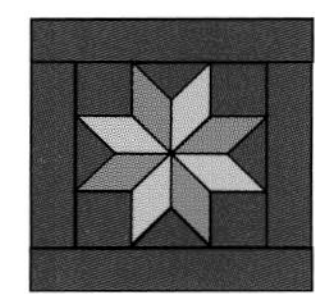

Corner Star Block Diagrams

Pieced Border Assembly

1. From remaining strip set segments, make 60 pieced diamonds.

2. Referring to *Border Unit Diagrams*, join 2 cream print #2 I triangles and 1 pieced diamond to make 1 Border Unit. In the same manner, join 2 cream print #2 I triangles and 1 red H diamond to make 1 red Border Unit. Join 2 cream print #2 I triangles and 1 gold diamond to make 1 gold Border Unit. Make 60 Pieced Diamond Border Units, 28 red Border Units, and 28 gold Border Units.

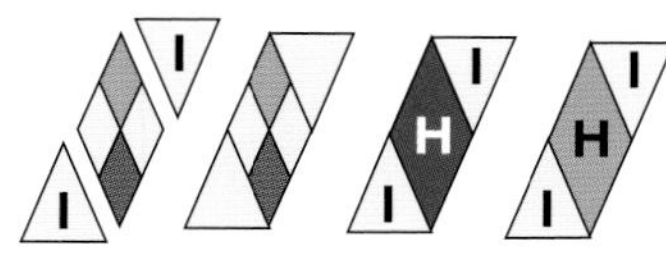

Border Unit Diagrams

3. Join 1 cream print #2 I triangle, 1 J triangle, 1 J triangle reversed, and 1 gold H diamond to make a Border End Unit as shown in *Border End Unit Diagrams.* Make 4 gold Border End Units and 4 red Border End Units.

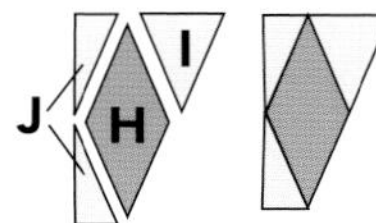

Border End Unit Diagrams

4. Referring to *Quilt Top Assembly Diagram*, lay out 15 Pieced Diamond Border Units, 7 Red Border units, 7 gold Border Units, 1 red Border End Unit, and 1 gold Border End Unit. Join to make 1 pieced border.
5. Add 1 (2¼" × 68⅛") cream print #2 strip to border to complete 1 pieced outer border. Make 4 pieced outer borders.

Quilt Top Assembly Diagram

Quilt Assembly

1. Referring to *Quilt Top Assembly Diagram*, lay out Star blocks and sashing strips. Join into rows; join rows to complete quilt center.
2. Add cream print #1 side inner borders to quilt center. Add top and bottom inner borders to quilt.
3. Add outer borders to sides of quilt.
4. Add Corner Star blocks to each end of remaining outer borders. Add borders to quilt.

Finishing

1. Divide backing into 3 (2½-yard) lengths. Join panels lengthwise.
2. Layer backing, batting, and quilt top; baste. Quilt as desired. Quilt shown was quilted with allover meandering *(Quilting Diagram).*
3. Join 2¼"-wide red print strips into 1 continuous piece for straight-grain French-fold binding. Add binding to quilt.

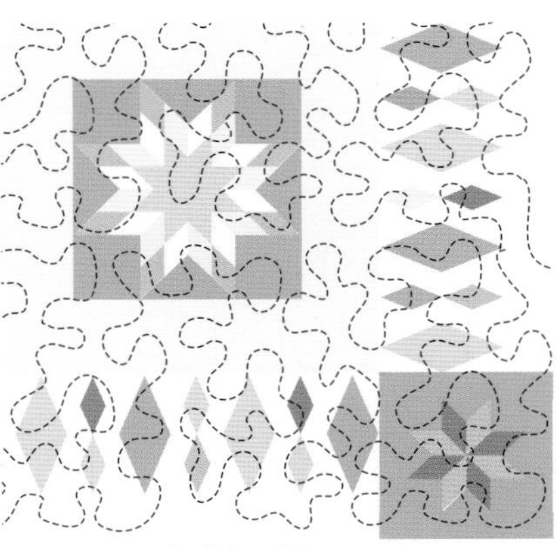
Quilting Diagram

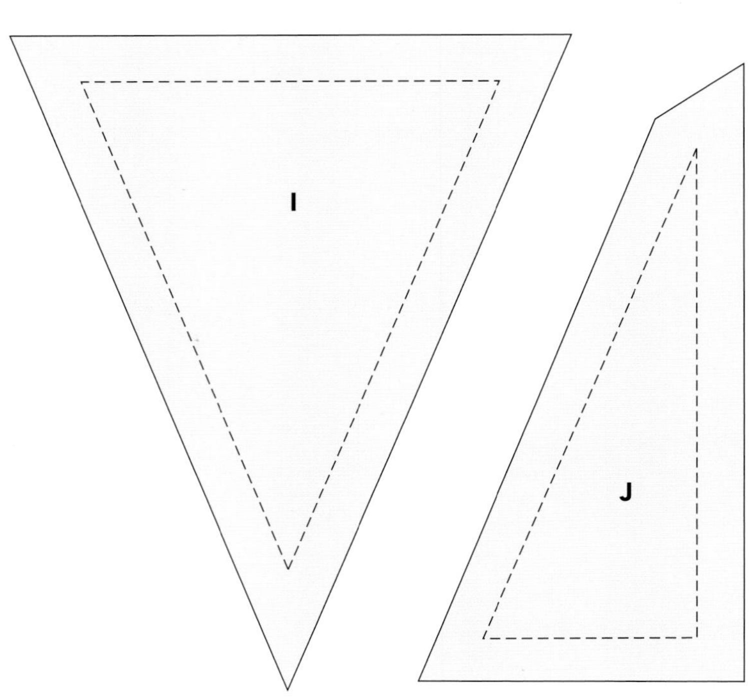

WEB EXTRA

To download size options and *Quilt Top Assembly Diagrams* for this project visit our Web site at www.FonsandPorter.com/sowingsizes

TRIED & TRUE

This traditional pattern also looks great in contemporary fabrics. We used batiks from Robert Kaufman Fabrics for our version.

DESIGNER

Former art teacher Sandy Klop has been making quilts for over thirty years. She creates and markets her own patterns under the name American Jane Patterns and designs fabrics for Moda. ⋇

QUILT DESIGNED BY **Pat Sloan**. PIECED BY **Kathy Norton**. MACHINE QUILTED BY **Heidi Pridemore.**

ARABELLA'S Courtyard

This medallion-style quilt features a variety of traditional blocks that are combined nicely in rich, warm colors.

PROJECT RATING: INTERMEDIATE

Size: 87" × 87"

MATERIALS

NOTE: Fabrics in the quilt shown are by P&B Textiles.

2¼ yards dark green print for outer border

1¼ yards green print for border #2 and center medallion

½ yard light green print for border #2

⅝ yard red print #1 for border #1

¾ yard red print #2 for center medallion

⅝ yard red print #3 for border #3

1 yard red print #4 for border #5

1 yard yellow print for border #5

2 yards orange print # 1 for border #2 and center medallion

⅝ yard orange print #2 for border #1

¾ yard black print #1 for border #4

⅞ yard black print #2 for binding

Fons & Porter Half & Quarter Ruler (optional)

7⅞ yards backing fabric

King-size quilt batting

Cutting

Measurements include ¼" seam allowances. Border strips are exact length needed. You may want to make them longer to allow for piecing variations.

> Sew **Smart**™
> **To cut A and D triangles for triangle-squares and B triangles for Hourglass Units, use the Fons & Porter Half & Quarter Ruler. If you are not using the Fons & Porter Half & Quarter Ruler, use the cutting NOTE instructions given here. —Marianne**

For instructions on using the Fons & Porter Half & Quarter Ruler, see page 107.

From dark green print, cut:

- 9 (8"-wide) strips. Piece strips to make 2 (8" × 87½") top and bottom outer borders and 2 (8" × 72½") side outer borders.

From green print, cut:

- 4 (2½"-wide) strips. From strips, cut 4 (2½" × 20½") F rectangles.
- 10 (2½"-wide) strips. From strips, cut 224 half-square A triangles. **NOTE:** If NOT using the Fons & Porter Half & Quarter Ruler to cut the A triangles, cut 9 (2⅞"-wide) strips. From strips,

cut 112 (2⅞") squares. Cut squares in half diagonally to make 224 half-square A triangles.

From light green print, cut:

- 4 (2½"-wide) strips. From strips, cut 96 half-square A triangles. **NOTE:** If NOT using the Fons & Porter Half & Quarter Ruler to cut the A triangles, cut 4 (2⅞"-wide) strips. From strips, cut 48 (2⅞") squares. Cut squares in half diagonally to make 96 half-square A triangles.

From red print #1, cut:

- 7 (2½"-wide) strips. From 1 strip, cut 12 (2½") C squares. Remaining strips are for strip sets.

From red print #2, cut:

- 1 (2½"-wide) strip. From strip, cut 4 (2½") C squares.
- 1 (4½"-wide) strip. From strip, cut 4 half-square D triangles. **NOTE:** If NOT using the Fons & Porter Half & Quarter Ruler to cut the D triangles, cut 1 (4⅞"-wide) strip. From strip, cut 2 (4⅞") squares. Cut squares in half diagonally to make 4 half-square D triangles.
- 5 (2½"-wide) strips. From strips, cut 104 half-square A triangles. **NOTE:** If NOT using the Fons & Porter Half & Quarter Ruler to cut the A triangles, cut 4 (2⅞"-wide) strips. From strips, cut 52 (2⅞") squares. Cut squares in half diagonally to make 104 half-square A triangles.

From red print #3, cut:

- 7 (2½"-wide) strips. Piece strips to make 2 (2½" × 60½") top and bottom border #3 and 2 (2½" × 56½") side border #3.

From red print #4, cut:

- 11 (2½"-wide) strips. From strips, cut 128 quarter-square B triangles. **NOTE:** If NOT using the Fons & Porter Half & Quarter Ruler to cut the B triangles, cut 5 (5¼"-wide) strips. From strips, cut 32 (5¼") squares. Cut squares in half diagonally in both directions to make 128 quarter-square B triangles.

From yellow print, cut:

- 11 (2½"-wide) strips. From strips, cut 128 quarter-square B triangles. **NOTE:** If NOT using the Fons & Porter Half & Quarter Ruler to cut the B triangles, cut 5 (5¼"-wide) strips. From strips, cut 32 (5¼") squares. Cut squares in half diagonally in both directions to make 128 quarter-square B triangles.

From orange print #1, cut:

- 13 (2½"-wide) strips. From strips, cut 208 (2½") C squares.
- 1 (4½"-wide) strip. From strip, cut 4 half-square D triangles. **NOTE:** If NOT using the Fons & Porter Half & Quarter Ruler to cut the D triangles, cut 1 (4⅞"-wide) strip. From strip, cut 2 (4⅞") squares. Cut squares in half diagonally to make 4 half-square D triangles.
- 8 (2½"-wide) strips. From strips, cut 200 half-square A triangles. **NOTE:** If NOT using the Fons & Porter Half & Quarter Ruler to cut the A triangles, cut 8 (2⅞"-wide) strips. From strips, cut 100 (2⅞") squares. Cut squares in half diagonally to make 200 half-square A triangles.

From orange print #2, cut:

- 7 (2½"-wide) strips. From 1 strip, cut 12 (2½") C squares. Remaining strips are for strip sets.

From black print #1, cut:

- 1 (4½"-wide) strip. From strip, cut 4 (4½") E squares.
- 8 (2½"-wide) strips. Piece strips to make 2 (2½" × 64½") top and bottom border #4 and 2 (2½" × 60½") side border #4.

From black print #2, cut:

- 1 (2½"-wide) strip. From strip, cut 12 (2½") C squares.
- 10 (2¼"-wide) strips for binding.

Carpenter's Wheel Medallion Assembly

1. Join 1 red print #2 A triangle and 1 orange print #1 A triangle to make a small red/orange triangle-square *(Triangle-Square Diagrams)*. Make 88 small red/orange triangle-squares.

Triangle-Square Diagrams

2. In the same manner, using red print #2 and green print A triangles, make 16 small red/green triangle-squares. Make 112 orange triangle-squares using orange print #1 and green print A triangles.
3. Referring to *Carpenter's Wheel Diagrams*, lay out 16 small red/green triangle-squares, 48 small red/orange triangle-squares, 16 orange/green triangle-squares, 4 red print #2 C squares, and 16 orange print #1 C squares. Join into rows; join rows to complete Carpenter's Wheel block.

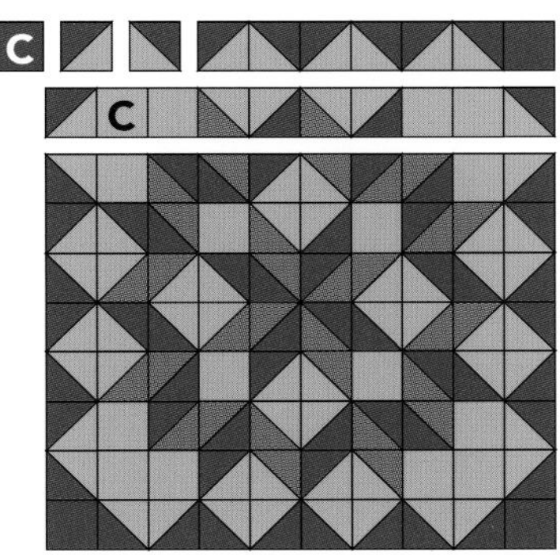

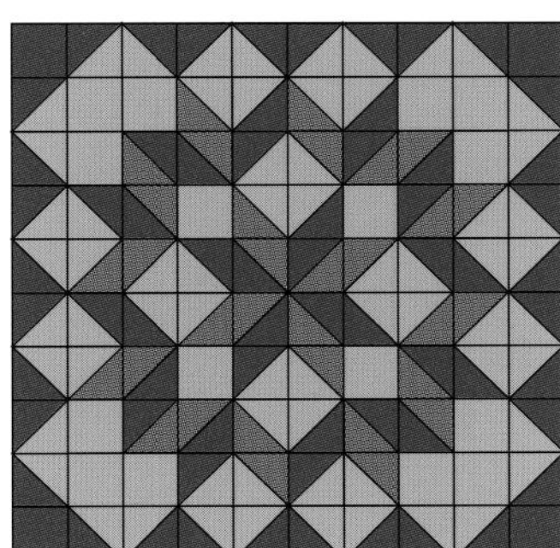
Carpenter's Wheel Diagrams

4. Lay out 10 small red/orange triangle-squares and 1 green print F rectangle as shown in *Medallion Border Diagram*. Join to make 1 Medallion Border. Make 4 Medallion Borders.

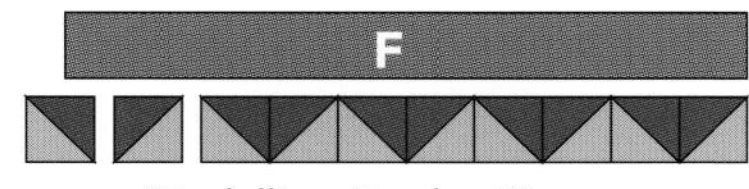

Medallion Border Diagram

5. Add 1 border to each side of Carpenter's Wheel.
6. Make 4 large red/orange triangle-squares, using red print #2 and orange print #1 D triangles.
7. Add 1 large red triangle-square to each end of remaining borders. Add borders to top and bottom of Carpenter's Wheel to complete quilt center.

Checkerboard Border Assembly

1. Join 2 orange print #2 strips and 1 red print #1 strip as shown in *Strip Set #1 Diagram*. Make 2 Strip Set #1. From strip sets, cut 28 (2½"-wide) #1 segments.

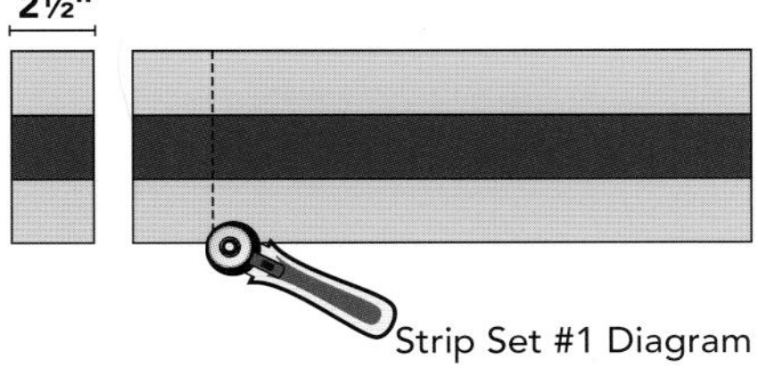

Strip Set #1 Diagram

2. In the same manner, join 2 red print #1 strips and 1 orange print #2 segment as shown in *Strip Set #2 Diagram*. Make 2 Strip Set #2. From strip sets, cut 28 (2½"-wide) #2 segments.

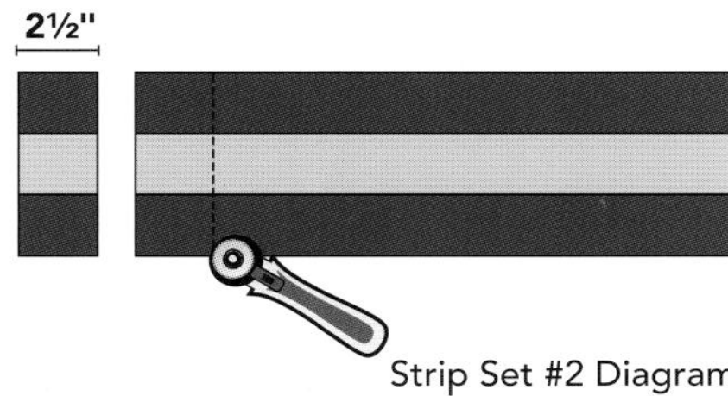

Strip Set #2 Diagram

3. Referring to *Quilt Top Assembly Diagram* on page 105, lay out 7 #1 segments and 7 #2 segments as shown. Join segments to make 1 Checkerboard border. Make 4 Checkerboard borders.
4. Lay out 3 black print #2 C squares, 3 orange print #2 C squares, and 3 red print #1 C squares as shown in *Checkerboard Corner Diagrams*. Join into rows; join rows to complete 1 Checkerboard Corner. Make 4 Checkerboard Corners.

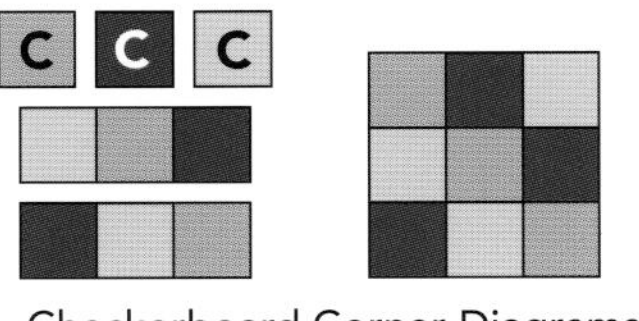

Checkerboard Corner Diagrams

Clay's Choice Block Border Assembly

1. Join 1 light green print A triangle and 1 green print A triangle to make a triangle-square *(Triangle-Square Diagrams)*. Make 96 light green triangle-squares.
2. Lay out 8 orange print #1 C squares, 4 light green triangle-squares, and 4 orange/green triangle-squares as shown in *Clay's Choice Block Assembly Diagram*. Join into rows; join rows to complete 1 Clay's Choice block *(Clay's Choice Block Diagram)*. Make 24 Clay's Choice blocks.

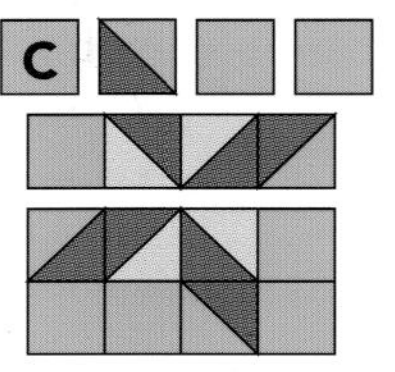

Clay's Choice Block Assembly Diagram

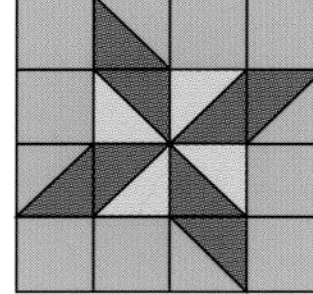

Clay's Choice Block Diagram

3. Referring to *Quilt Top Assembly Diagram*, join 5 Clay's Choice blocks as shown to make 1 Clay's Choice side border. Make 2 Clay's Choice side borders.
4. In the same manner, join 7 Clay's Choice blocks as shown to make Clay's Choice top border. Repeat for Clay's Choice bottom border.

Hourglass Unit Border Assembly

1. Lay out 2 yellow print B triangles and 2 red print #4 B triangles as shown in *Hourglass Unit Diagrams*. Join triangles to make 1 Hourglass Unit. Make 64 Hourglass Units.

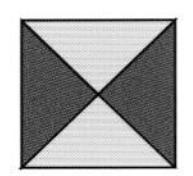

Hourglass Unit Diagrams

2. Referring to *Quilt Top Assembly Diagram*, join 16 Hourglass Units as shown to make 1 Hourglass Unit border. Make 4 Hourglass Unit borders.

Quilt Assembly

1. Referring to *Quilt Top Assembly Diagram*, add 1 Checkerboard Border to each side of quilt center. Add 1 Checkerboard Corner to each end of remaining Checkerboard borders. Add borders to quilt.
2. Add Clay's Choice side borders to quilt. Repeat for Clays Choice top and bottom borders.
3. Repeat for red print border #3 and black print border #4.
4. Add 1 Hourglass border to each side of quilt. Add 1 black print #1 E square to each end of remaining Hourglass borders. Add borders to top and bottom of quilt.
5. Add dark green print side outer borders to quilt. Add dark green print top and bottom outer borders to quilt.

Finishing

1. Divide backing into 3 (2⅝-yard) lengths. Join panels lengthwise.
2. Layer backing, batting, and quilt top; baste. Quilt as desired. Quilt shown was quilted in the ditch, with meandering in Carpenter's Wheel, Clay's Choice border, and border #6, and with a diagonal grid in Checkerboard border *(Quilting Diagram)*.
3. Join 2¼"-wide black print strips into 1 continuous piece for straight-grain French-fold binding. Add binding to quilt.

Quilting Diagram

WEB EXTRA

To download size options and *Quilt Top Assembly Diagrams* for this project visit our Web site at www.FonsandPorter.com/arabellasizes

E

#4

#3

Quilt Top Assembly Diagram

DESIGNER

Pat Sloan is a prolific quilter, author, teacher, and fabric designer. Her quilts appear in many publications and she teaches on line, on cruises, and in classrooms in several countries. ⁕

Cutting Half-Square and Quarter-Square Triangles

Easily cut half-square and quarter-square triangles from strips of the same width with the Fons & Porter Half & Quarter Ruler.

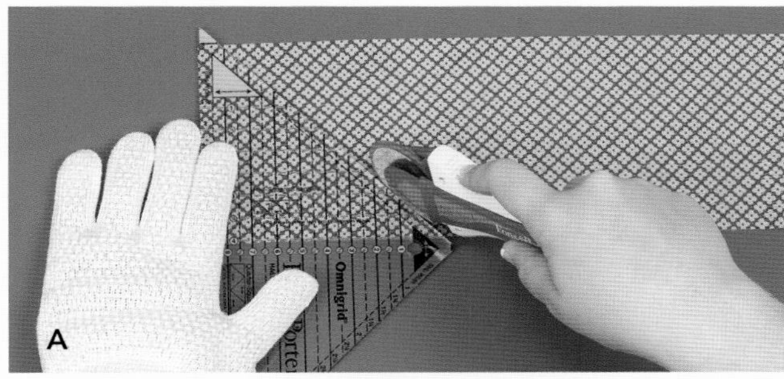

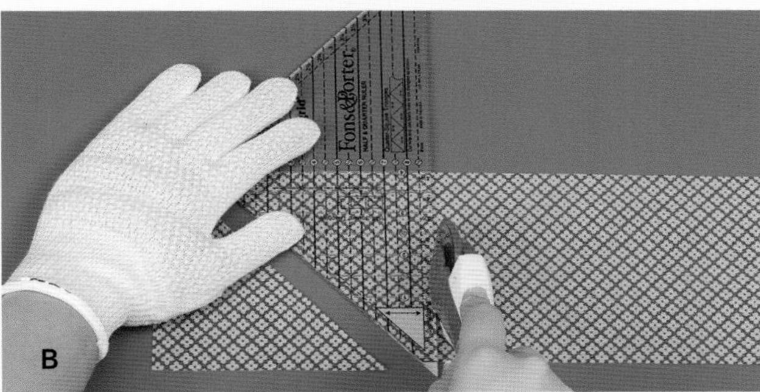

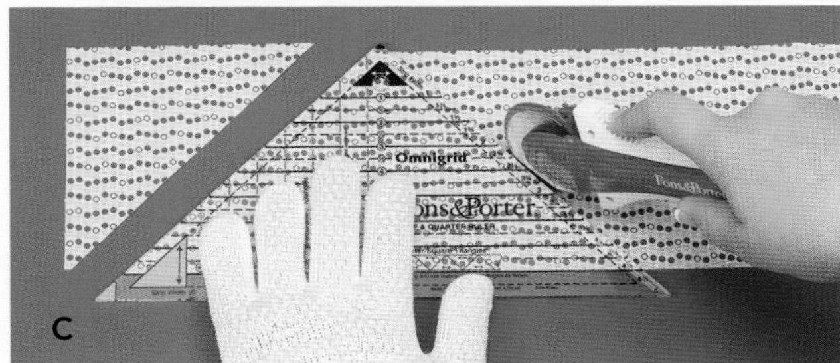

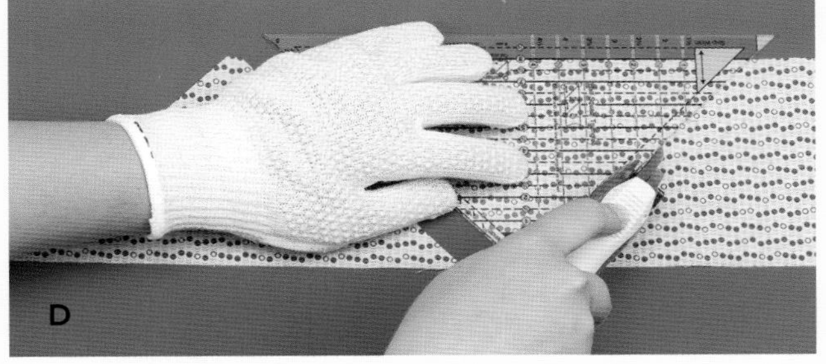

Cutting Half-Square Triangles

1. Straighten the left edge of 2½"-wide fabric strip. Place the 2½" line of the Fons & Porter Half & Quarter Ruler on the bottom edge of strip, aligning left edge of ruler with straightened edge of strip. The yellow tip of ruler will extend beyond top edge of strip.
2. Cut along right edge of ruler to make 1 half-square triangle *(Photo A)*.
3. Turn ruler and align 2½" line with top edge of strip. Cut along right edge of ruler *(Photo B)*.
4. Repeat to cut required number of half-square triangles.

Cutting Quarter-Square Triangles

1. Place Fons & Porter Half & Quarter Ruler on 2½"-wide fabric strip, with 2½" line along bottom edge. The black tip of ruler will extend beyond top edge. Trim off end of strip along left edge of ruler.
2. Cut along right edge of ruler to make 1 quarter-square triangle *(Photo C)*.
3. Turn ruler and align 2½" line along top edge of strip. Cut along right edge of ruler *(Photo D)*.
4. Repeat to cut required number of quarter-square triangles.

NOTE: Cut half-square D triangles in the same manner, using 4½"-wide fabric strip and 4½" line on ruler.

Luminosity Stars

Quilt artist Jeri Riggs created this attractive wall quilt of kaleidoscopic hexagons as a way to play with the infinite motif combinations in the fabrics she chose.

MIRROR Images

• Cutting pieces so the same fabric motif is repeated exactly in each piece creates kaleidoscopic effects in patchwork blocks. • To select images to repeat, reflect the designs in the print first by placing two design mirrors which are attached at one side atop the fabric to audition print areas. (See *Sew Easy: Mirror Images* on page 112.) • Medium- and large-scale prints that use a variety of colors work best when you are creating mirrored motifs.

PROJECT RATING: CHALLENGING

Size: 47½" × 45½"

Blocks: 23 (9½") Hexagon Star blocks

MATERIALS

NOTE: Fabrics in the quilt shown are by Paula Nadelstern for Benartex.

¾ yard each of 7 assorted "busy" motif fabrics for star point diamonds

¼ yard each of 11 assorted "quiet" fabrics for star edge diamonds

½ yard each of 2 fabrics for border pieces and binding

Fons & Porter's 60° Diamonds Template (optional)

Template material

3 yards backing fabric

Twin-size batting

Cutting

Make templates for diamond and border piece from patterns on page 113. Make holes in templates at points indicated by dots on patterns. Measurements include ¼" seam allowances.

From each star point fabric, cut:

- 4 sets of 6 star point diamonds. (Position template on a specific motif and cut 1 diamond. Cut 5 additional identical diamonds.)

From each edge diamond fabric, cut:

- 2 (2⅞"-wide) strips. From strips, cut 18 diamonds, using diamond template.

From each border fabric, cut:

- 6 border pieces.
- 3 (2¼"-wide) strips for binding.

Block Assembly

1. For each Hexagon Star block, choose 6 matching star point diamonds and 6 matching edge diamonds.

2. On each diamond and border piece, mark dots through holes in templates.

3. Referring to *Star Point Unit Diagrams,* join 3 matching star point diamonds, stitching from dot to dot. Backstitch at dots, leaving seam allowance free beyond dots. In the same manner, set 2 edge diamonds into openings between star points to complete 1 Star Point Unit. Make 2 Star Point Units.

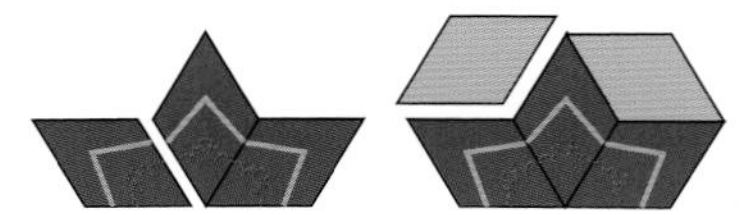

Star Point Unit Diagrams

4. Lay out 2 Star Point Units and 2 edge diamonds as shown in *Block Assembly Diagram.* Join Star Point Units; set edge diamonds into openings between star points to complete 1 Hexagon Star block *(Block Diagram).* Make 23 blocks.

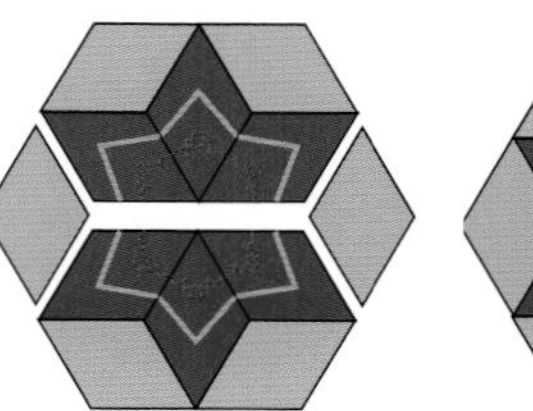

Block Assembly Diagram

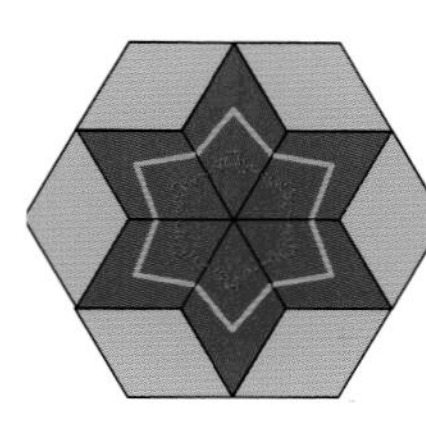

Block Diagram

5. For each Half Star, choose 3 matching star point diamonds and 4 matching edge diamonds. Mark dots on diamonds.

6. Referring to *Half Star Diagram,* join 3 matching star point diamonds, leaving seam allowance free beyond dots. Set 2 edge diamonds into openings between star points. Join 1 edge diamond to each outside edge of star point unit.

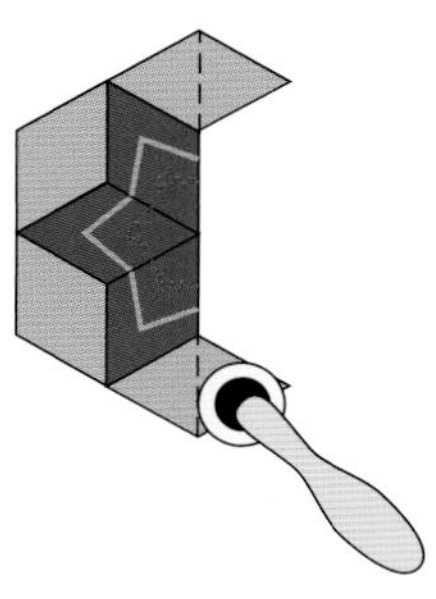

Half Star Diagram

7. Trim edge diamonds as shown to complete 1 Half Star. Make 4 Half Stars.

Quilt Assembly

1. Referring to *Quilt Top Assembly Diagram,* lay out blocks, Half Stars, and border pieces. Join in diagonal rows. Join rows to complete quilt center.

2. Trim border pieces even with edges of quilt.

Quilting and Finishing

1. Divide backing fabric into 2 (1½-yard) lengths. Cut 1 piece in half lengthwise to make 2 narrow panels. Join 1 narrow panel to wider panel. Remaining panel is extra and may be used to make a hanging sleeve.

2. Layer backing, batting, and quilt top; baste. Quilt as desired. Quilt shown was quilted with a small arc on both sides of each seam.

3. Join 3 matching 2¼"-wide binding strips into 1 continuous piece for straight-grain French-fold binding. Repeat with remaining 3 binding strips. Add binding to quilt, using each color to bind 2 sides.

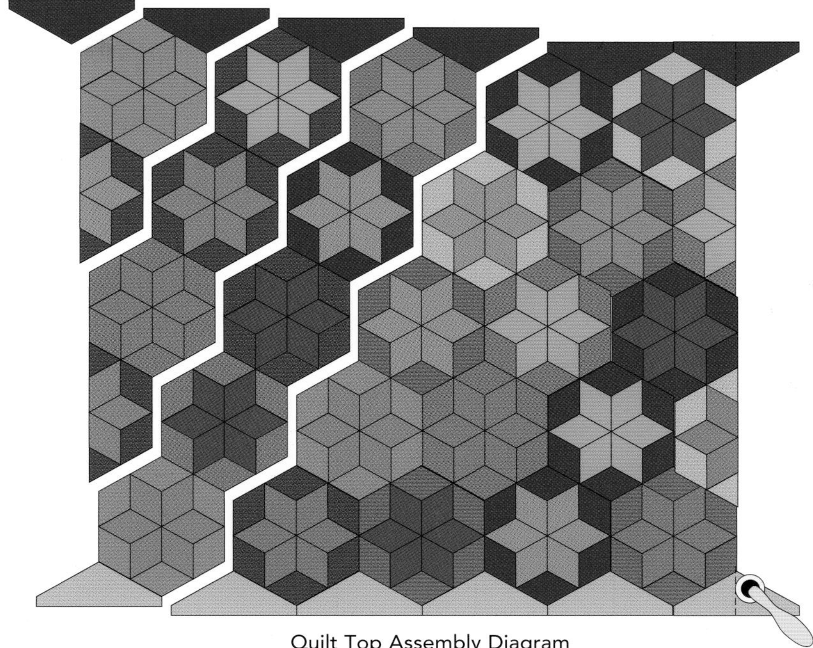

Quilt Top Assembly Diagram

DESIGNER

Jeri Riggs' original design quilts have won many awards, have been shown in national quilt exhibitions, and are in private collections around the world.

Sew *Easy*™ Mirror Images

If you are cutting many stars from the same fabric, as in the quilt at right, try this speedy technique to cut sets of 6 identical diamonds. Large-scale fabrics or novelty prints work well for this method.

1. Focusing on a specific motif in your fabric to find the repeat, cut 6 sections of fabric which are exactly alike *(Photo A)*.
2. Stack the 6 layers so that the motifs are perfectly lined up. Push a flatheaded pin through each layer in exactly the same spot to align layers *(Photo B)*. Pin layers in several places to keep them from slipping when cutting.
3. Position template on fabric pieces and cut through all layers *(Photo C)*. Repeat to cut required number of pieces for project.
4. Lay out 1 group of 6 diamonds to make a star *(Photo D1)*. The same group of pieces make a totally different star when the diamonds are turned in the opposite direction *(Photo D2)*.
5. Join diamonds and add setting pieces to complete 1 Hexagon Star Block *(Photo E)*.

A

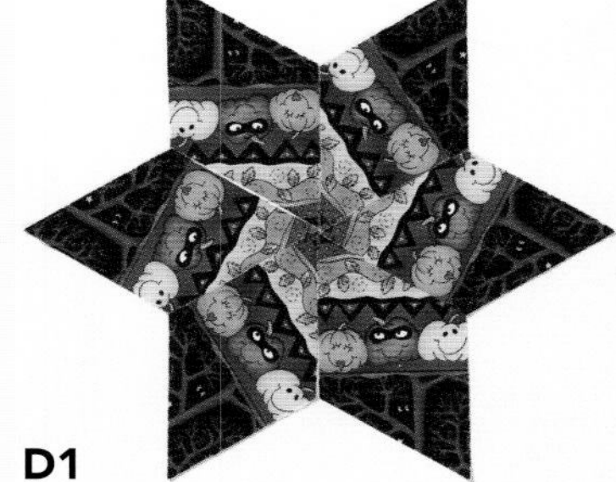

D1

B

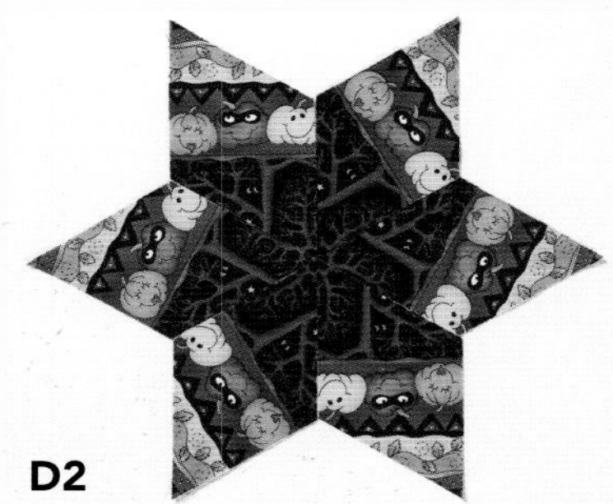

D2

C

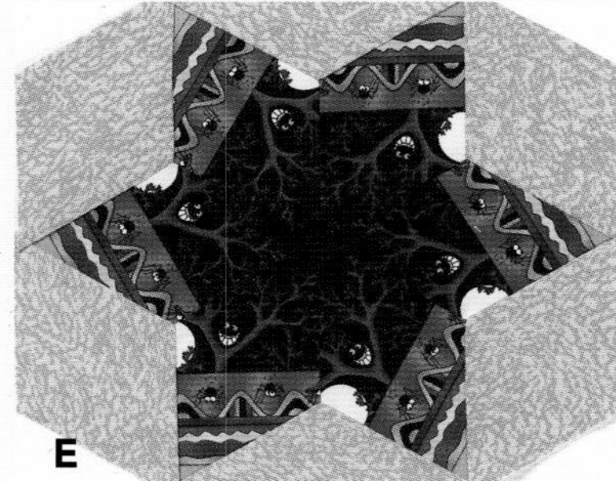

E

Sew **Smart**™

Design mirrors which are attached at one side can be moved around the fabric to find an area that will make an interesting block.

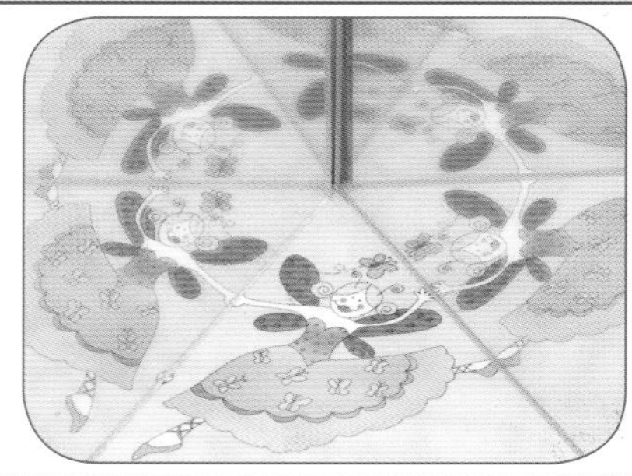

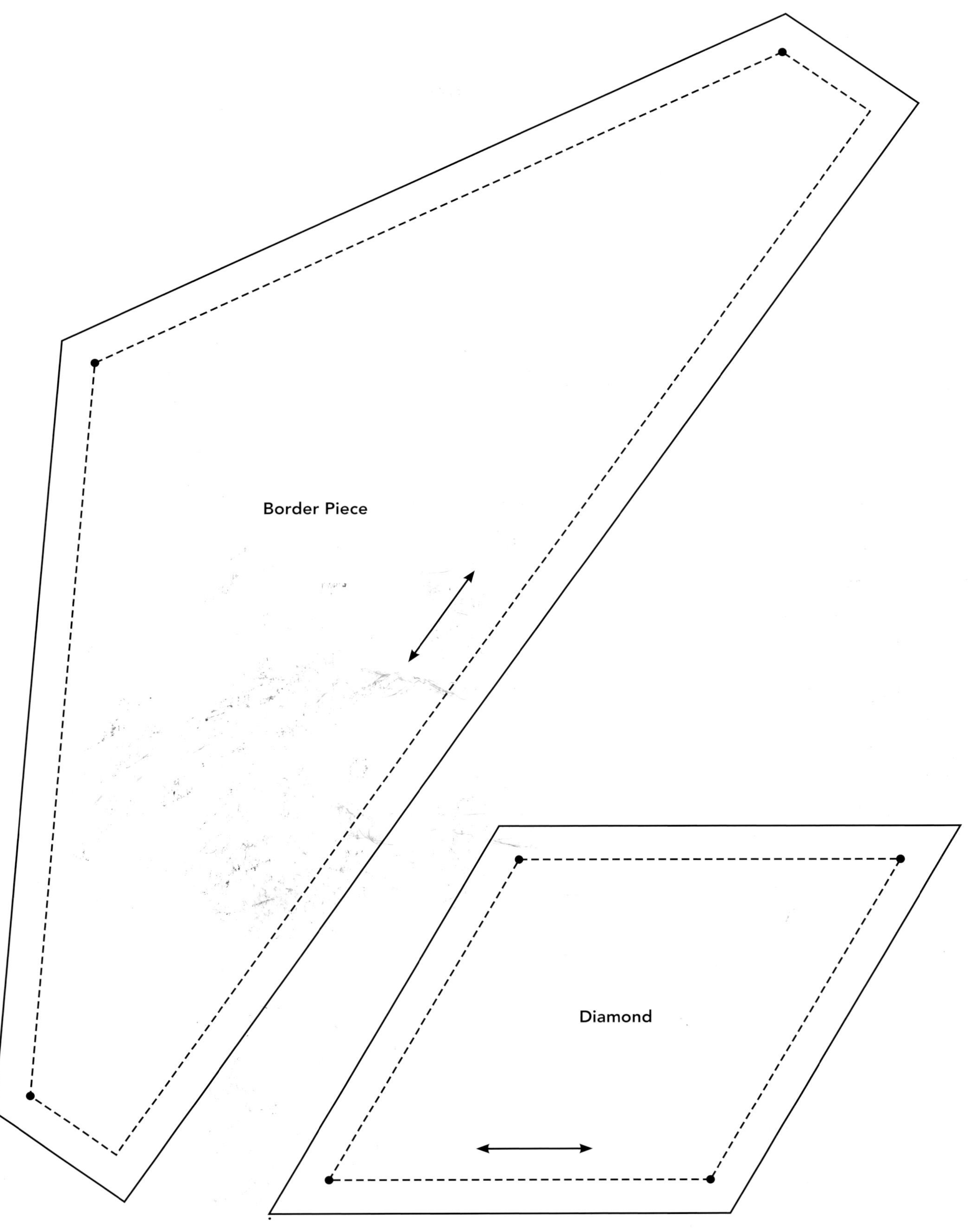
Border Piece
Diamond

Winter Stars

Designer Dereck Lockwood of Chico, California, used elegant, rather formal printed fabrics and a diagonal set to create this stunning bed quilt. The border stripe gives the impression of multiple borders without the work. See *Sew Easy: Making Split Diamonds* on page 116 for step-by-step instructions for cutting and piecing the star points.

PROJECT RATING: CHALLENGING

Size: 90¼" × 115"

Blocks: 18 (14½") Winter Star blocks

MATERIALS

Fabrics in the quilt shown are by Maywood Fabrics.

3 yards black print #1 for blocks, sashing strip sets, and binding

1¼ yards black print #2 for blocks and sashing squares

1 yard red print #1 for blocks

1 yard red print #2 for blocks

3¾ yards tan print for blocks and setting triangles

1 yard green floral print for blocks

2 yards red floral print for sashing strip sets

6 yards border stripe print (3½ yards if not using a pattern that must be centered on each border.)

Fons & Porter Split Diamond Template Set (optional)

Template material

8 yards backing fabric

King-size quilt batting

Cutting

NOTE: Cutting for this quilt is tricky. Be sure to read *Sew Easy: Making Split Diamonds* on page 116 before beginning.

If you are not using the Fons & Porter Split Diamond Template Set, make templates from the patterns on page 119 and mark lines on fabric before cutting. Measurements include ¼" seam allowances.

From black print #1, cut:

- 12 (2⅜"-wide) strips. From strips, cut 72 A half diamonds. (See *Sew Easy: Making Split Diamonds* on page 116 for cutting instructions.)
- 48 (1"-wide) strips for strip sets.
- 11 (2¼"-wide) strips for binding.

From black print #2, cut:

- 3 (3½"-wide) strips. From strips, cut 31 (3½") sashing squares.
- 12 (2⅜"-wide) strips. From strips, cut 72 A half diamonds.

From red print #1, cut:

- 12 (2⅜"-wide) strips. From strips, cut 72 A half diamonds.

From red print #2, cut:

- 12 (2⅜"-wide) strips. From strips, cut 72 A half diamonds.

From tan print, cut:

- 3 (21¾"-wide) strips. From strips, cut 3 (21¾") squares and 2 (11⅛") squares. Cut 21¾" squares in half diagonally in both directions to make 12 quarter-square side setting triangles (2 are extra). Cut 11⅛" squares in half diagonally to make 4 half-square corner setting triangles.
- 4 (7¼"-wide) strips. From strips, cut 18 (7¼") squares. Cut squares in half diagonally in both directions to make 72 quarter-square C triangles.
- 6 (5⅛"-wide) strips. From strips, cut 36 (5⅛") squares. Cut squares in half diagonally to make 72 half-square B triangles. (Since B and C triangles are the same size, you may want to label them as you cut.)

From green floral print, cut:

- 6 (5⅛"-wide) strips. From strips, cut 36 (5⅛") squares. Cut squares in half diagonally to make 72 half-square B triangles.

From red floral print, cut:

- 24 (2½"-wide) strips for strip sets.

Sew *Easy*™ Making Split Diamonds

The Split Diamond Template Set makes easy work of cutting and piecing the diamonds for *Winter Stars* on page 114. The half diamonds are cut oversized and joined; the diamond is then cut from that piece. If you do not have the template set, make your own templates from the patterns on page 119.

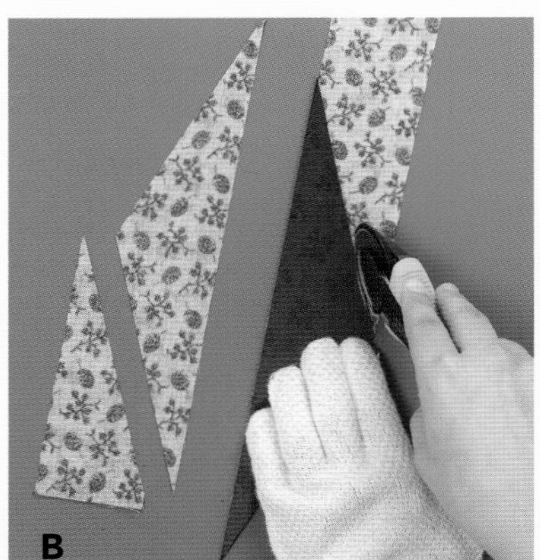

B

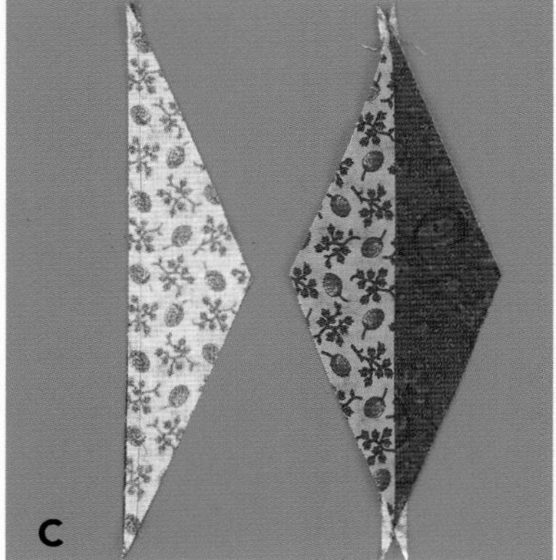

C

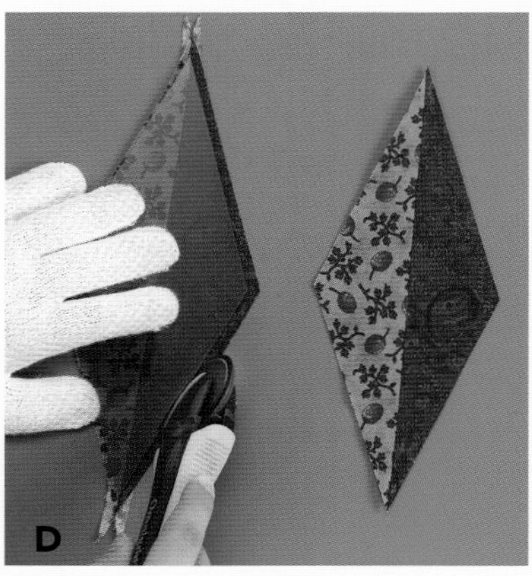

D

Cutting Triangles

1. Cut required number of (2⅜"-wide) strips for half diamonds.

2. Align long edge of Half Diamond Template with bottom edge of strip and cut half diamond *(Photo A)*.

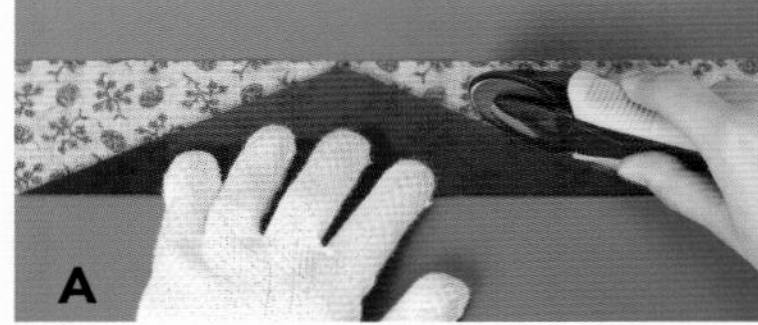

A

3. Align long edge of Half Diamond Template with top edge of strip and cut another triangle *(Photo B)*. Continue cutting half diamonds in this manner until you have the number needed.

Making Diamonds

1. Join 2 contrasting half diamonds to make 1 oversized diamond *(Photo C)*.

2. Align Diamond Cutting Template on pieced diamond with top and bottom points on the seam line. Cut around Diamond Cutting Template *(Photo D)*.

From border stripe print, cut:

- 2 (9"-wide) **lengthwise** strips, centering a red stripe in each one. If you are not using a border stripe, cut 4 (9"-wide) **lengthwise** strips. From strips, cut 2 (9" × 120") side borders and 2 (9" × 95") top and bottom borders. Borders are oversized and will be trimmed later.

Quilt Top Assembly Diagram

Block Assembly

1. Referring to *Sew Easy: Making Split Diamonds* on page 116, join 1 red print #1 A half diamond and 1 black print #1 A half diamond to make a split diamond. Make 4 split diamonds from these fabrics.
2. In the same manner, make 4 split diamonds using red print #2 and black print #2.
3. Use diamond template to trim pieced diamond to correct size.
4. Referring to *Sew Easy: Set In Seams* on page 73 and *Star Point Unit Diagram,* join 1 split diamond of each color combination. Set in 1 C triangle between the red star points to complete 1 star point unit. Make 4 star point units.

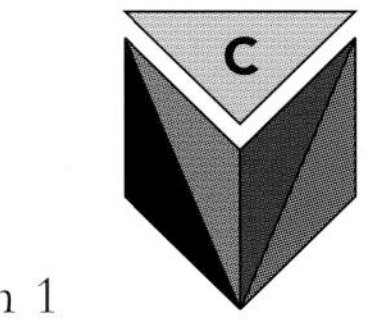

Star Point Unit Diagram

5. Join 1 tan print B triangle and 1 green print B triangle to make a triangle-square. Make 4 triangle-squares.
6. Lay out star point units and triangle-squares as shown in *Block Assembly Diagram.* Join 2 star point units; set in 1 triangle-square between black star points. Repeat for remaining star point units. Join the 2 star point unit assemblies and set in triangle-squares between the black star points to complete 1 Winter Star block *(Block Diagram).* Make 18 blocks.

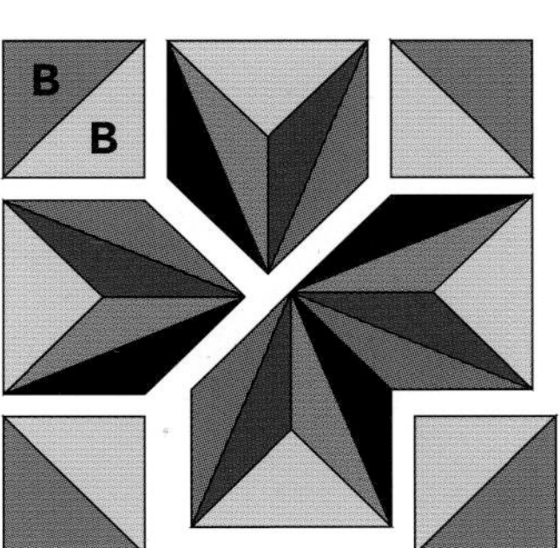

Block Assembly Diagram

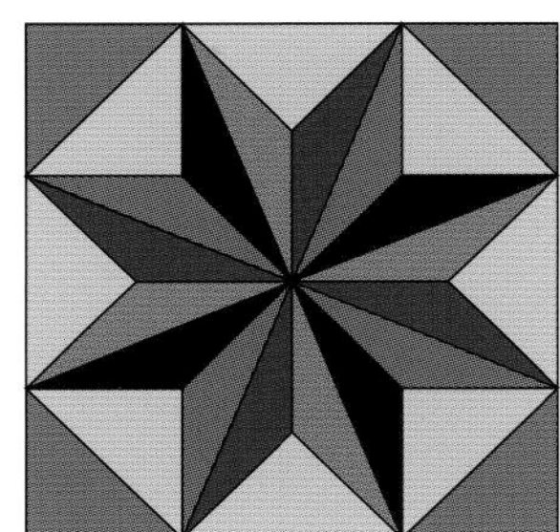
Block Diagram

Quilt Assembly

1. Join 1 (2½"-wide) red floral print strip and 2 (1"-wide) black print #1 strips as shown in *Strip Set Diagram*. Make 24 strip sets. From strip sets, cut 48 (15"-long) segments.

Strip Set Diagram

2. Lay out blocks, sashing strips, sashing squares, and setting triangles as shown in *Quilt Top Assembly Diagram*. Join into diagonal rows; join rows to complete quilt center. Trim corners of setting squares even with edges of quilt center.
3. Add borders to quilt center, mitering corners. See *Sew Easy: Mitered Borders* on page 23.

Finishing

1. Divide backing fabric into 3 (2⅔-yard) pieces. Join pieces to make quilt back. Seams will run horizontally.
2. Layer backing, batting, and quilt top; baste. Quilt as desired. Quilt shown is stitched in the ditch in the stars, has fan motifs in the block corners and has feather motifs surrounded by stippling in the tan setting triangles.
3. Join 2¼"-wide black print #1 strips into 1 continuous piece for straight-grain French-fold binding. Add binding to quilt.

TRIED & TRUE

A fantastic fusion of florals delights the eye in this block made with spring and summer colors. Fabrics are by P&B Textiles.

DESIGNER

A quilter since 1973, Dereck Lockwood has won numerous awards for his quilts. ⁕

Half Diamond Template

Diamond Cutting Template

Sunburst

High contrast fabrics showcase designer Marti Michell's precision patchwork. Template patterns for the Sunburst block are on page 125; however, we suggest you make life easier by using Marti's acrylic templates. Buy them at your favorite quilt shop.

PROJECT RATING: CHALLENGING

Size: 53" × 53"

Blocks: 9 (11¼") Sunburst blocks and 64 (3¾") Nine Patch blocks

MATERIALS

8 fat quarters★ assorted navy prints for blocks
1 fat quarter★ red print for blocks
4 yards white or cream fabric for background and binding
3⅓ yards backing fabric
½ yard lightweight washable interfacing for lining
From Marti Michell Perfect Patchwork Template Set F to rotary cut Sunburst block pieces (optional)
Template material
Twin-size batting
★fat quarter = 18" × 20"

Cutting

Make templates for the three D circles from the patterns on page 125. You will test them later to see which works best with your blocks.

If you are not using purchased template set, make templates for patterns A, B, and C on page 125. Make holes in templates at dots on patterns. As you cut pieces with A, B, and C templates, mark dots onto fabric pieces through holes in templates. Use dots to align pieces and as indicators of where to start and stop stitching.

Measurements include ¼" seam allowances.

From each navy or red fat quarter, cut:

- 2 (1⅞"-wide) strips. From strips, cut 16 A diamonds using diamond template.
- 4 (1¾"-wide) strips for strip sets.
- 1 (6") square for D circle.

From white or cream print, cut:

- 3 (11¾"-wide) strips. From strips, cut 9 (11¾") background squares and 2 (3¾") squares. Cut 3¾" squares in half diagonally to make 4 half-square G triangles.
- 2 (6⅞"-wide) strips. From strips, cut 9 (6⅞") squares. Cut squares in half diagonally in both directions to make 36 quarter-square F triangles.
- 4 (4¼"-wide) strips. From strips, cut 36 (4¼") E squares.
- 12 (1¾"-wide) strips for strip sets. Cut each strip in half to make 24 (20"-long) strips.
- 7 (2"-wide) strips. From strips, cut 144 B pieces.
- 4 (2⅛"-wide) strips. From strips, cut 144 C pieces.
- 6 (2¼"-wide) strips for binding.

Nine Patch Block Assembly

1. Referring to *Dark Strip Set Diagram* join 2 dark strips and 1 light strip to make 1 dark strip set. Make 12 dark strip sets. From strip sets, cut 128 (1¾"-wide) segments.

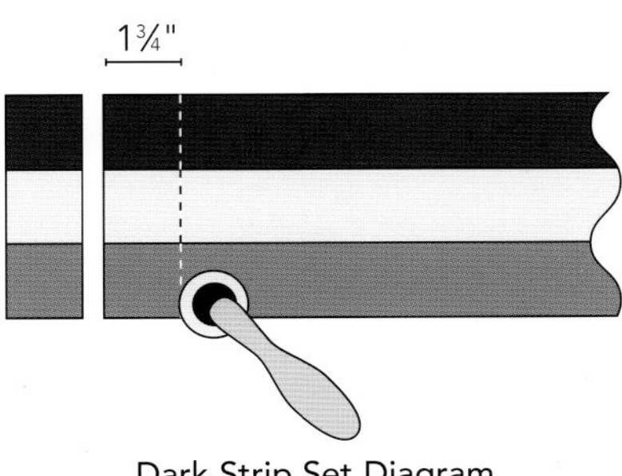

Dark Strip Set Diagram

2. Referring to *Light Strip Set Diagram,* join 2 light strips and 1 dark strip to make 1 light strip set. Make 6 light strip sets. From strip sets, cut 64 (1¾"-wide) segments.

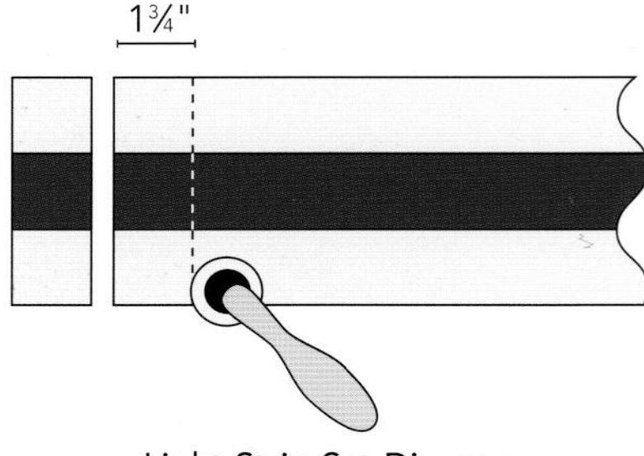

Light Strip Set Diagram

3. Referring to *Nine Patch Diagrams,* join 2 dark segments and 1 light segment to make Nine Patch block. Make 64 Nine Patch blocks.

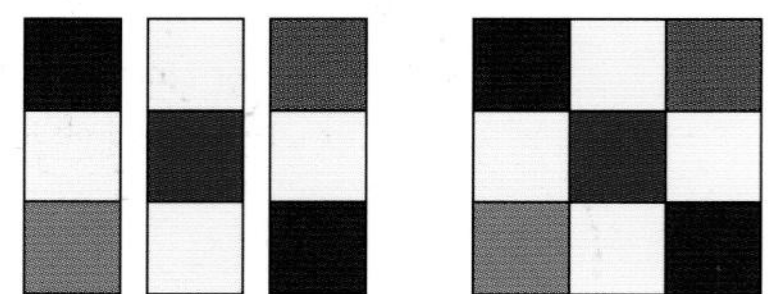

Nine Patch Diagrams

Sunburst Block Assembly

1. Choose 1 set of 16 matching A diamonds to make 1 block. Lay out 1 A diamond, 1 B piece, and 1 C piece, right sides facing up, as shown in *Unit Layout Diagram.* Put pieces right sides together just before you sew.

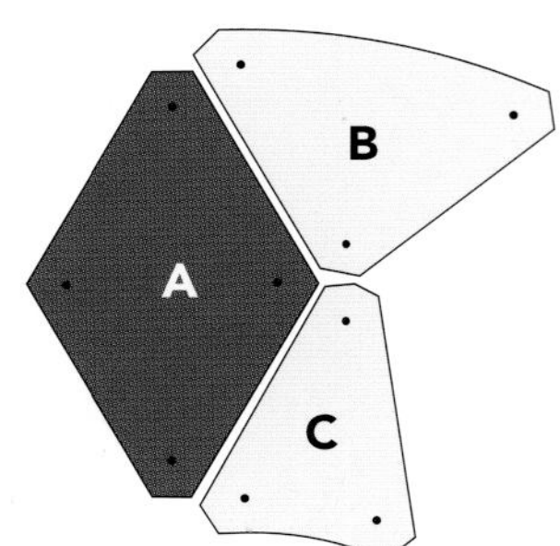

Unit Layout Diagram

2. Join C to A, stitching from edge to edge *(A/C Assembly Diagram).* Press seam allowance away from diamond.

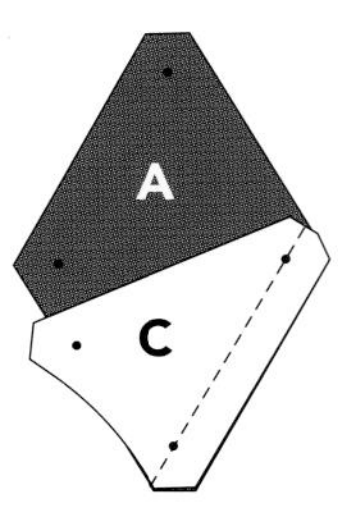

A/C Assembly Diagram

3. Paying careful attention to add B to right side of diamond, place pieces so that diamond is atop B and wrong side up. In this position, the previous stitching line on the diamond can be used as the starting guide to add B. Join A/C unit to B, stitching in direction indicated by arrow, from previous stitching line to outer edge as shown in *A/B/C Assembly Diagram* to make 1 A/B/C Unit *(A/B/C Unit Diagram).* Press seam allowance away from diamond. Make 16 A/B/C units.

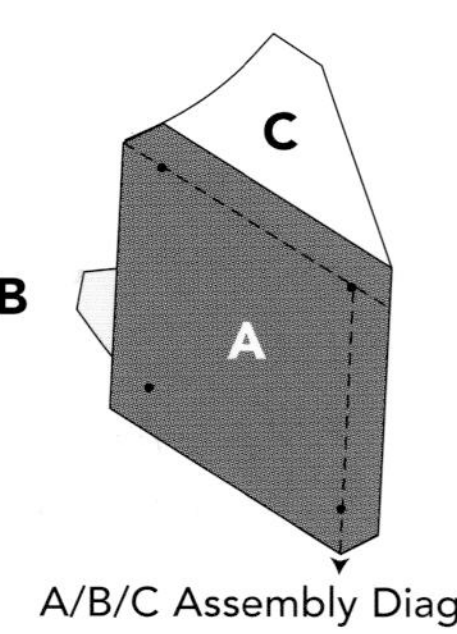

A/B/C Assembly Diagram

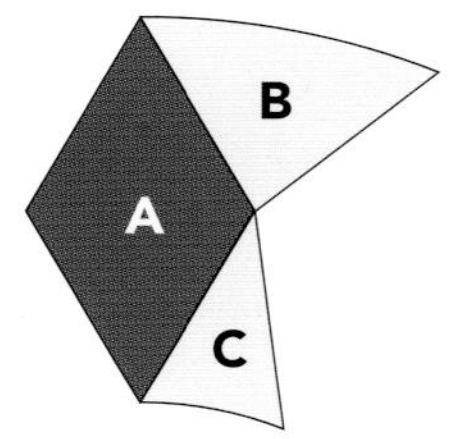

A/B/C Unit Diagram

4. Paying careful attention to position, pin B piece of 1 A/B/C unit to A diamond of another unit *(Joining Units Diagram 1).* Push seam allowance out of the way to expose the center dot where the 3 pieces of the first unit meet. Begin sewing at this dot and sew to the edge of the unit. Press seam allowance away from diamond.

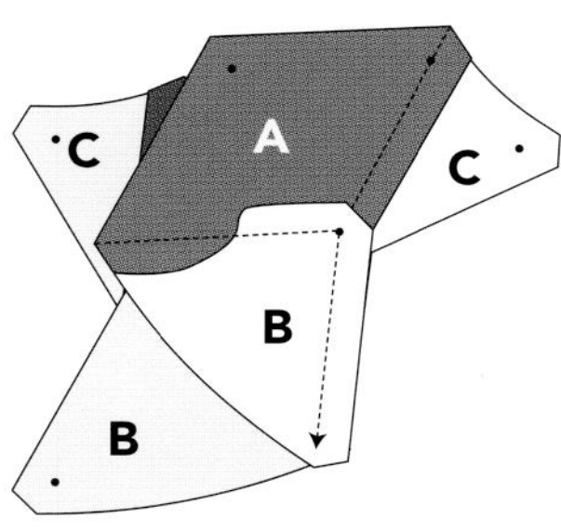

Joining Units Diagram 1

5. Finish joining the 2 units by pinning C piece to the same diamond. Sew from edge to center dot as indicated by arrow in *Joining Units Diagram 2.* Press

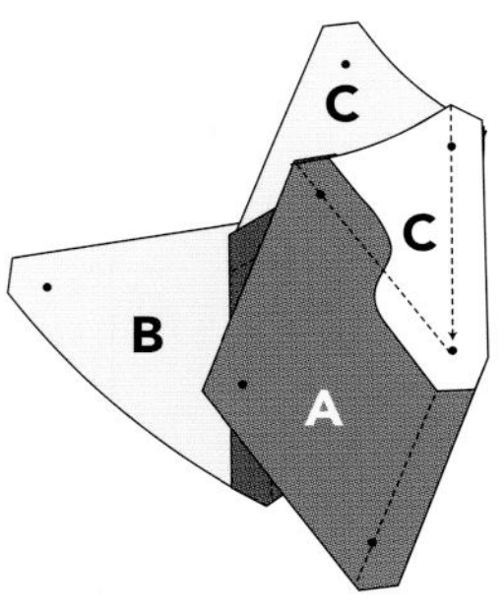

Joining Units Diagram 2

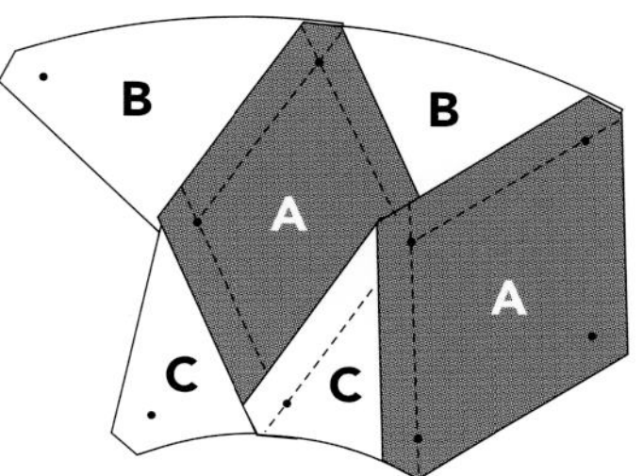

Joined Units Diagram

seam allowances toward diamond *(Joined Units Diagram).*

6. Continue to join A/B/C units in this manner until all units are joined into a ring. Press seam allowances consistently.
7. Stay-stitch ¼" around outside edge of ring. Press under seam allowance along stitching. Do not turn under edge on inside circle.
8. Fold 1 background square in quarters and finger crease. Center sunburst ring on square, aligning diamond points with crease lines on square. Appliqué outer edge of ring to background square. Baste inner edge of ring to background. (*Block Assembly Diagram*).

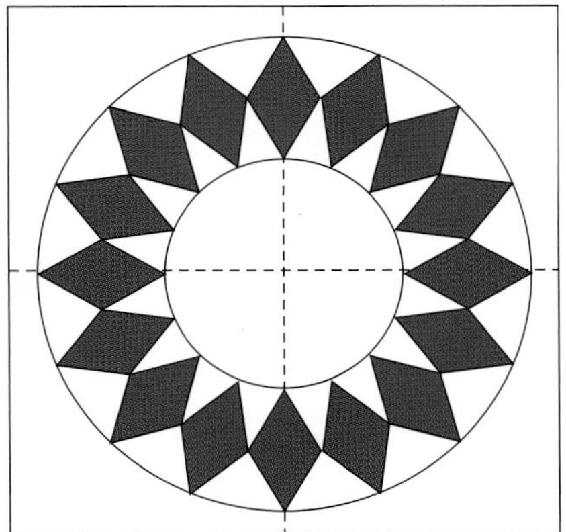

Block Assembly Diagram

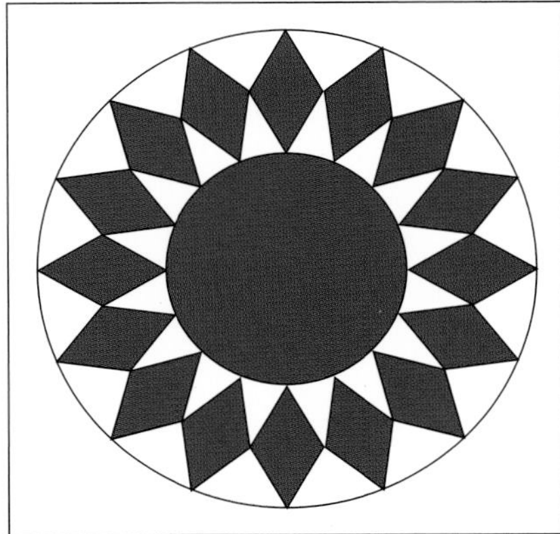

Sunburst Block Diagram

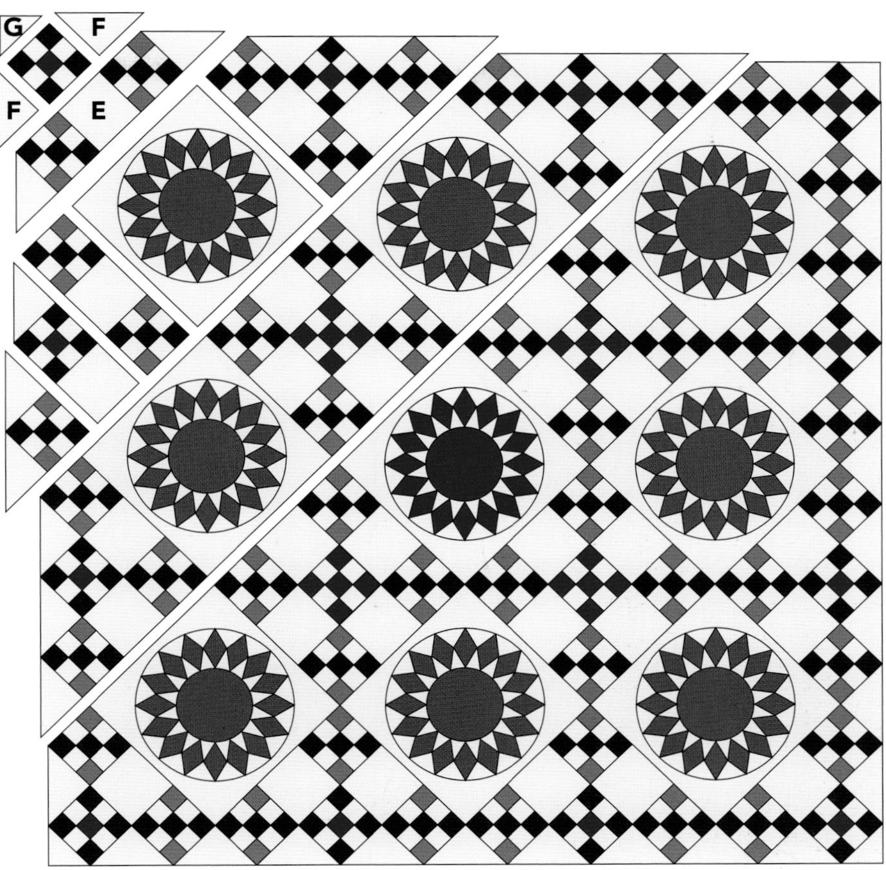

Quilt Top Assembly Diagram

9. Place each of the three circle templates over basted block to see which fits best. (Use the circle that will cover the seam allowance on the inside of the Sunburst ring—this is the line that is ¼" from the hole, not the raw edge of the hole!) You will need to check each block since they may vary. Use selected template to trace circle on wrong side of lining fabric. Cut a 1"–2" slit in the center of the lining. Place the lining right sides together with 6" center square. Using a small sewing machine stitch, stitch around entire circle on drawn line. Trim and clip seam allowance. Turn the circle right side out through silt. Center on Sunburst ring and appliqué to block center to complete block *(Sunburst Block Diagram).* Make 9 Sunset blocks.

Quilt Assembly

1. Referring to *Quilt Top Assembly Diagram*, lay out Sunburst blocks, Nine Patch blocks, E squares, and setting triangles.
2. Join pieces into units. Join units into diagonal rows; join rows to complete quilt.

Finishing

1. Divide backing fabric into 2 (1⅔-yard) pieces. Cut 1 piece in half lengthwise. Sew 1 narrow panel to 1 side of wide panel. Press seam allowance toward narrow panel. Remaining panel is extra and may be used to make a hanging sleeve.

2. Layer backing, batting, and quilt top; baste. Quilt as desired. Quilt shown was quilted in the ditch on Sunburst blocks and Nine Patch blocks with multi-pointed stars in the center of Sunburst blocks and looped tiara shapes in open background areas.

3. Join 2¼"-wide white strips into 1 continuous piece for straight-grain French-fold binding. Add binding to quilt.

TRIED & TRUE

Add extra interest to the center of a Starburst block by "fussy cutting" the circular center from a print fabric. Brilliant orange, navy, and yellow batiks make this Sunburst block glow like the sun.

DESIGNER

Marti Michell is well known among quilters for her From Marti Michell line of precision acrylic rotary cutting templates and rulers. She has written a number of books on strip piecing techniques, including *Quilting for People Who Don't Have Time to Quilt.* Marti is a recipient of the prestigious Silver Star Award given annually at International Quilt Festival in Houston. ⁕

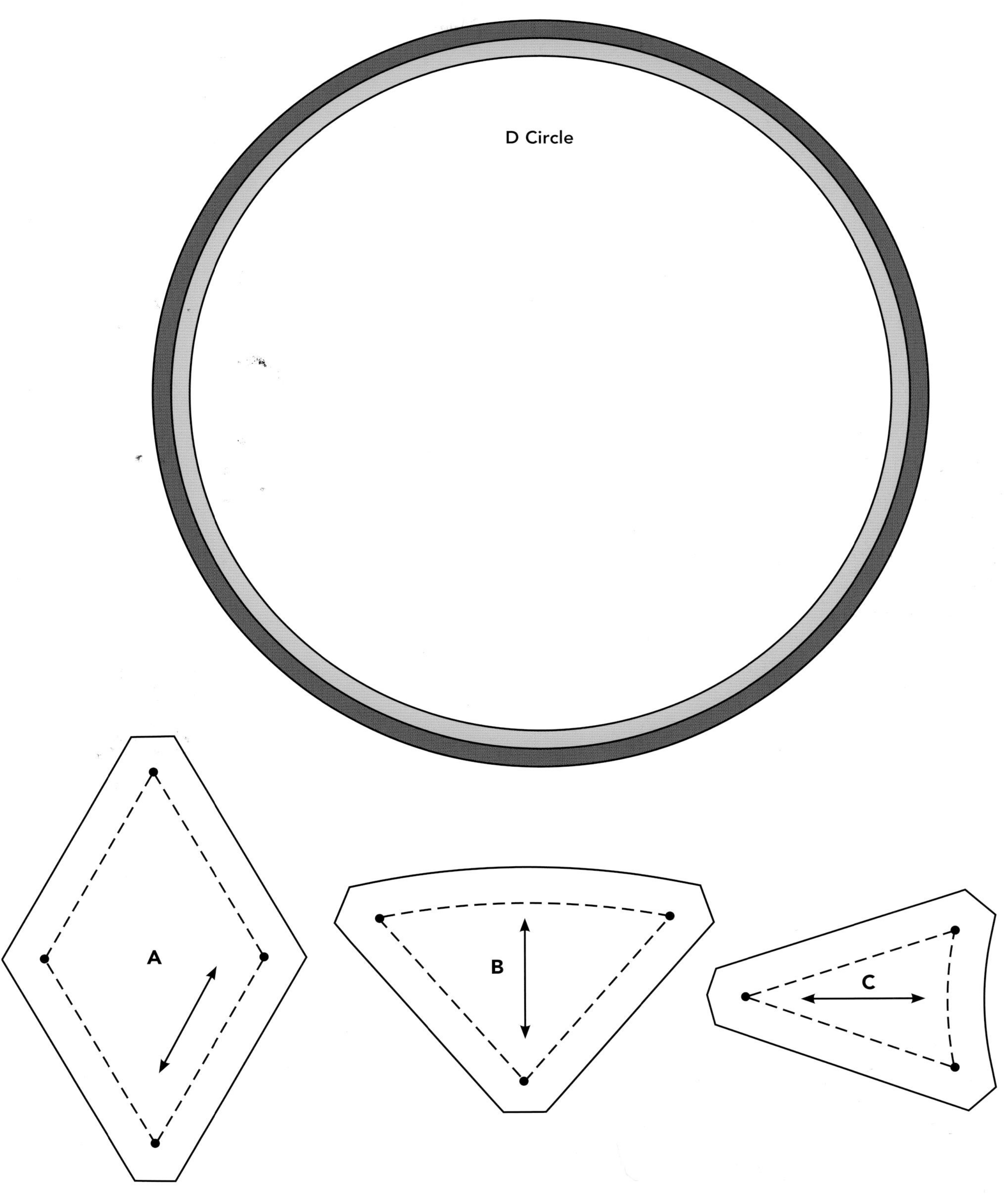
D Circle
A
B
C

Mariner's IN A PICKLE

If you like the challenge of making a quilt with complex geometrical piecing, this quilt is worth the effort!

PROJECT RATING: CHALLENGING

Size: 118" × 118"

Blocks: 16 (18") Mariner's Compass blocks and 116 Pickle Dish units

MATERIALS

2¾ yards **each** of 17 assorted purple, green, and blue prints and batiks
2 yards dark blue print for binding
Tracing paper
Template Material
14 yards backing fabric
King-size quilt batting

Cutting

Make templates for pieces A–D and foundation piecing patterns from pages 131–134. Pieces for foundation piecing are cut oversize.

> Sew **Smart**™
> To create more dimension, fussy cut the C and D pieces from a border print fabric. —Liz

From assorted prints, cut:

- 65 A.
- 29 sets of 4 matching B for Pickle Dish units.
- 29 sets of 8 matching C for Pickle Dish units.
- 16 sets of 4 matching D for compass points.
- 16 sets of 16 matching (1½" × 6½") E rectangles for foundation piecing compass points.
- 16 sets of 8 matching (1¾" × 8") F rectangles for foundation piecing compass points.
- 16 sets of 4 matching (2¼" × 8½") G rectangles for foundation piecing compass points.
- 16 sets of 32 matching (2¼" × 5") H rectangles for foundation piecing compass backgrounds.
- 29 sets of 48 matching (1½" × 3") I rectangles for foundation piecing pickle dish units.
- 29 sets of 40 matching (1¾" × 2¾") J rectangles and 16 (2½" × 2¾") K rectangles for foundation piecing pickle dish units.

From dark blue print, cut:

- 600" of 2¼"-wide bias strips. Join strips to make bias binding.

> Sew **Smart**™
> **For basic instructions on foundation piecing, see *Sew Easy: Paper Foundation Piecing* on page 135.**

Mariner's Compass Assembly

1. Trace 64 foundation patterns for Section 2 and Section 3, and 128 foundation patterns for Section 1, on pages 131–132.

2. Foundation piece sections in numerical order, using pieces E through H as indicated. Make 8 matching Section 1, 4 matching Section 2, and 4 matching Section 3.

3. Trim fabric even with outside edges of foundations.

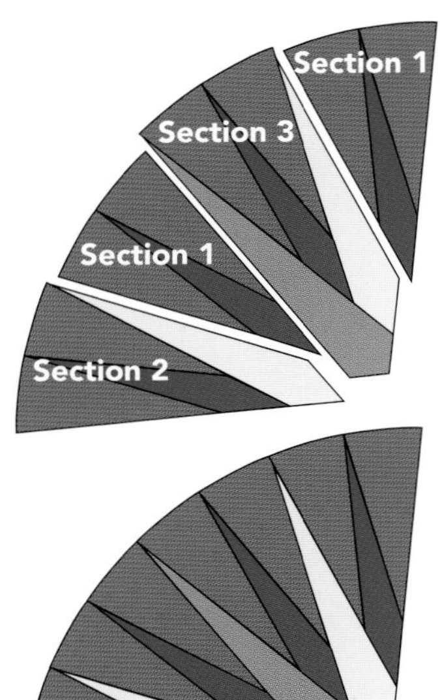

Segment Diagrams

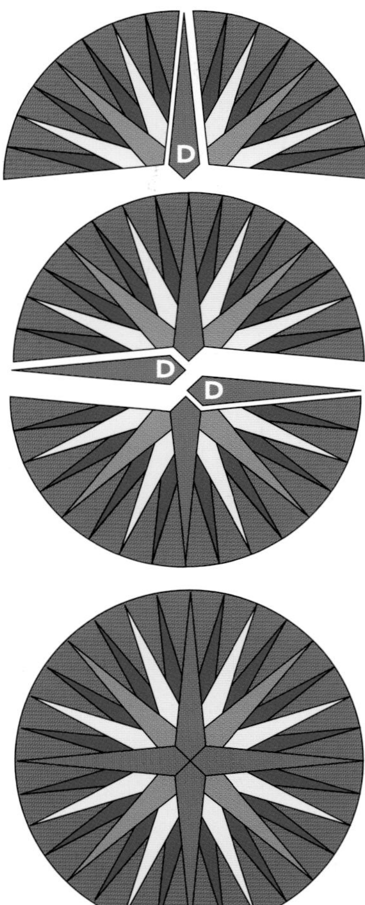

Compass Assembly Diagrams

4. Join 2 Section 1, 1 Section 2, and 1 Section 3 as shown in *Segment Diagrams*. Make 4 segments.
5. Join segments with 4 matching D compass points to complete 1 compass *(Compass Assembly Diagrams)*. Remove paper from back of compass. Make 16 Compass blocks.

Pickle Dish Assembly

1. Trace 232 sets of foundation patterns for Pickle Dish Arc on page 131.
2. Foundation piece Pickle Dish Arc in numerical order, using pieces I through K as indicated. Make 29 sets of 8 matching Pickle Dish Arcs.
3. Trim fabric even with outside edges of foundations.
4. Join 2 matching Pickle Dish Arcs, 2 matching C pieces, and 1 B as shown in *Pickle Dish Unit Assembly Diagrams* to make 1 Pickle Dish Unit. Make 29 sets of 4 matching Pickle Dish Units.

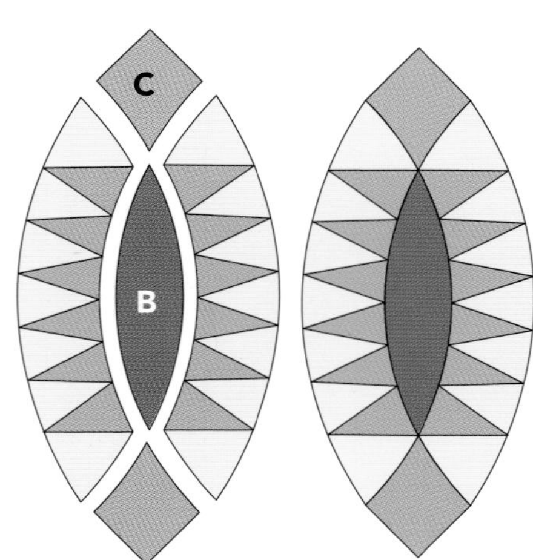

Pickle Dish Unit Diagrams

Quilt Assembly

1. Lay out Mariner's Compass blocks, Pickle Dish Units, and A pieces as shown in *Quilt Top Assembly Diagram*.
2. Make a Trimming Template by tracing red lines on C pattern on page 134. Trim Pickle Dish Units that will be joined to Mariner's Compass as shown in *Trimming Diagrams*. Do not trim Pickle Dish Units that will be on outer edge of quilt.
3. Join pieces into into rows. Join rows to complete quilt top.

Trimming Diagram

Finishing

1. Divide backing into 4 (3½-yard) lengths. Join panels lengthwise.
2. Layer backing, batting, and quilt top; baste. Quilt as desired. Quilt shown was quilted in the ditch in Compass blocks, with a feather design in A pieces, and with feathers and flames in Pickle Dish Units *(Quilting Diagram)*.
3. Add binding to quilt.

Quilt Top Assembly Diagram

Quilting Diagram

DESIGNER

Heather Kimpel Costen enjoys the challenge of making quilts with complex geometrical piecing. She worked as an engineer prior to becoming a stay-at-home mom. She often uses Ardco templates for piecing, and has had custom templates made for her own designs. Heather is also a longarm machine quilter. ⋇

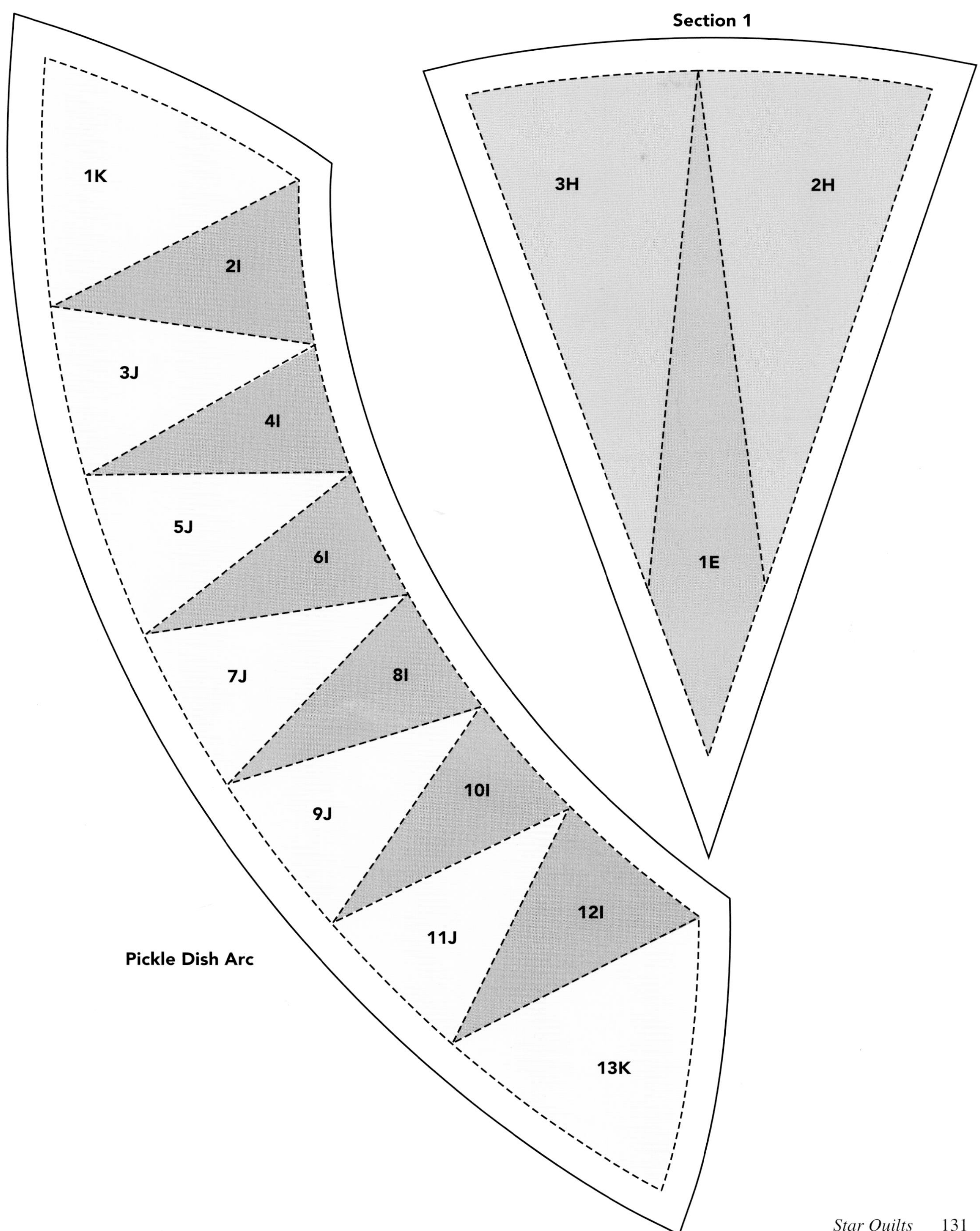
Section 1
3H
2H
1E
1K
2I
3J
4I
5J
6I
7J
8I
9J
10I
11J
12I
13K
Pickle Dish Arc

2H

3H

1E

4F

Section 2

Section 3

5G

4F

1E

3H

2H

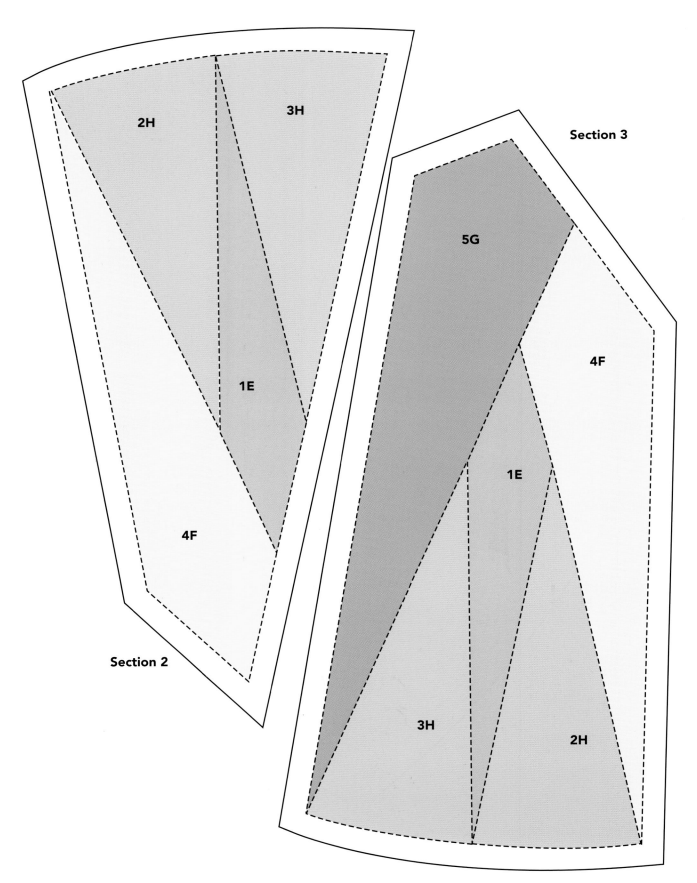

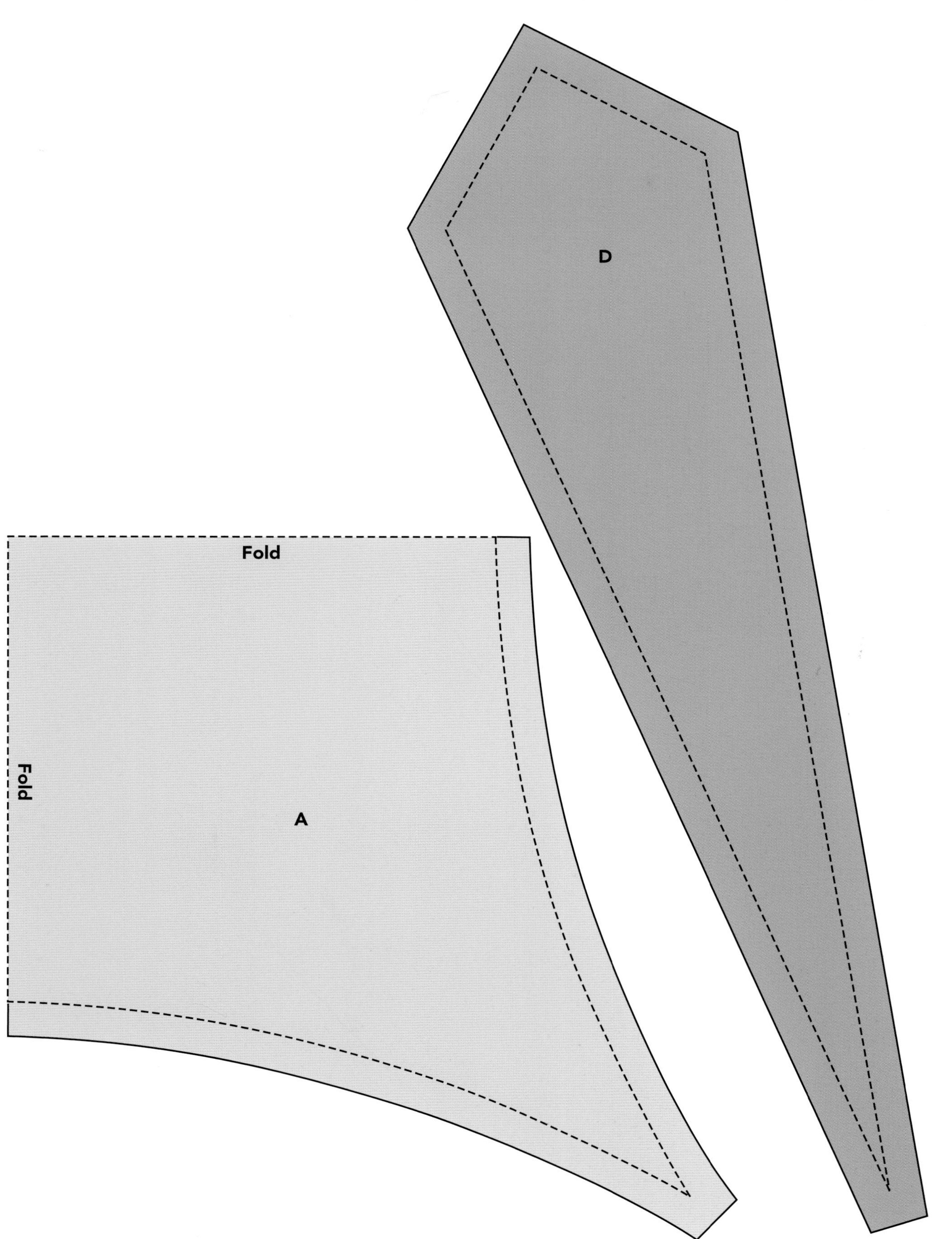
D
Fold
Fold
A

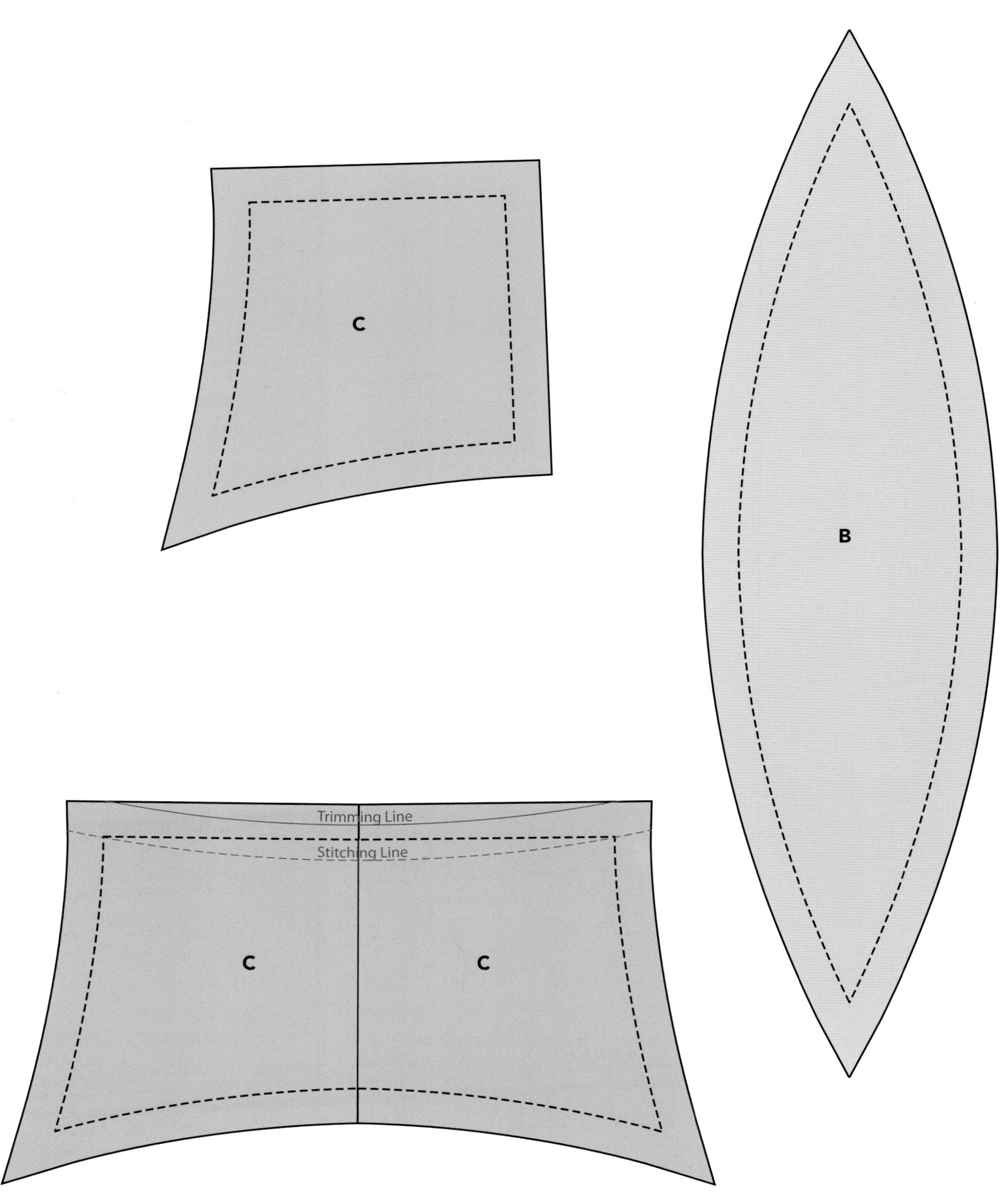
C
B
Trimming Line
Stitching Line
C
C

Sew *Easy*™ Paper Foundation Piecing

Paper foundation piecing is ideal for small, intricate designs or designs with odd angles and sizes of pieces. Eliminate tracing the patterns by using Fons & Porter's Printed Foundation Sheets.

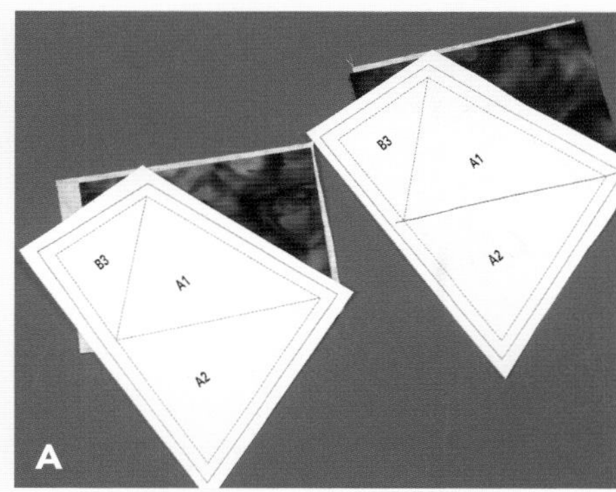

A

B

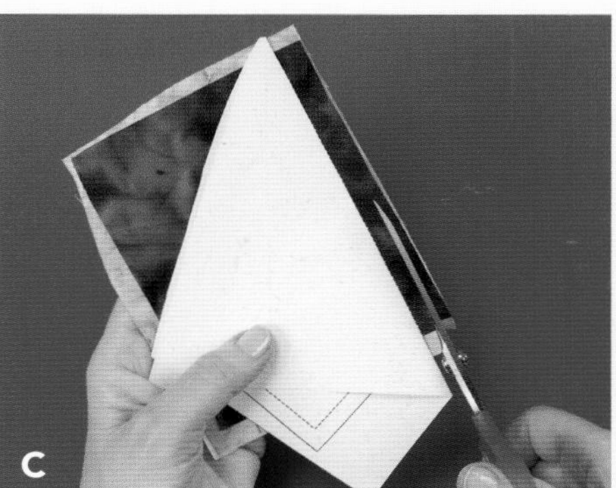
C

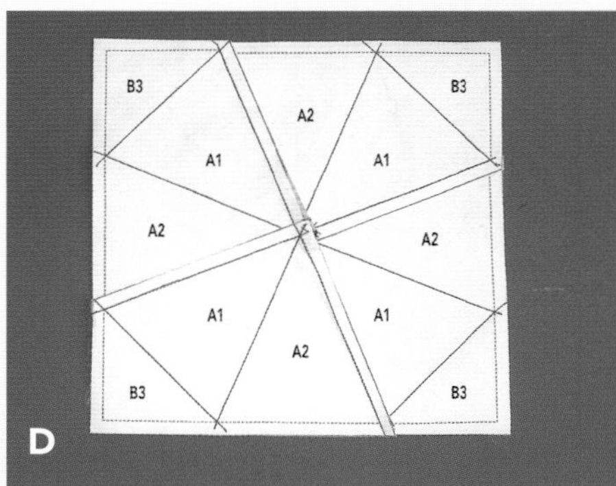

D

1. Using ruler and pencil, trace the outline of all shapes and the outer edge of the foundation pattern onto tracing paper. Number the pieces to indicate the stitching order. Using fabric pieces that are larger than the numbered areas, place fabrics for #1 and #2 right sides together. Position paper pattern atop fabrics with printed side of paper facing you *(Photo A)*. Make sure the fabric for #1 is under that area and that edges of fabrics extend ¼" beyond stitching line between the two sections.
2. Using a short machine stitch so papers will tear off easily later, stitch on line between the two areas, extending stitching into seam allowances at ends of seams.
3. Open out pieces and press or finger press the seam *(Photo B)*. The right sides of the fabric pieces will be facing out on the back side of the paper pattern.
4. Flip the work over and fold back paper pattern on stitched line. Trim seam allowance to ¼", being careful not to cut paper pattern *(Photo C)*.
5. Continue to add pieces in numerical order until pattern is covered. Use rotary cutter and ruler to trim excess paper and fabric along outer pattern lines.
6. Join pieced sections to complete block *(Photo D)*.
7. Carefully tear off foundation paper.

QUILT BY **Brenda Henning**. MACHINE QUILTED BY **Norma Kindred**.

SPICE ISLANDS Compass

Among the most evocative of quilt pattern names, Mariner's Compass was inspired by navigation motifs on ancient ocean maps. Designer Brenda Henning chose beautiful batiks in the colors of cinnamon, paprika, cayenne, ginger, and more.

PROJECT RATING: CHALLENGING

Size: 81" × 81"

Blocks: 9 (18") Mariner's Compass blocks

MATERIALS

12 fat quarters★ assorted medium/dark purple, rust, gold, and orange prints for compass points and centers

9 fat quarters★ assorted light cream, tan, peach, lavender, and beige prints for compass point accents

4½ yards light tan print for block backgrounds

2¾ yards medium tan print for sashing, inner border, and pieced outer border

3½ yards dark brown print for block borders, pieced outer border, and binding

That Patchwork Place Papers for Foundation Piecing or tracing paper

Template material

Fons & Porter Quarter Inch Seam Marker (optional)

7½ yards backing fabric

Queen-size quilt batting

★fat quarter = 18" × 20"

Cutting

Two methods are given for making triangle-squares. Read all instructions carefully before cutting.

Make templates for Compass Background and Compass Center from patterns on page 142. Foundation piecing patterns are on pages 142–143. Measurements include ¼" seam allowances. Border strips are exact length needed. You may want to make them longer to allow for piecing variations.

Sew **Smart**™

For basic instructions on foundation piecing, see *Sew Easy: Paper Foundation Piecing* on page 135.

From assorted medium/dark print fat quarters, cut:

- 9 matching sets of 8 (2¾" × 7½") B rectangles for compass points.
- 9 matching sets of 8 (2¼" × 5") C rectangles for compass points.
- 9 matching sets of 16 (1½" × 3½") D rectangles for compass points.
- 9 Compass Centers.

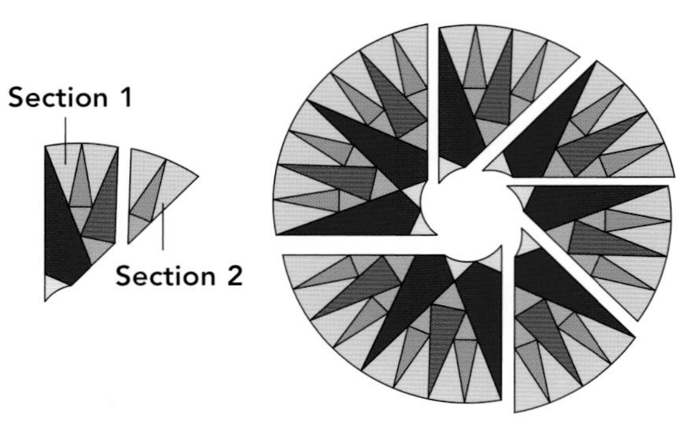

Segment Diagram   Compass Diagram

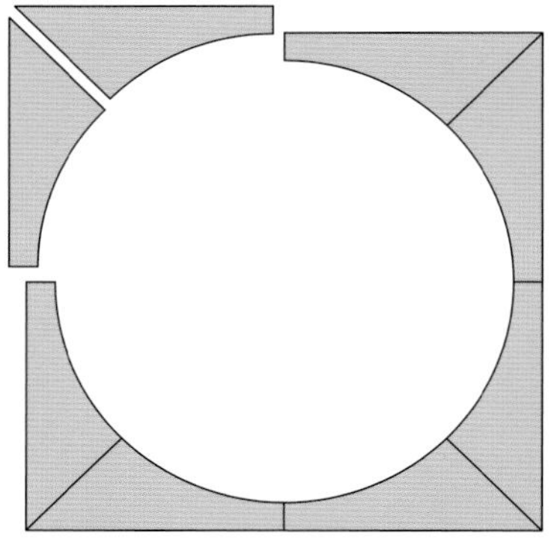

Background Assembly Diagram

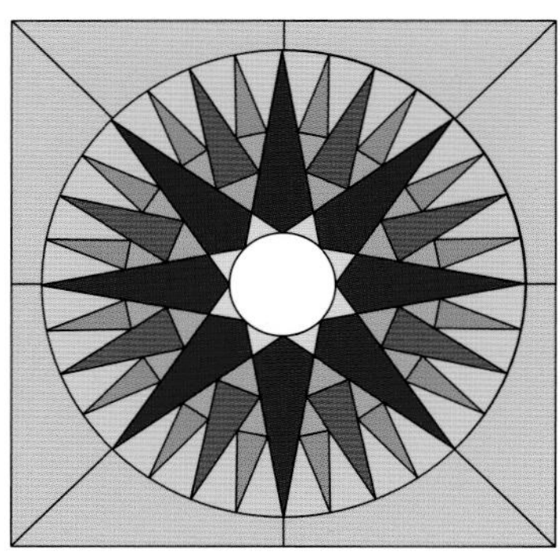

Block Center Assembly Diagram

From assorted light print fat quarters, cut:

- 9 matching sets of 16 (2½") E squares for compass.
- 9 matching sets of 8 (2½") F squares for compass.
- 9 matching sets of 8 (2½") G squares for compass.

From light tan print, cut:

- 12 (4¼"-wide) strips. From strips, cut 36 Compass Background and 36 Compass Background reverse.
- 18 (3¾"-wide) strips. From strips, cut 288 (3¾" × 2½") A rectangles for compass points background.
- 15 (2⅜"-wide) strips. From strips, cut 234 (2⅜") squares. Cut squares in half diagonally to make 468 half-square I triangles.

> Sew **Smart**™
>
> **For a quicker method of making triangle-squares, do not cut the I and J triangles from squares. Refer to *Sew Easy: Quick Triangle-Squares* on page 74.**

From medium tan print, cut:

- 5 (3⅞"-wide) strips. From strips, cut 50 (3⅞") squares. Cut squares in half diagonally to make 100 half-square J triangles.
- 12 (2⅜"-wide) strips. From strips, cut 192 (2⅜") squares. Cut squares in half diagonally to make 384 half-square I triangles.
- 17 (2"-wide) strips. From strips, cut 6 (2" × 21½") vertical sashing strips. Piece remaining strips to make 2 (2" × 66½") horizontal sashing strips, 2 (2" × 66½") top and bottom inner borders, and 2 (2" × 69½") side inner borders.
- 1 (4¼") square. Cut square in half diagonally in both directions to make 4 quarter-square K triangles.

From dark brown print, cut:

- 6 (3⅞"-wide) strips. From strips, cut 52 (3⅞") squares. Cut squares in half diagonally to make 104 half-square J triangles.
- 27 (2⅜"-wide) strips. From strips, cut 426 (2⅜") squares. Cut squares in half diagonally to make 852 half-square I triangles.
- 9 (2¼"-wide) strips for binding.
- 1 (4¼") square. Cut square in half diagonally in both directions to make 4 quarter-square K triangles.

Mariner's Compass Assembly

1. Trace 72 sets of foundation patterns for Section 1 and Section 2 on pages 142–143.
2. Foundation piece sections in numerical order, using pieces A through G as indicated. Make 8 matching Section 1 and Section 2.
3. Trim fabric around outside edges of foundations.
4. Join Section 1 and Section 2 as shown in *Segment Diagram*. Make 8 segments. Join segments to make 1 compass *(Compass Diagram)*. Remove paper from back of compass.
5. Join 1 Compass Background and 1 Compass Background reverse. Make 4 background units. Join units to complete block background *(Background Assembly Diagram)*.

Block Assembly Diagram

Block Diagram

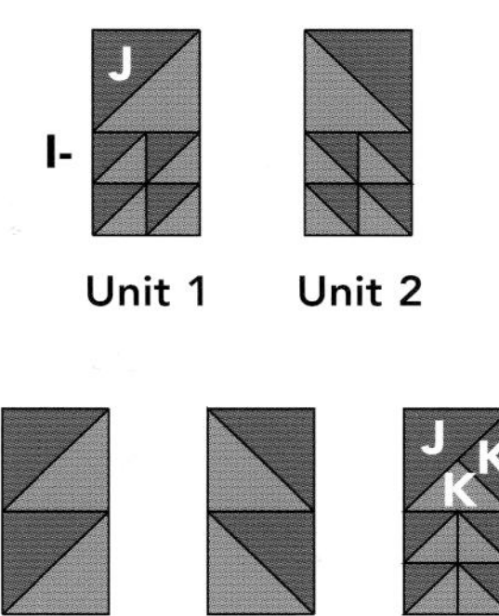

Border Unit Diagrams

> **Sew Smart™**
> **To reduce bulk, press seams open when joining background pieces. Press seam toward background after joining background to compass. —Liz**

6. Place pieced background atop compass, right sides facing. Match seams of pieced background to large B points. Pin and stitch the background and compass together *(Block Center Assembly Diagram).*
7. Appliqué 1 Compass Center on compass.

Block Assembly

1. Join 1 light tan I triangle and 1 dark brown I triangle to make 1 triangle-square. Make 52 light tan/dark brown I triangle-squares.
2. Join 12 I triangle-squares as shown in *Block Assembly Diagram* to make 1 Block Side Border. Make 2 Block Side Borders.
3. Join 14 I triangle-squares as shown to make top border. Repeat for bottom border.
4. Add side borders to block center. Add top and bottom borders to complete block *(Block Diagram).* Make 9 Mariner's Compass blocks.

Pieced Border Assembly

1. Join medium tan I triangles and dark brown I triangles to make 384 I triangle-squares.
2. In the same manner, join medium tan J triangles and dark brown J triangles to make 100 J triangle-squares.
3. Referring to *Border Unit Diagrams*, lay out 4 I triangle-squares and 1 J triangle-square as shown. Join to complete 1 Unit 1. Make 46 Unit 1.
4. In the same manner, make 46 Unit 2.
5. Lay out 2 J triangle-squares as shown. Join to complete 1 Unit 3. Make 2 Unit 3.
6. In the same manner, make 2 Unit 4.
7. Lay out 4 I triangle-squares, 1 medium tan K triangle, 1 dark brown K triangle, and 1 dark brown J triangle as shown. Join to complete 1 Unit 5. Make 4 Unit 5.
8. Referring to *Quilt Top Assembly Diagram* on page 140, lay out 11 Unit 1, 11 Unit 2, and 1 Unit 5 as shown. Join to make 1 pieced side border. Repeat for opposite side border.
9. In the same manner, join 12 Unit 1, 12 Unit 2, 1 Unit 3, 1 Unit 4, and 1 Unit 5 as shown to make top border. Repeat for bottom border.

Quilt Assembly

1. Lay out blocks and sashing strips as shown in *Quilt Top Assembly Diagram* on page 140.
2. Join into rows; join rows to complete quilt center.
3. Add tan top and bottom inner borders to quilt center. Add tan side inner borders to quilt.
4. Add pieced side borders to quilt. Add pieced top and bottom borders to quilt.

Finishing

1. Divide backing fabric into 3 (2½-yard) lengths. Divide one piece in half lengthwise to make two narrow panels. Join one narrow panel to 2 wider panels. Remaining panel is extra and may be used to make a hanging sleeve.

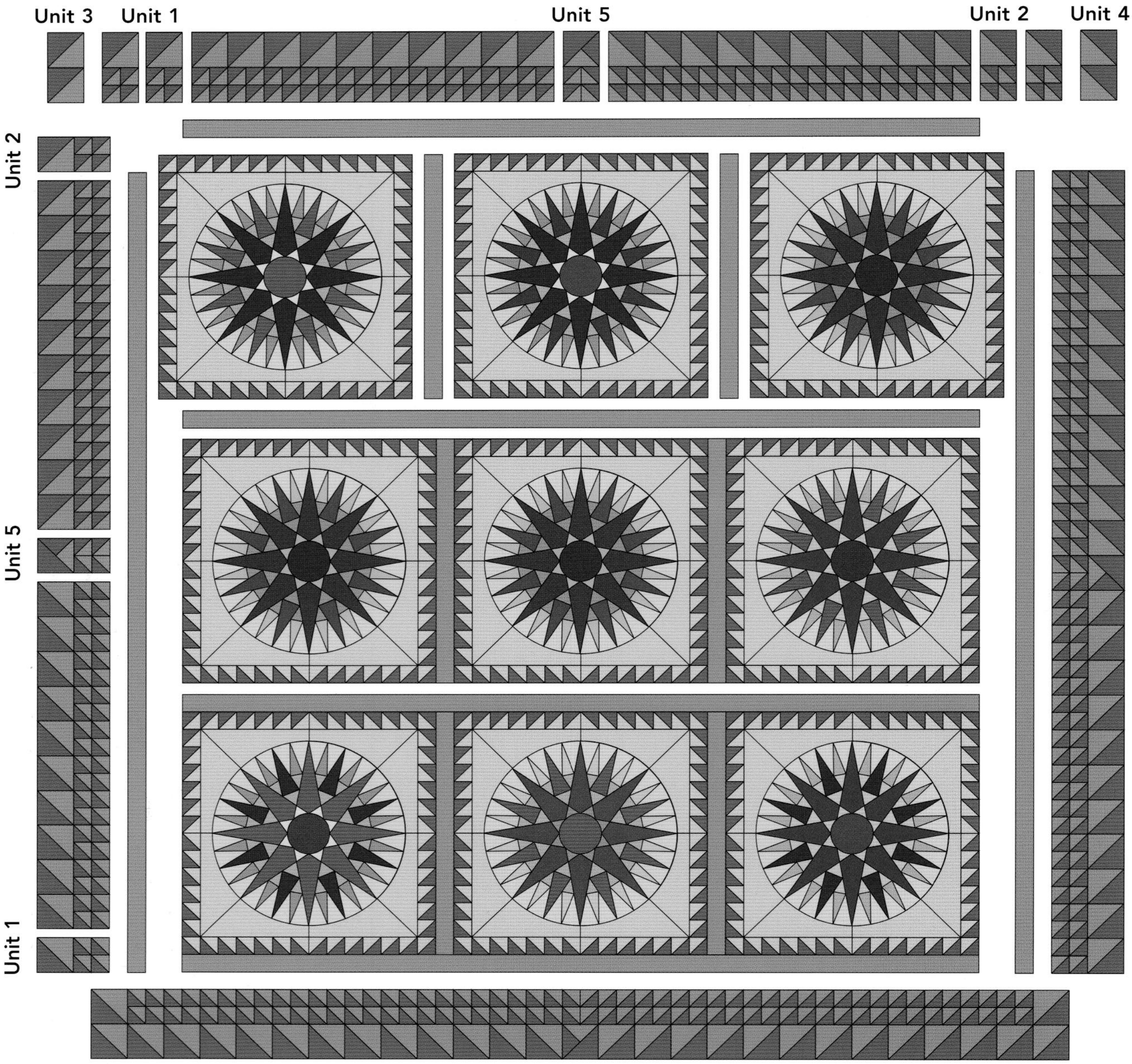

Unit 3 Unit 1 Unit 5 Unit 2 Unit 4

Unit 2 Unit 5 Unit 1

Quilt Top Assembly Diagram

2. Layer backing, batting, and quilt top; baste. Quilt as desired. Quilt shown was machine quilted with a radiating sunburst in each block and waves in the sashing and borders *(Quilting Diagram)*.

3. Join 2¼"-wide dark brown strips into 1 continuous piece for straight-grain French-fold binding. Add binding to quilt.

Quilting Diagram

DESIGNER

Brenda Henning is known for her graphic pieced quilts as well as her colorful stained glass designs. Her latest endeavor is Triangulations™ 2.0 software for printing pre-drawn grids for constructing half-square and quarter-square triangle units. Look for Brenda's book *Mariner's Compass Quilts: Reach for the Stars.* ⁂

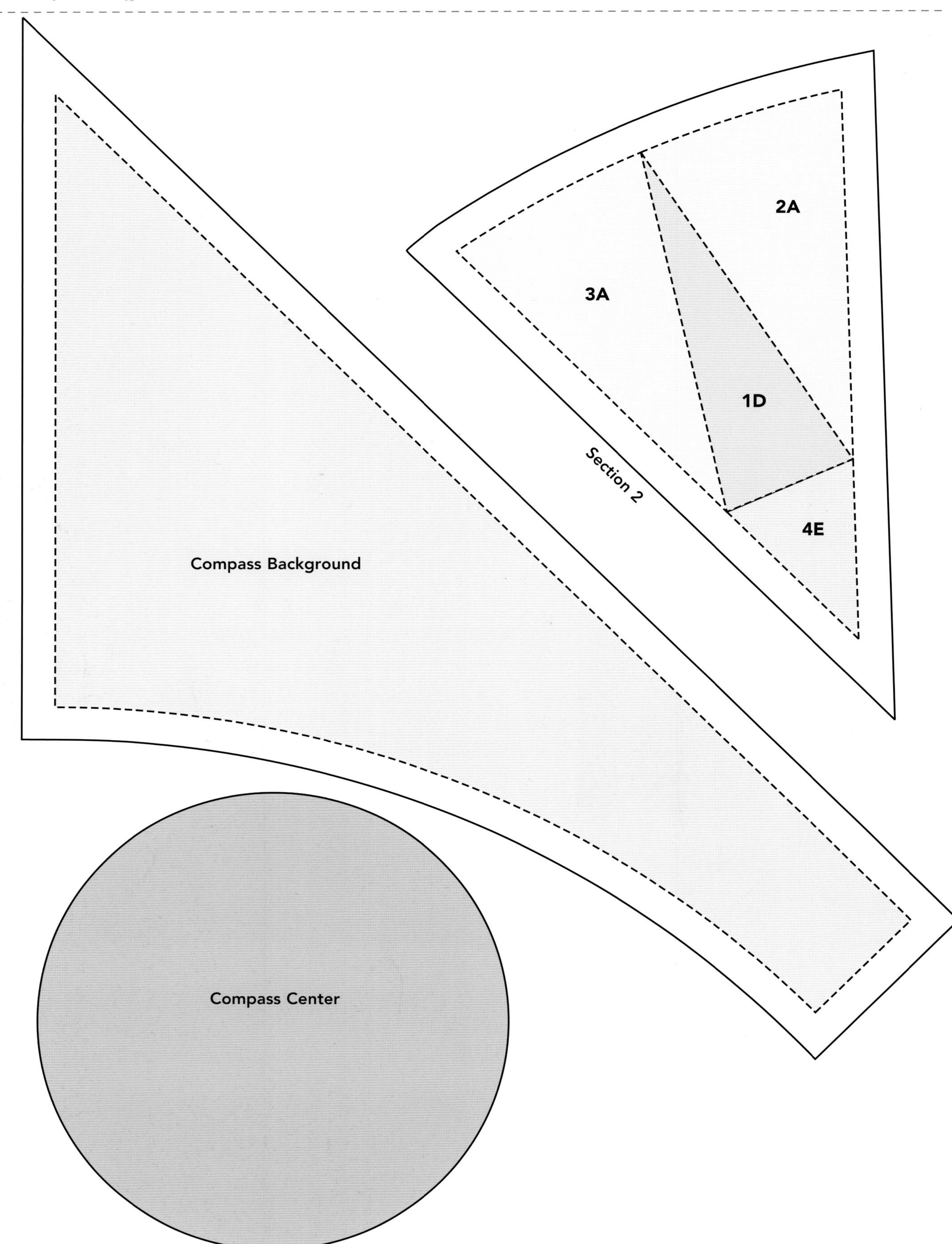
2A
3A
1D
Section 2
4E
Compass Background
Compass Center

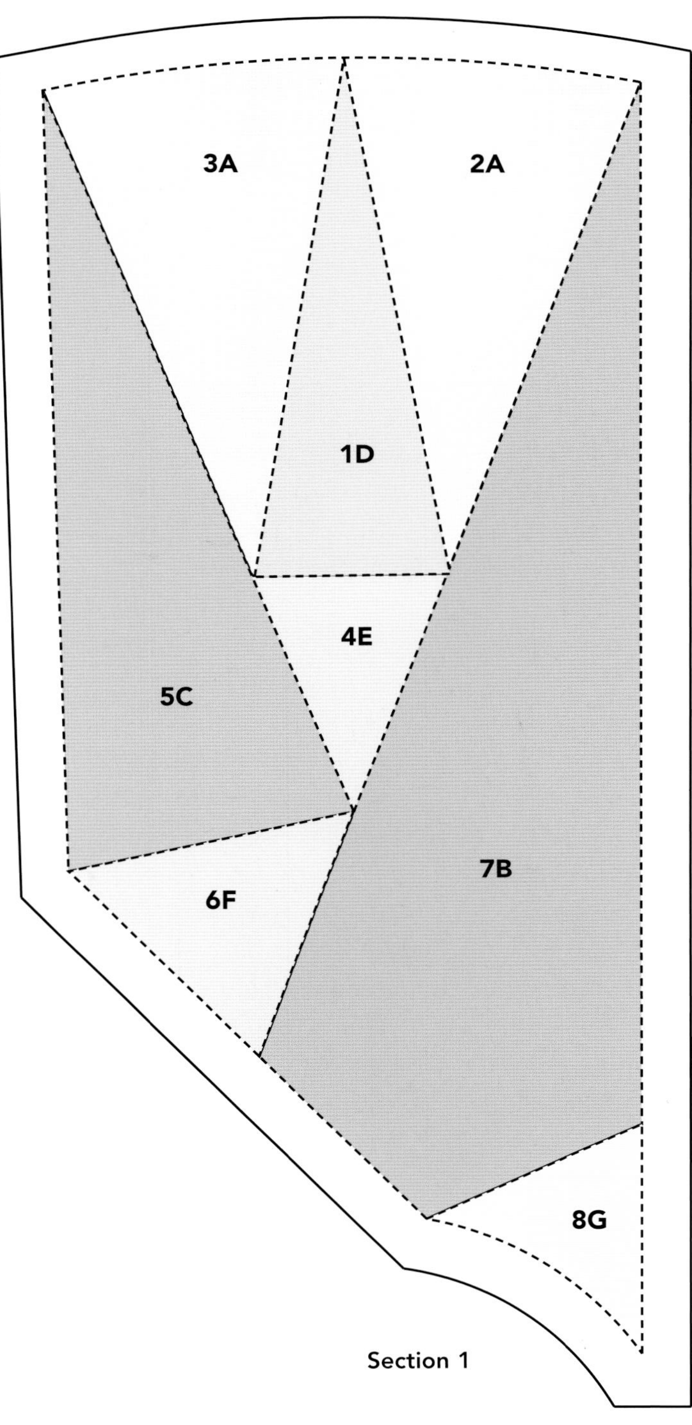

TRIED & TRUE

We made a more traditional block using reproduction fabrics by Windham Fabrics.

Storm at Sea

The allover design of *Storm at Sea* is created from three patchwork units. Strategic placement of the yellow fabric catches the eye and creates great movement.

PROJECT RATING: INTERMEDIATE

Size: 40" × 52"

MATERIALS

10 fat quarters★ assorted light/medium batiks in yellow, orange, green, and blue

6 fat quarters★ assorted dark batiks in red, purple, green, and blue

⅜ yard blue batik for binding

Template material or Storm at Sea Template Set

2¾ yards backing fabric

Crib-size quilt batting

★fat quarter = 18" × 20"

Cutting

Measurements include ¼" seam allowances. Patterns for the G diamond and H triangles are on page 147. You will have some extra pieces so you can arrange the colors to get a look that is pleasing to you.

From each light/medium fat quarter, cut:

- 1 (4⅞"-wide) strip. From strip, cut 3 (4⅞") squares. Cut squares in half diagonally to make 6 half-square F triangles.
- 2 (4½"-wide) strips. From strips, cut 2 (4½") D squares and 4 G diamonds.
- 1 (2⅞"-wide) strip. From strip, cut 4 (2⅞") squares and 2 (2½") A squares. Cut 2⅞" squares in half diagonally to make 8 half-square C triangles.

From each dark fat quarter, cut:

- 1 (5¼"-wide) strip. From strip, cut 2 (5¼") squares. Cut squares in half diagonally in both directions to make 8 quarter-square E triangles.
- 2 (4½"-wide) strips. From strips, cut 11 pairs of H triangles. (Place strips with right sides together so you will be cutting two mirror image pieces at one time.)
- 1 (3¼"-wide) strip. From strip, cut 4 (3¼") squares. Cut squares in half diagonally in both directions to make 16 quarter-square B triangles.

From blue batik, cut:

- 5 (2¼"-wide) strips for binding.

> Sew **Smart**™
>
> **For best results, lay out the entire quilt on a design wall before beginning to piece the units. Rearrange colors to create a design you like.**

Unit Assembly

1. Choose 1 light/medium A square, 4 dark B triangles, and 4 light/medium C triangles.

2. Lay out pieces as shown in *Unit 1 Diagrams* on page 146. Join B triangles to A square. Join C triangles to center unit to complete 1 Unit 1. Make 20 Unit 1.

3. In the same manner, join 1 light/medium D square, 4 dark E triangles, and 4 light/medium F triangles to make 1 Unit 2 (*Unit 2 Diagrams*). Make 12 Unit 2.

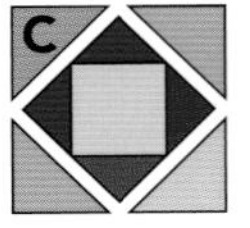

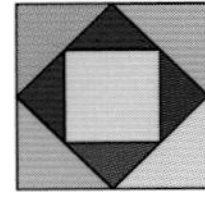

Unit 1 Diagrams

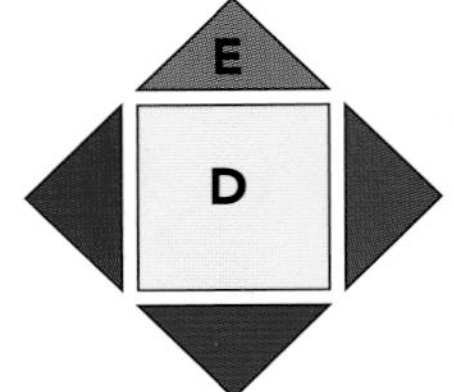

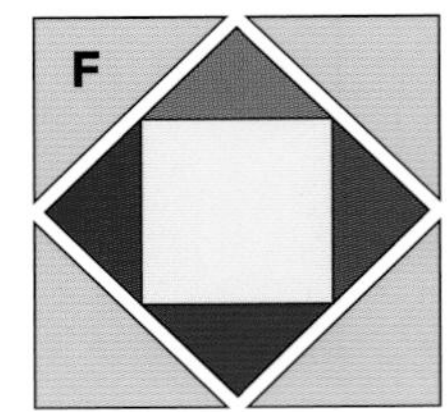

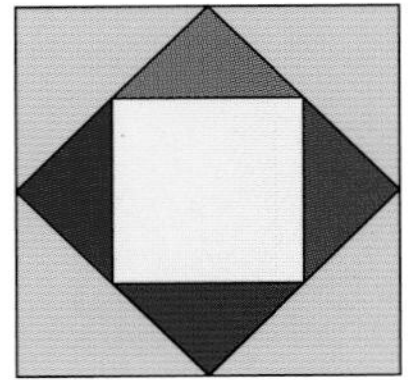

Unit 2 Diagrams

Unit 3 Diagrams

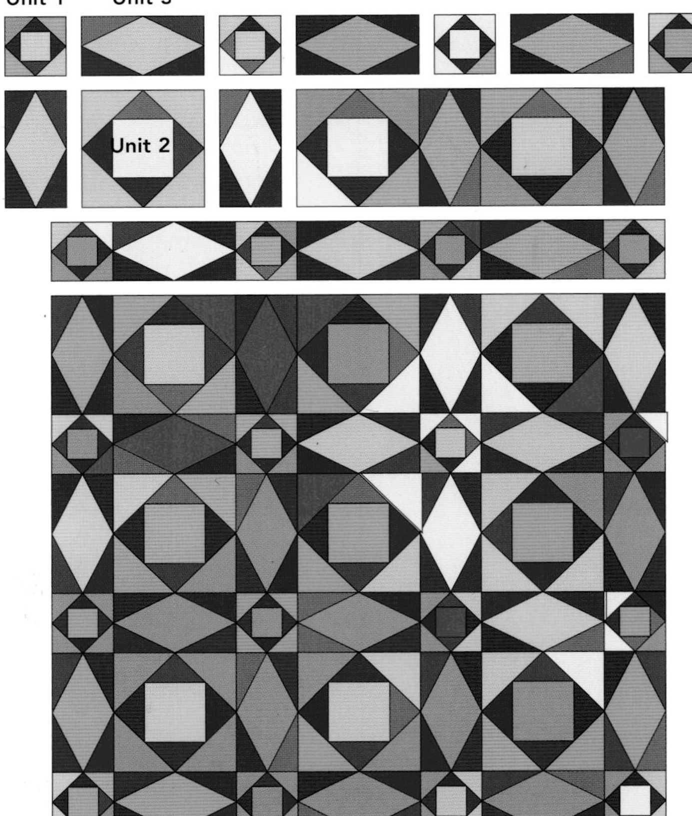

Quilt Top Assembly Diagram

4. Choose 1 light/medium G diamond, 2 dark H triangles, and 2 dark H reverse triangles.
5. Lay out pieces as shown in *Unit 3 Diagrams*. Join pieces to complete 1 Unit 3. Make 31 Unit 3.

Quilt Assembly

1. Referring to *Quilt Top Assembly Diagram* and photo on page 145, lay out Units 1–3 as shown.
2. Join into horizontal rows; join rows to complete quilt top.

Finishing

1. Divide backing fabric into 2 (1⅜-yard) pieces. Join panels lengthwise. Seam will run horizontally.
2. Layer backing, batting, and quilt top; baste. Quilt as desired. Quilt shown was quilted with straight lines creating a grid.
3. Join 2¼"-wide blue batik strips into 1 continuous piece for straight-grain French-fold binding. Add binding to quilt.

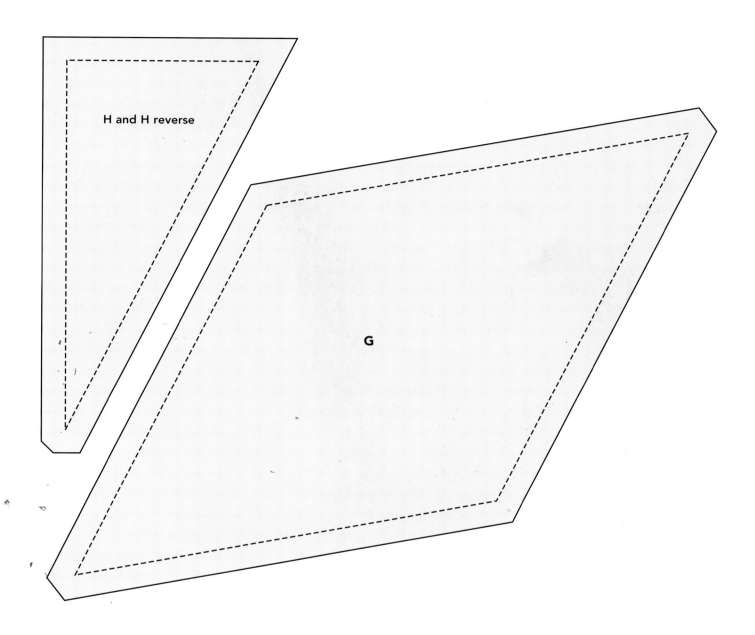

H and H reverse

G

DESIGNER

John Flynn considers himself a problem solver. "The more disagreeable the task, the more opportunity there is to streamline the process," says John. "Working out the most efficient way to perform sewing tasks is actually my favorite part of quilting." His development of laser cut quilt kits is just one way he has been improving the efficiency of quiltmaking. Another is his no-baste machine quilting system for the home sewing machine. ⁂

PROJECT BY **Cindy Hathaway**.

Ozark Star Table Topper

Make this easy table topper in an afternoon. But plan to make more than one—your friends and family will surely want one too!

PROJECT RATING: INTERMEDIATE

Size: 20" × 18½"

MATERIALS

1 fat eighth★ green print #1 for center

1 fat quarter★★ green print #2 for outer diamonds

1 fat quarter★★ tan print

1 fat eighth★ black print

1 fat eighth★ rust print

¼ yard black solid for binding

Fons & Porter Hexagons Ruler (optional)

Fons & Porter 60° Diamonds Ruler (optional)

Fons & Porter 60° Pyramids Ruler (optional)

¾ yard backing fabric

26" square quilt batting

★fat eighth = 9" × 20"

★★fat quarter = 18" × 20"

Cutting

Measurements include ¼" seam allowances. Instructions are written for using the Fons & Porter Hexagons, Diamonds, and Pyramids Rulers. See *Sew Easy: Cutting 60° Diamonds & Pyramids* on page 152 and *Sew Easy: Cutting Hexagons* on page 153 for instructions on using these rulers. If not using the Fons & Porter Rulers, make templates from patterns on pages 150–151.

From green print #1, cut:

- 1 (5½"-wide) strip. From strip, cut 1 Hexagon.

From green print #2, cut:

- 3 (5½"-wide) strips. From strips, cut 6 large Diamonds.

From tan print, cut:

- 4 (3"-wide) strips. From strips, cut 18 Pyramids.

From black print, cut:

- 2 (3"-wide) strips. From strips, cut 6 small Diamonds.

From rust print, cut:

- 2 (3"-wide) strips. From strips, cut 6 small Diamonds.

From black solid, cut:

- 2 (2¼"-wide) strips for binding.

Table Topper Assembly

1. Join green print #1 Hexagon and 3 tan print Pyramids as shown in *Unit 1 Diagrams*.

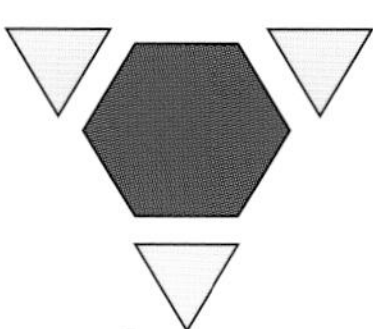

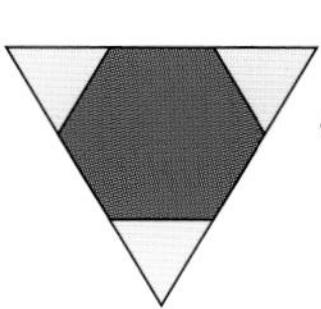

Unit 1 Diagrams

2. Join 2 black print Diamonds and 1 tan print Pyramid as shown in *Unit 2 Diagrams*. Make 3 Unit 2.

Unit 2 Diagrams

3. Join 1 rust print small Diamond and 2 tan print Pyramids as shown in *Unit 3 Diagrams*. Make 6 Unit 3.

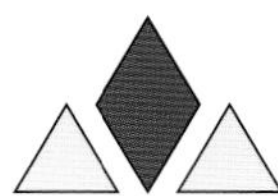

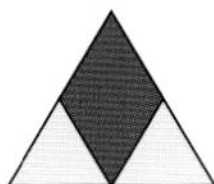

Unit 3 Diagrams

4. Join 1 Unit 3 and 2 green print #2 large Diamonds as shown in *Unit 4 Diagrams*. Make 3 Unit 4.

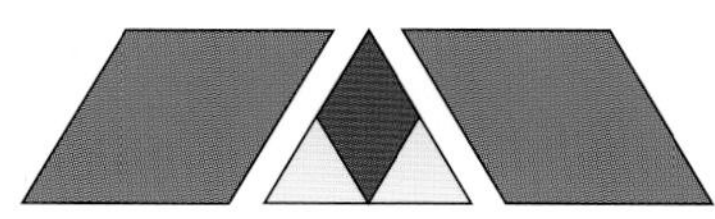

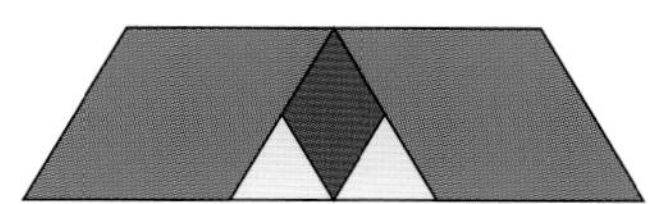

Unit 4 Diagrams

5. Lay out Units 1, 2, 3, and 4 as shown in *Table Topper Assembly Diagram*. Join units in numerical order to complete table topper.

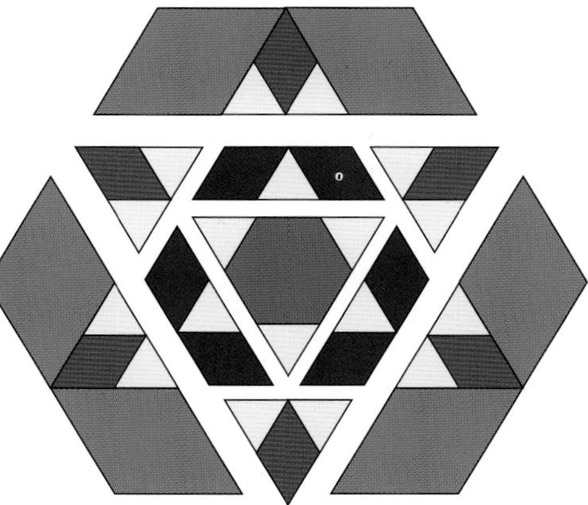

Quilt Top Assembly Diagram

Finishing

1. Layer backing, batting, and quilt top; baste. Quilt as desired. Quilt shown was quilted in the ditch and with parallel lines in outer diamonds *(Quilting Diagram)*.

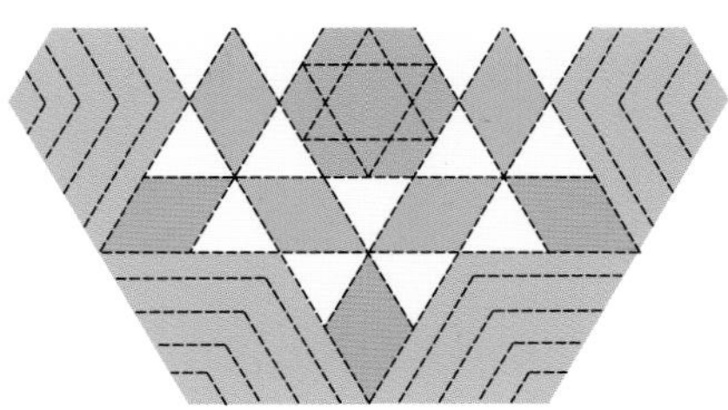

Quilting Diagram

2. Join 2¼"-wide black solid strips into 1 continuous piece for straight-grain French-fold binding. Add binding to quilt. ✱

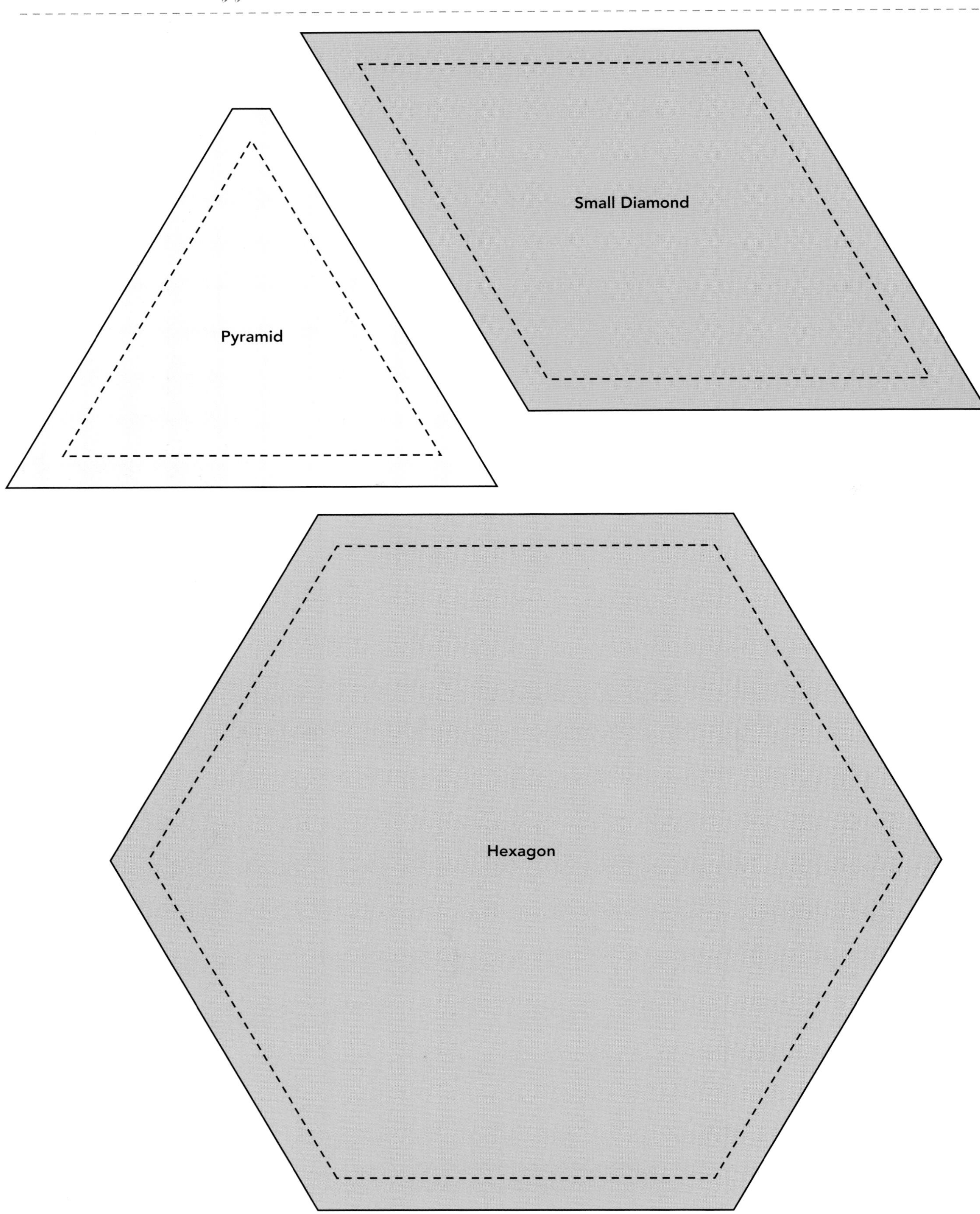
Small Diamond
Pyramid
Hexagon

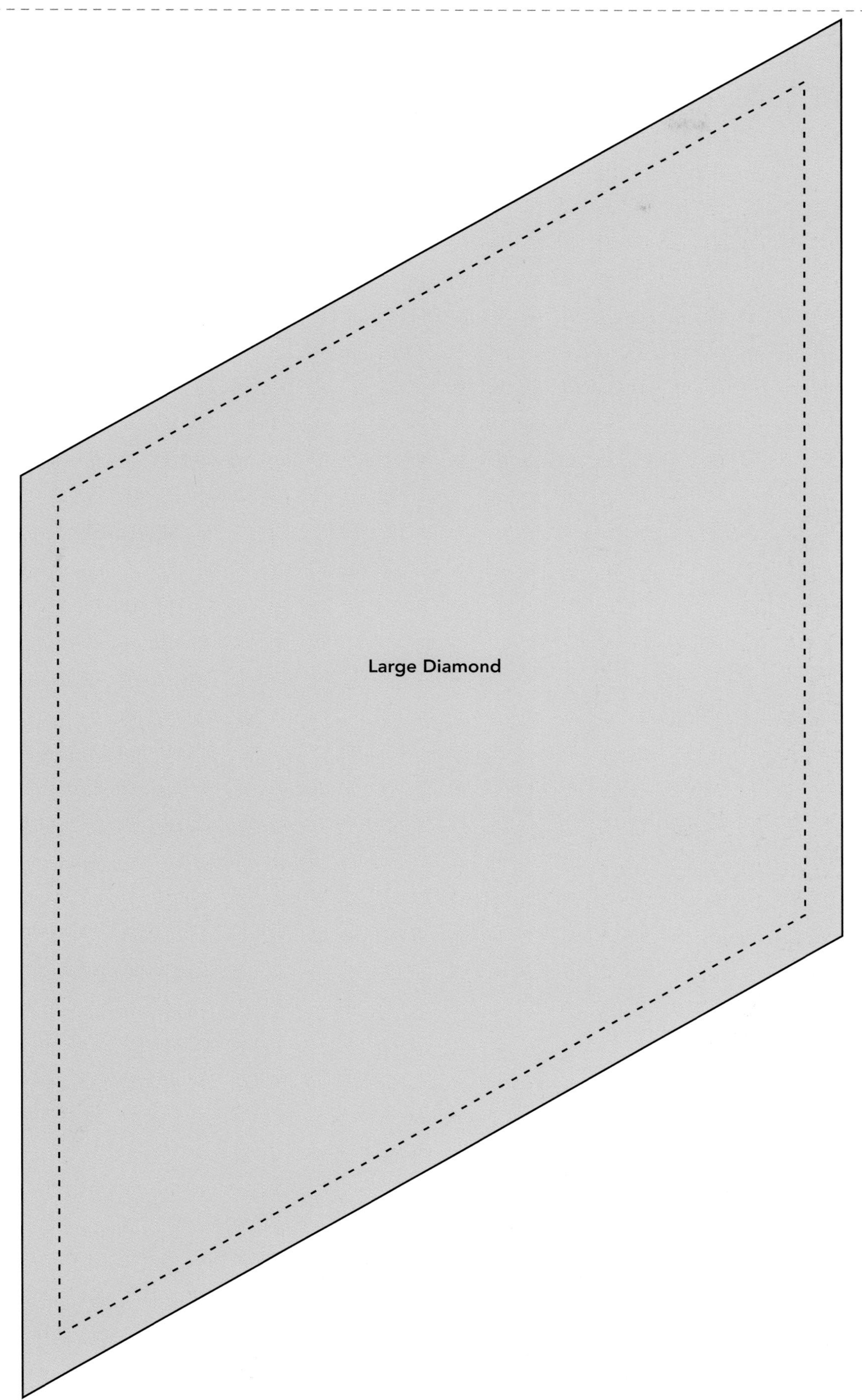
Large Diamond

Sew *Easy*™ Cutting 60° Diamonds & Pyramids

Use the Fons & Porter 60° Diamonds Ruler and 60° Pyramids Ruler to make easy work of cutting pieces for *Ozark Star Table Topper*.

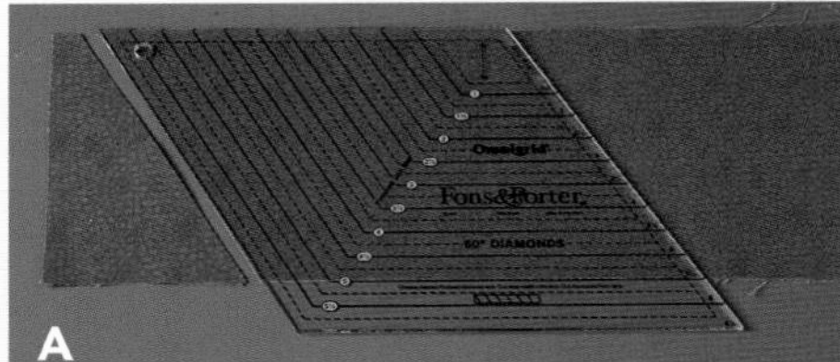
A

B

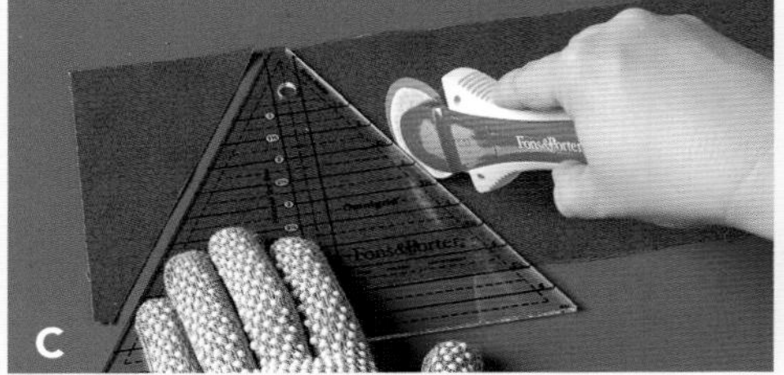
C

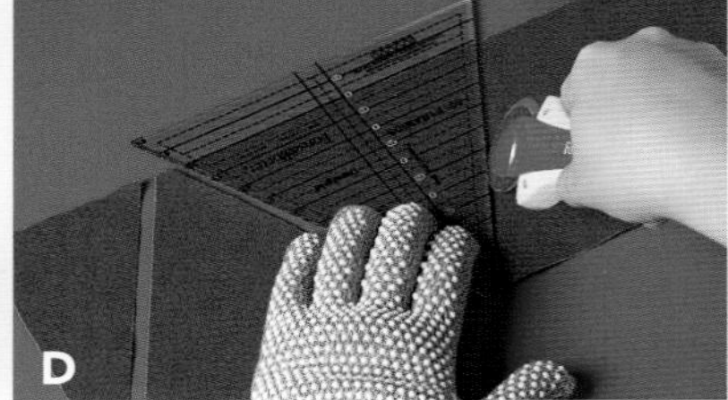
D

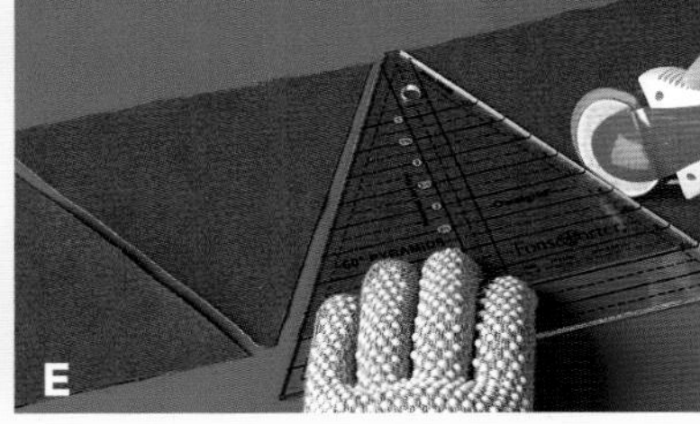
E

Diamonds

1. To cut diamonds, cut strip desired width (for Ozark Star Table Topper, cut strips 5½" wide for large diamonds and 3" wide for small diamonds).
2. Referring to strip width numbers along lower section of Fons & Porter 60° Diamonds ruler, find the solid black line on the ruler that corresponds to the width of strip you cut.
3. Beginning at left end of fabric strip, place ruler so bottom solid line for desired size diamond is aligned with bottom edge of strip, and cut along left side of ruler *(Photo A).*

Sew **Smart**™

To cut the maximum number of pieces from a fabric strip, open out the strip so you will be cutting through a single layer. To cut many pieces, layer several strips and cut them at the same time. —Liz

4. Move ruler to the right; align desired line of ruler with slanted edge and bottom edge of strip. Cut along right slanted edge of ruler to cut diamond *(Photo B).*
5. Repeat Step #4 to cut required number of diamonds.

Pyramids

1. To cut pyramids, cut strip desired width (for Ozark Star Table Topper, cut strips 3" wide).
2. Referring to strip width numbers along lower section of Fons & Porter 60° Pyramids ruler, find the solid black line on the ruler that corresponds to the width of strip you cut.
3. Beginning at left end of fabric strip, place ruler atop strip so solid line on ruler is along bottom edge of fabric strip. Trim along left slanted edge of ruler.

Sew **Smart**™

If you cut left handed, work from the right end of the fabric strip and begin by cutting along the right edge of the ruler. —Marianne

4. Cut along right slanted edge of ruler to cut one pyramid triangle *(Photo C).*
5. To cut second pyramid triangle, rotate ruler so solid line is on top edge of strip and angled side of ruler is aligned with slanted edge of strip. Cut along slanted edge of ruler *(Photo D).*
6. Continue in this manner to cut required number of Pyramids *(Photo E).*

Sew *Easy*™ Cutting Hexagons

Cutting hexagons is easy with the Fons & Porter Hexagons Ruler. Follow these simple instructions to cut pieces for *Ozark Star Table Topper*.

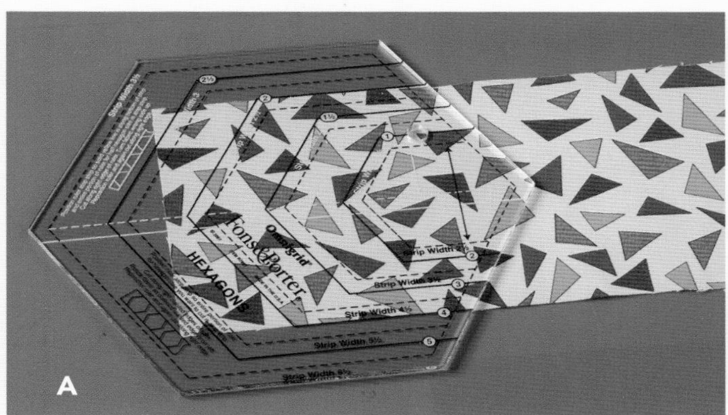
A

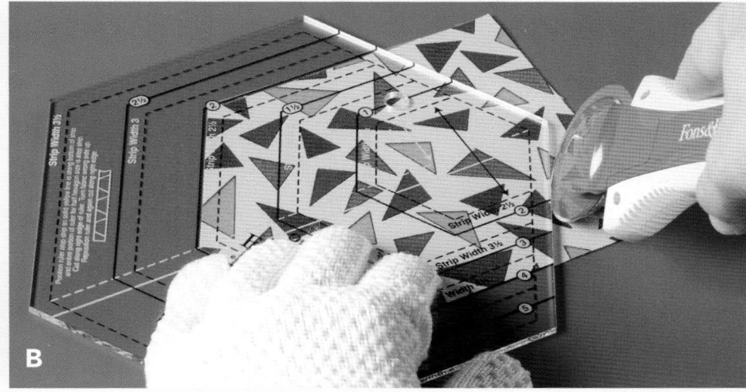
B

1. To cut hexagons, cut strip desired width (for *Ozark Star Table Topper*, strip width is 5½").
2. Refer to numbers along lower section of ruler and find the solid black line on the Hexagons Ruler that corresponds to the width of strip you cut.
3. Beginning at left end of fabric strip, place ruler so top and bottom solid lines for desired-size hexagon are aligned with top and bottom edges of strip and entire desired-size hexagon shape is atop strip *(Photo A)*. Cut along right slanted edges of ruler.

Sew Smart™

To cut the maximum number of pieces from a fabric strip, open out the strip so you will be cutting through a single layer. To cut many pieces, layer several strips and cut them at the same time. —Liz

4. Remove ruler and rotate the fabric piece you just cut so slanted edges are to your left. Reposition ruler atop fabric so correct solid lines are aligned with cut slanted edges. Cut along right slanted edges of ruler to complete cutting hexagon *(Photo B)*.
5. Repeat Steps #3 and #4 to cut additional hexagons.

Sew Smart™

To avoid having to rotate fabric, work on a small cutting mat and turn the mat. —Marianne

QUILT BY **Virginia A. Walton**. MACHINE QUILTED BY **Betty Sandiferd**.

Uneven Star

Designer Virginia Walton made this dynamic quilt using her Multi-Angle, Wedge Ruler. See *Sew Easy: Uneven Star Point Units* on page 159 for detailed instructions for cutting and stitching the star points in this quilt.

PROJECT RATING: INTERMEDIATE

Size: 52" × 60"

MATERIALS

NOTE: Fabrics in the quilt shown are by Benartex.

1½ yards multicolor print for blocks, outer border, and binding

13 fat eighths* assorted prints in gold, green, red, orange, blue, brown, rust, purple, aqua, and yellow for blocks

2¾ yards ivory solid for background

Multi-Angle, Wedge Ruler (optional) or template material

3¼ yards backing fabric

Twin-size quilt batting

*fat eighth = 9" × 20"

Cutting

Measurements include ¼" seam allowances. Border strips are exact length needed. You may want to make them longer to allow for piecing variations. If NOT using Multi-Angle, Wedge Ruler, make template plastic Trimming Guide from pattern on page 157. B, C, and D pieces are all cut over-sized and will be trimmed after Star Point Units are pieced.

From multicolor print, cut:

- 2 (4½"-wide) strips. From strips, cut 13 (4½") A squares.
- 6 (3½"-wide) strips. Piece strips to make 2 (3½" × 54½") side outer borders and 2 (3½" × 52½") top and bottom outer borders.
- 7 (2¼"-wide) strips for binding.

From ivory solid cut:

- 7 (5"-wide) strips. From strips, cut 52 (5") squares. Trim squares as shown in *Trimming Diagrams* (using Multi-Angle, Wedge Ruler and following instructions in *Sew Easy: Uneven Star Point Units* on page 159), or trim using Trimming Guide to make B piece.

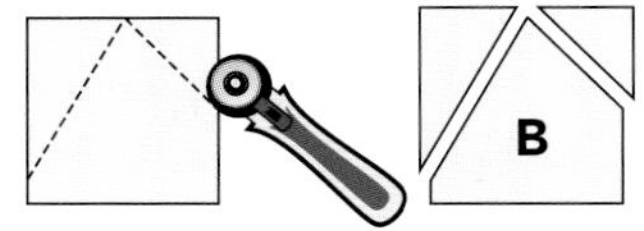

Trimming Diagrams

- 10 (4½"-wide) strips. From strips, cut 4 (4½" × 24½") G rectangles, 2 (4½" × 20½") F rectangles, 4 (4½" × 12½") E rectangles, and 32 (4½") A squares.
- 6 (1½"-wide) strips. Piece strips to make 2 (1½" × 52½") side inner borders and 2 (1½" × 46½") top and bottom inner borders.

From each fat eighth, cut:

- 1 (4"-wide) strip. From strip, cut 2 (4" × 6½") rectangles. Cut rectangles in half diagonally to make 4 C triangles *(Rectangle Cutting Diagrams)*.

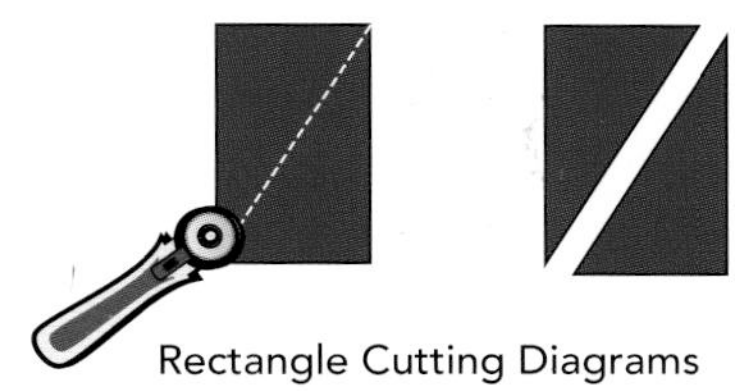
Rectangle Cutting Diagrams

- 1 (3"-wide) strip. From strip, cut 2 (3") squares. Cut squares in half diagonally to make 4 half-square D triangles.

Star Point Unit Assembly

1. Choose 1 set of 4 B pieces, 4 matching D triangles, and 2 pairs of matching C triangles for each set of Star Point Units.

2. Referring to *Sew Easy: Uneven Star Point Units*, make 13 sets of Star Point Units *(Star Point Unit Diagrams* on page 156*)*.

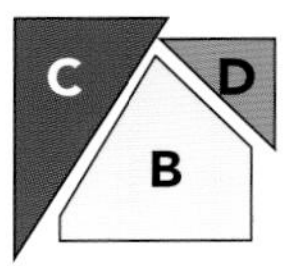

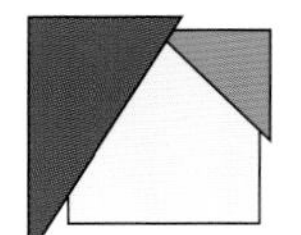
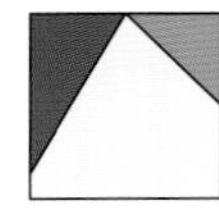

Star Point Unit Diagrams

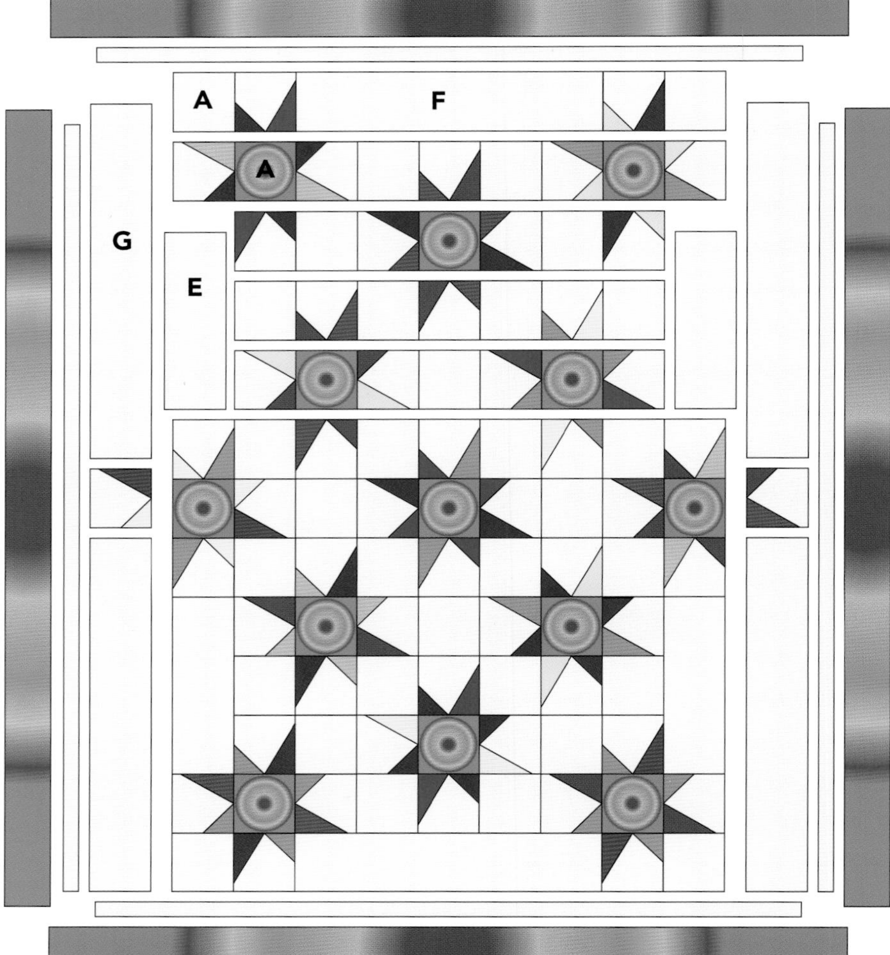

Quilt Top Assembly Diagram

Quilt Assembly

1. Lay out Star Point Units, A squares, and E, F, and G rectangles as shown in *Quilt Top Assembly Diagram.* Join in sections, join sections to complete quilt center.
2. Add ivory side inner borders to quilt center. Add top and bottom inner borders to quilt.
3. Repeat for multicolor print outer borders.

Finishing

1. Divide backing into 2 (1⅝-yard) lengths. Cut 1 piece in half lengthwise to make 2 narrow panels. Join 1 narrow panel to each side of wider panel; press seam allowances toward narrow panels.
2. Layer backing, batting, and quilt top; baste. Quilt as desired. Quilt shown was quilted with an allover swirl design using variegated thread *(Quilting Diagram).*
3. Join 2¼"-wide multicolor print strips into 1 continuous piece for straight-grain French-fold binding. Add binding to quilt.

Quilting Diagram

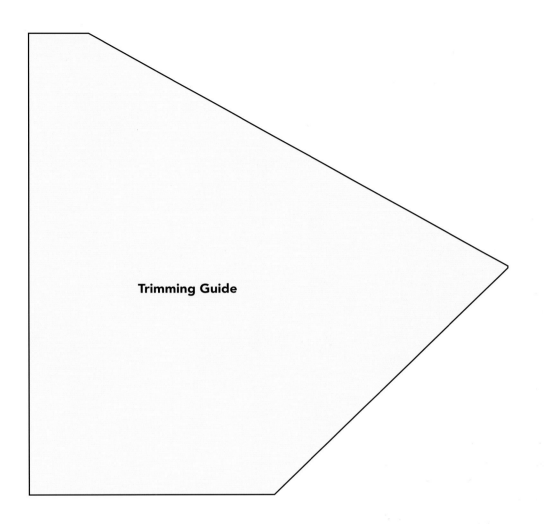

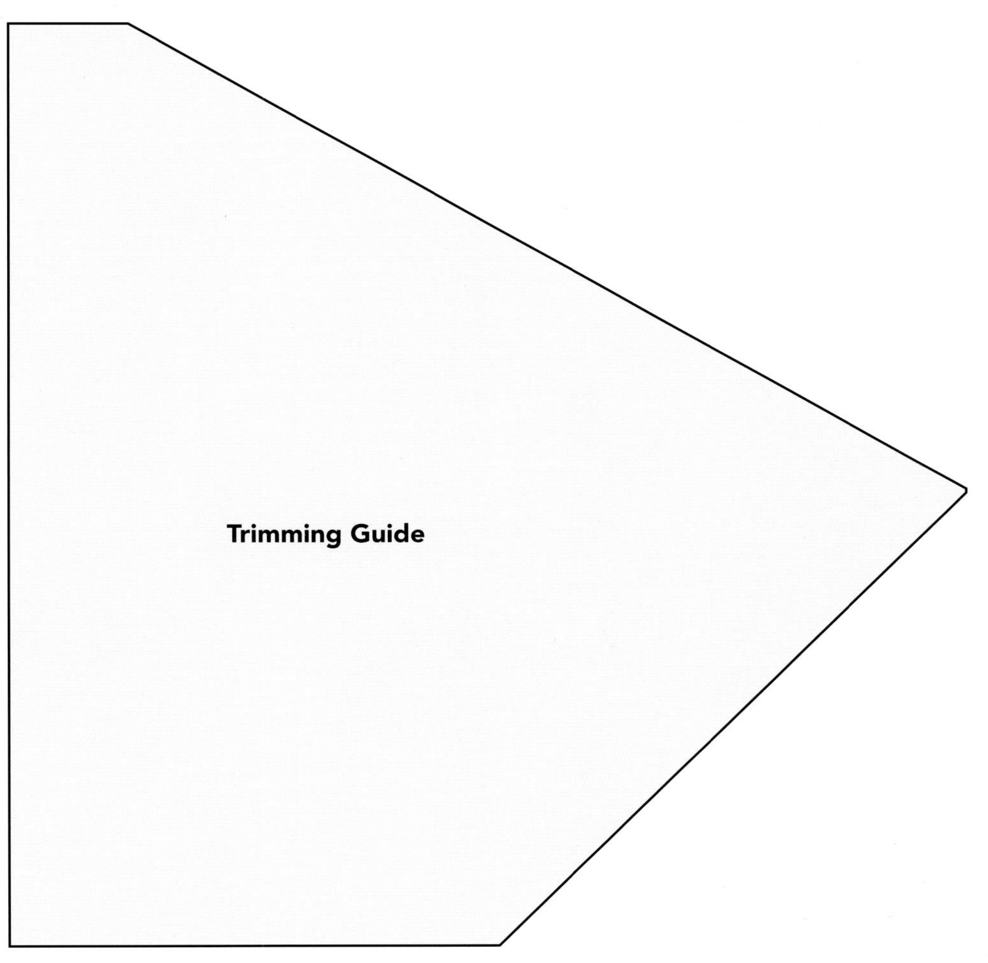

TRIED & TRUE

Soft greens prints by Connecting Threads are perfect for a monochromatic version of this block.

DESIGNER

Virginia Walton is an artist and teacher who specializes in easy sewing machine techniques such as her "No Pins" curved piecing method. She is the inventor of the Creative Curves Rulers, the Creative Curves Ellipse Rulers, Creative Curves Kaleidoscope Ruler, and the Multi-Angle, Wedge Ruler. She can be seen on QNNtv.com's Web site demonstrating the new Multi-Angle, Wedge Ruler & Sampler Pattern in the free videos section. ⁕

Sew *Easy*™ Uneven Star Point Units

Use Virginia Walton's Multi-Angle, Wedge Ruler to cut Uneven Star Point Units for the *Uneven Star* quilt on page 154.

If using Multi-Angle, Wedge Ruler, read *General Cutting and Sewing Instructions* provided with the ruler.

> Sew **Smart**™
> **For an even better understanding of how to use this ruler, view the three-part video *Creative Curves* on QNNtv.com (in the Free Video section of the Web site). —Marianne**

1. Fold 5" square in half; press crease; unfold.
2. Trim 45° angle. Place 45° line on ruler on crease and corner of ruler at edge of square. Trim as shown *(Photo A)*. If NOT using the Multi-Angle ruler, use the Trimming Guide on page 157 to trim 45° and 60° angles.

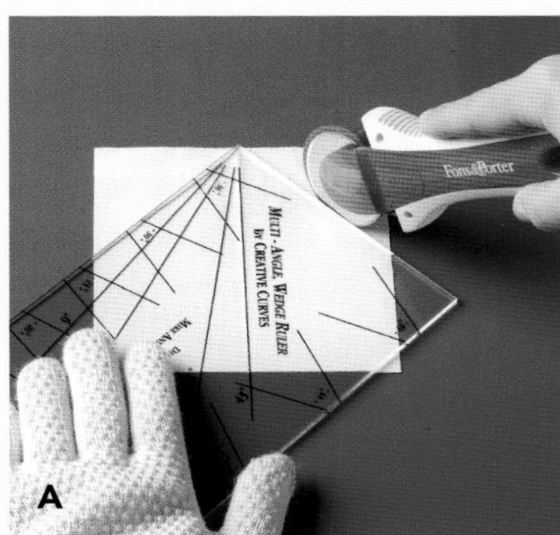

A

3. Turn ruler wrong side facing up. Place 60° line on ruler on crease and corner of ruler at edge of square. Trim as shown *(Photo B)*.

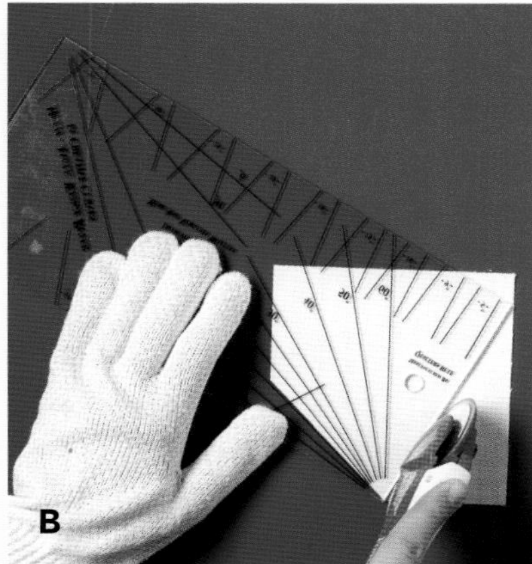
B

4. Add D triangle to trimmed B piece. Add C triangle to B *(Photo C)*.

> Sew **Smart**™
> **Both D and C triangles are over size and will be trimmed to complete Star Point Units. —Virginia**

5. Trim Star Point Unit to 4½"-square. Trim sides first, aligning 2¼" line on ruler on the crease. Trim top next, aligning ¼" line of ruler on point *(Photo D)*. Trim bottom.
6. Repeat to make 1 set of 4 Star Point Units.

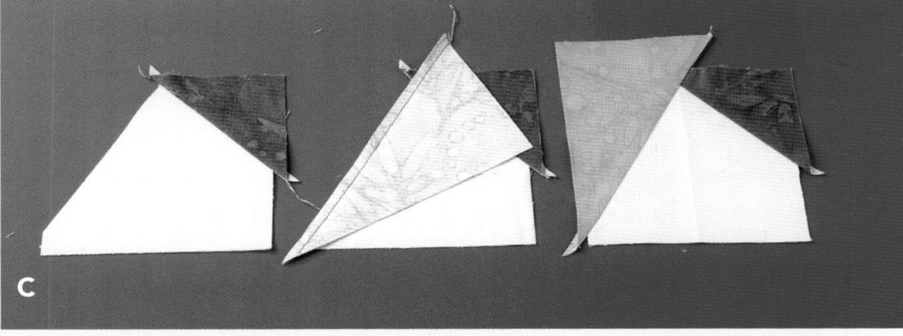
C

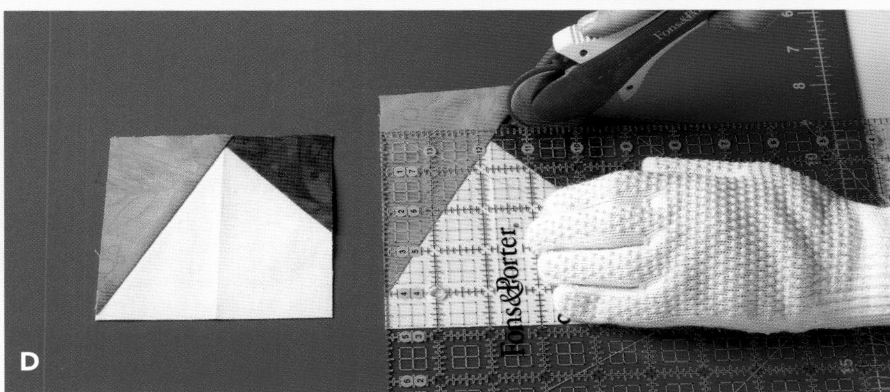

D

QUILT BY **Janet Pittman**.

Slanted Stars

After seeing another quilt in a slanted star pattern, Iowa quiltmaker Janet Pittman drafted her own stars and made this autograph quilt for her son's graduation. We've provided some helpful hints for organizing a signature quilt on page 162.

PROJECT RATING: EASY

Size: 64" × 96"

MATERIALS

5¼ yards beige print for background
18 fat quarters* assorted plaid fabrics
⅞ yard plaid fabric for binding
5¾ yards backing fabric
Queen-size quilt batting
*fat quarter = 18" × 20"

Cutting

Measurements include ¼" seam allowances. Border strips are exact length needed. You may want to make them longer to allow for piecing variations.

From beige print, cut:

- 35 (4½"-wide) strips. From strips, cut 273 (4½") A squares.
- 8 (2½"-wide) strips. Piece strips to make 2 (2½" × 92½") side borders and 2 (2½" × 64½") top and bottom borders.

From each fat quarter, cut:

- 4 (4½") A squares.
- 26 (2½") B squares.

From plaid fabric, cut:

- 2½"-wide bias strips. Join to make about 350" of bias binding.

Unit Assembly

1. Referring to *Unit 1 Diagrams*, place 1 plaid B square atop 1 beige print A square, right sides facing. Stitch diagonally from corner to corner. Trim ¼" beyond stitching. Press open to reveal triangle. Make 150 Unit 1.

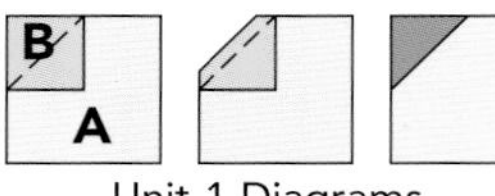

Unit 1 Diagrams
Make 150

2. Referring to *Unit 2 Diagrams*, place 1 plaid B square atop 1 beige print A square, right sides facing. Stitch diagonally from corner to corner. Trim ¼" beyond stitching. Press open to reveal triangle. Repeat on opposite corner. Make 87 Unit 2.

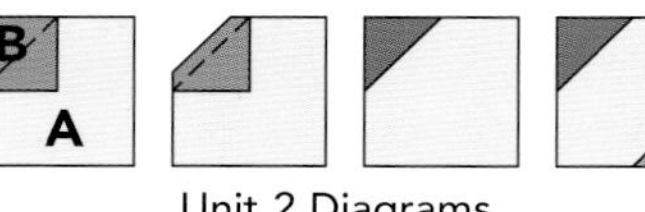

Unit 2 Diagrams
Make 87

3. Referring to *Unit 3 Diagrams*, place 1 plaid B square atop 1 plaid A square, right sides facing. Stitch diagonally from corner to corner. Trim ¼" beyond stitching. Press open to reveal triangle. Repeat on opposite corner. Make 72 Unit 3.

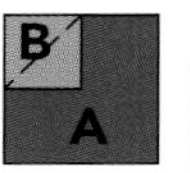

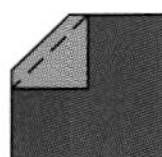

Unit 3 Diagrams
Make 72

Quilt Assembly

1. Referring to *Quilt Top Assembly Diagram*, lay out Units 1, 2, and 3 and beige print A squares as shown. (Use some Unit 2 blocks as signature blocks if desired.)
2. Join into horizontal rows; join rows to complete quilt center.
3. Add beige print side borders to quilt center. Add beige print top and bottom borders to quilt.

Finishing

1. Divide backing fabric into 2 (2⅞-yard) pieces. Cut one piece in half lengthwise. Join 1 narrow panel to each side of wider panel. Press seam allowances toward narrow panels.
2. Layer backing, batting, and quilt top; baste. Quilt as desired. Quilt shown was quilted in the ditch around the stars and with a continuous double heart motif in the background and star centers.
3. Add binding to quilt.

A LONG WAY FROM HOME
TOM BROKAW · A LONG WAY FROM HOME

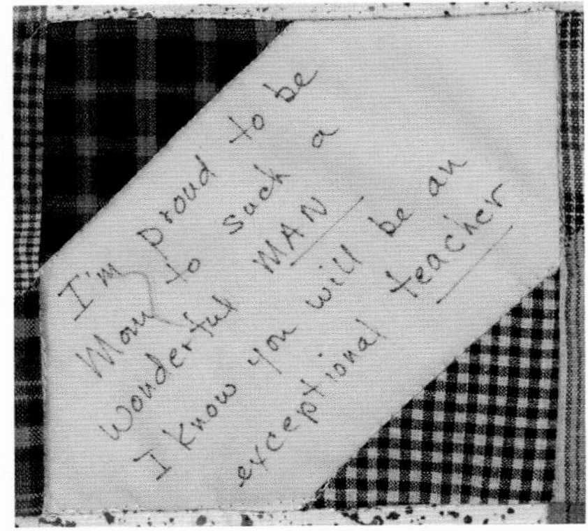

Completing a signature quilt

to commemorate an important event in someone's life takes careful organization. Begin early enough so you can get all of the signatures and still have time to finish the quilt by your deadline. Allow about 12 weeks for the project from start to finish (longer if you will be hand quilting). Use our tips and timeline to make your project a success.

TIPS

- Choose a patchwork block that has an area large enough for signatures. Find a block that has a patchwork area you can construct while you you are waiting for signature pieces to be returned.
- Plan to leave the signature areas on some blocks blank to be signed later.
- Select a light-colored fabric for the signature area so writing will show.

TIMELINE

Week 1

- Plan your quilt design.
- Buy fabric and fabric marking pens to send with signature pieces.
- If you don't plan to quilt the project yourself, schedule an appointment with a machine quilter.

Continued on page 163.

Unit 2
A
Unit 3
Unit 1

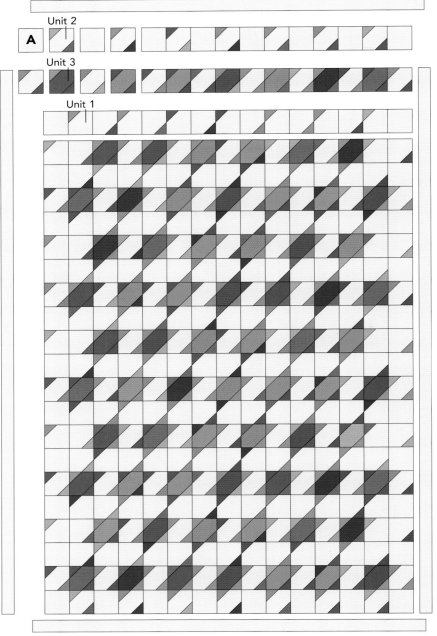

Quilt Top Assembly Diagram

DESIGNER

Janet Pittman of West Des Moines, Iowa, translates her love of fabric to art quilts and quilt patterns. ☼

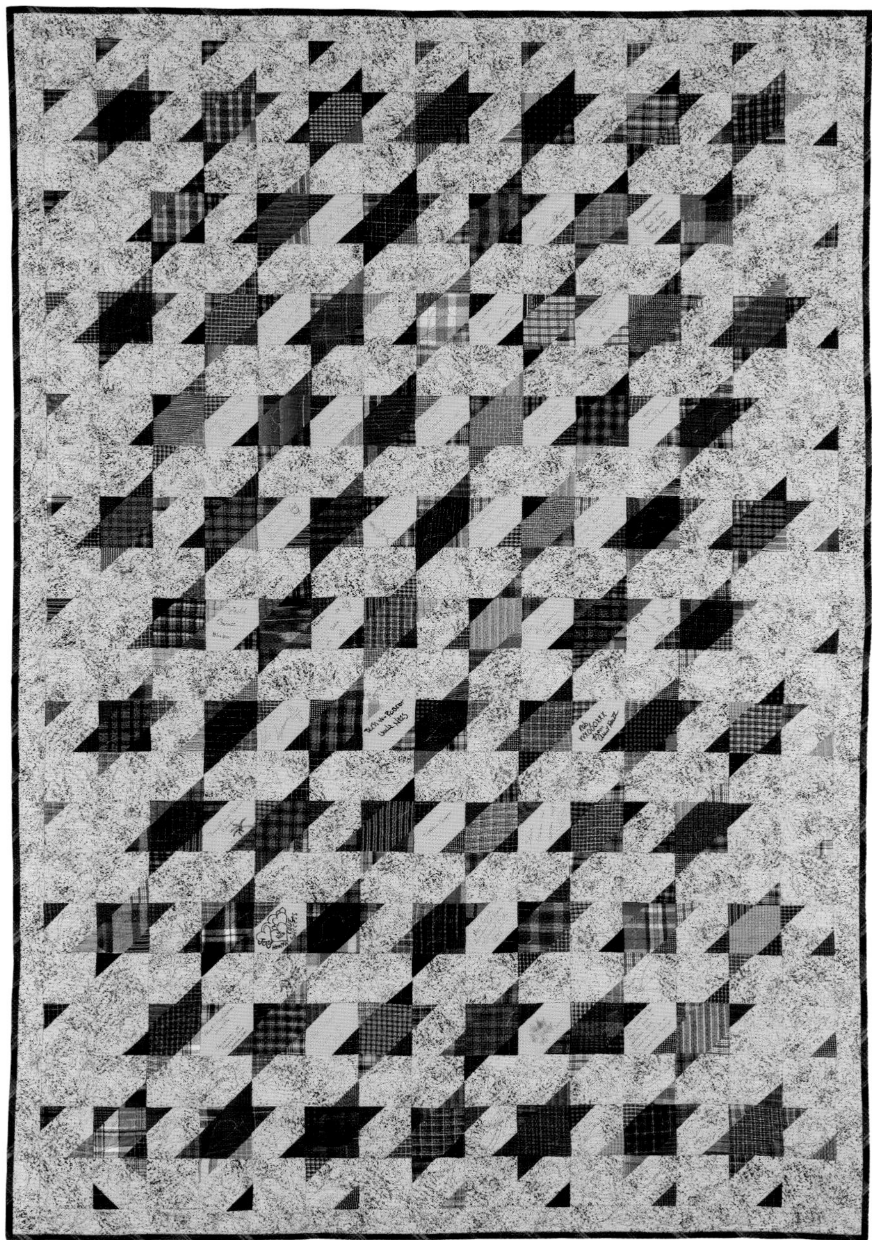

TRIED & TRUE

Try a brighter look with fabrics such as these by P&B Textiles.

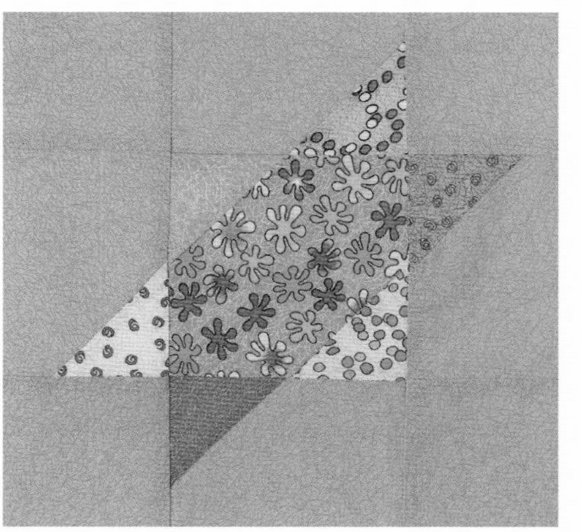

Week 2

- Cut freezer paper pieces the finished size of signature patches. (For *Slanted Stars*, cut 4" squares of freezer paper.) Press shiny side of a freezer paper piece to the wrong side of each signature patch to stabilize fabric. Cut enough signature pieces so each person can have an extra in case he/she makes a mistake.
- Write instructions for signing to include when you send the fabric pieces. Warn people to write only in areas backed by freezer paper.
- List signatures you want; mail prepared fabric, pens, instructions, and stamped return envelopes to those on your list. Include a deadline for returning pieces.

Week 3

- Make other parts of the quilt.

Week 4

- Start calling people to remind them to return their signed pieces.
- Continue sewing other sections.

Weeks 5 & 6

- As signatures arrive, remove freezer paper and heat set signatures by pressing with a hot, dry iron.
- Assemble blocks.

Weeks 7 & 8

- Join blocks to complete quilt top and mark quilting designs.

Week 9 to final week

- Quilt the quilt or deliver it to the machine quilter.
- Make binding and quilt label.

Final week

- Stitch binding to quilt and sew label to back.

Sew Smart™

Mail pens in a box or padded envelope to prevent breakage which could damage fabric.

General Instructions

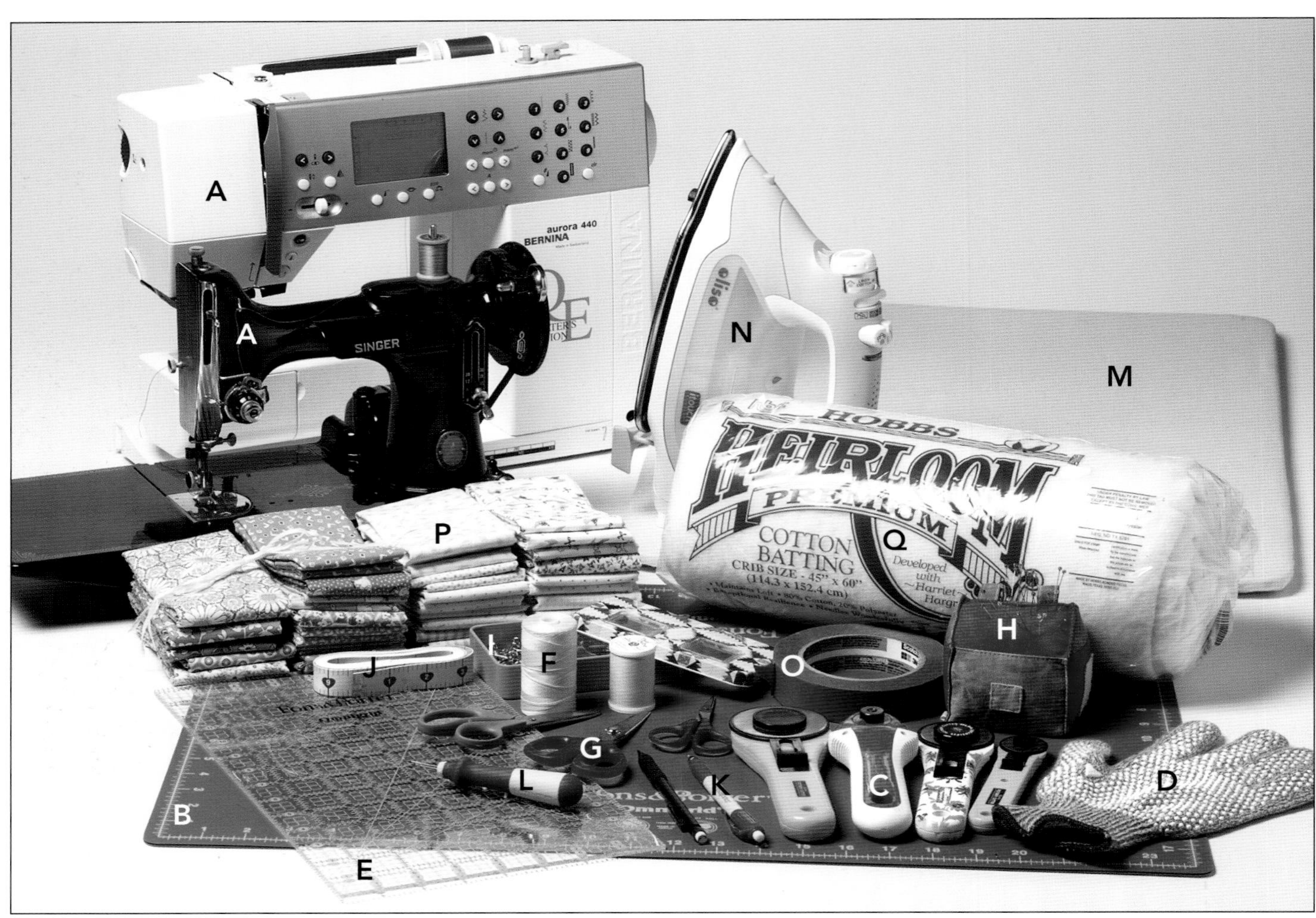

Basic Supplies

You'll need a **sewing machine (A)** in good working order to construct patchwork blocks, join blocks together, add borders, and machine quilt. We encourage you to purchase a machine from a local dealer, who can help you with service in the future, rather than from a discount store. Another option may be to borrow a machine from a friend or family member. If the machine has not been used in a while, have it serviced by a local dealer to make sure it is in good working order. If you need an extension cord, one with a surge protector is a good idea.

A **rotary cutting mat (B)** is essential for accurate and safe rotary cutting. Purchase one that is no smaller than 18" × 24". Rotary cutting mats are made of "self-healing" material that can be used over and over.

A **rotary cutter (C)** is a cutting tool that looks like a pizza cutter, and has a very sharp blade. We recommend starting with a standard size 45mm rotary cutter. Always lock or close your cutter when it is not in use, and keep it out of the reach of children.

A **safety glove** (also known as a *Klutz Glove)* **(D)** is also recommended. Wear your safety glove on the hand that is holding the ruler in place. Because it is made of cut-resistant material, the safety glove protects your non-cutting hand from accidents that can occur if your cutting hand slips while cutting.

An acrylic **ruler (E)** is used in combination with your cutting mat and rotary cutter. We recommend the Fons & Porter

8" × 14" ruler, but a 6" × 12" ruler is another good option. You'll need a ruler with inch, quarter-inch, and eighth-inch markings that show clearly for ease of measuring. Choose a ruler with 45-degree-angle, 30-degree-angle, and 60-degree-angle lines marked on it as well.

Since you will be using 100% cotton fabric for your quilts, use **cotton or cotton-covered polyester thread (F)** for piecing and quilting. Avoid 100% polyester thread, as it tends to snarl.

Keep a pair of small **scissors (G)** near your sewing machine for cutting threads.

Thin, good quality **straight pins (H)** are preferred by quilters. The pins included with pin cushions are normally too thick to use for piecing, so discard them. Purchase a box of nickel-plated brass **safety pins** size #1 **(I)** to use for pin-basting the layers of your quilt together for machine quilting.

Invest in a 120"-long dressmaker's **measuring tape (J)**. This will come in handy when making borders for your quilt.

A 0.7–0.9mm mechanical **pencil (K)** works well for marking on your fabric.

Invest in a quality sharp **seam ripper (L)**. Every quilter gets well-acquainted with her seam ripper!

Set up an **ironing board (M)** and **iron (N)** in your sewing area. Pressing yardage before cutting, and pressing patchwork seams as you go are both essential for quality quiltmaking. Select an iron that has steam capability.

Masking **tape (O)** or painter's tape works well to mark your sewing machine so you can sew an accurate ¼" seam. You will also use tape to hold your backing fabric taut as you prepare your quilt sandwich for machine quilting.

The most exciting item that you will need for quilting is **fabric (P)**. Quilters generally prefer 100% cotton fabrics for their quilts. This fabric is woven from cotton threads, and has a lengthwise and a crosswise grain. The term "bias" is used to describe the diagonal grain of the fabric. If you make a 45-degree angle cut through a square of cotton fabric, the cut edges will be bias edges, which are quite stretchy. As you learn more quiltmaking techniques, you'll learn how bias can work to your advantage or disadvantage.

¼ yard versus Fat Quarter

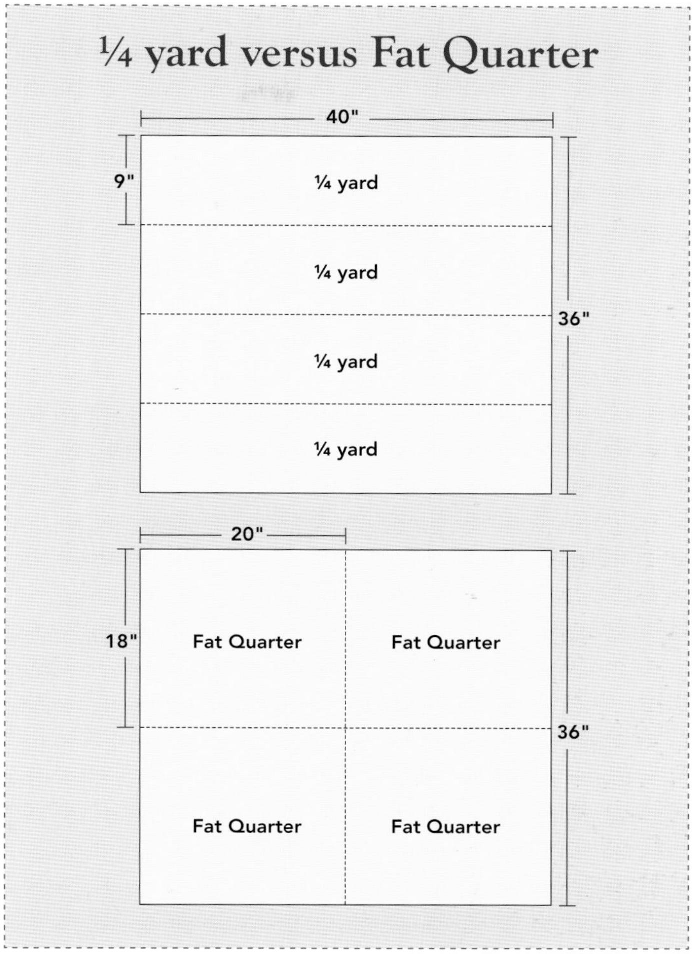

Fabric is sold by the yard at quilt shops and fabric stores. Quilting fabric is generally about 40"–44" wide, so a yard is about 40" wide by 36" long. As you collect fabrics to build your own personal stash, you will buy yards, half yards (about 18" × 40"), quarter yards (about 9" × 40"), as well as other lengths.

Many quilt shops sell "fat quarters," a special cut favored by quilters. A fat quarter is created by cutting a half yard down the fold line into two 18" × 20" pieces (fat quarters) that are sold separately. Quilters like the nearly square shape of the fat quarter because it is more useful than the narrow regular quarter yard cut.

Batting (Q) is the filler between quilt top and backing that makes your quilt a quilt. It can be cotton, polyester, cotton-polyester blend, wool, silk, or other natural materials, such as bamboo or corn. Make sure the batting you buy is at least six inches wider and six inches longer than your quilt top.

Accurate Cutting

Measuring and cutting accuracy are important for successful quilting. Measure at least twice, and cut once!

Cut strips across the fabric width unless directed otherwise.

Cutting for patchwork usually begins with cutting strips, which are then cut into smaller pieces. First, cut straight strips from a fat quarter:

1. Fold fat quarter in half with selvage edge at the top (*Photo A*).

2. Straighten edge of fabric by placing ruler atop fabric, aligning one of the lines on ruler with selvage edge of fabric (*Photo B*). Cut along right edge of ruler.

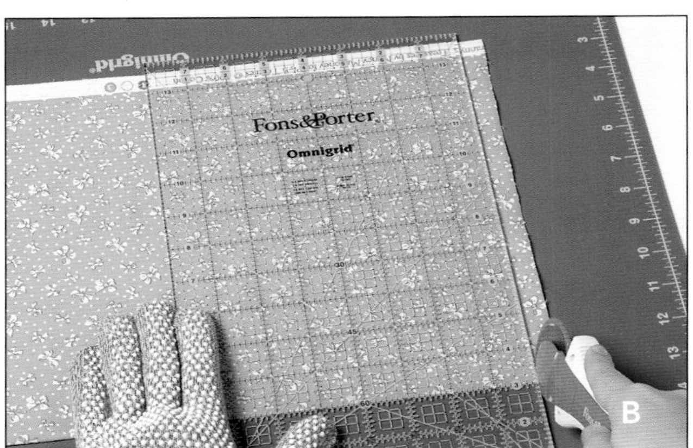

3. Rotate fabric, and use ruler to measure from cut edge to desired strip width (*Photo C*). Measurements in instructions include ¼" seam allowances.
4. After cutting the required number of strips, cut strips into squares and label them.

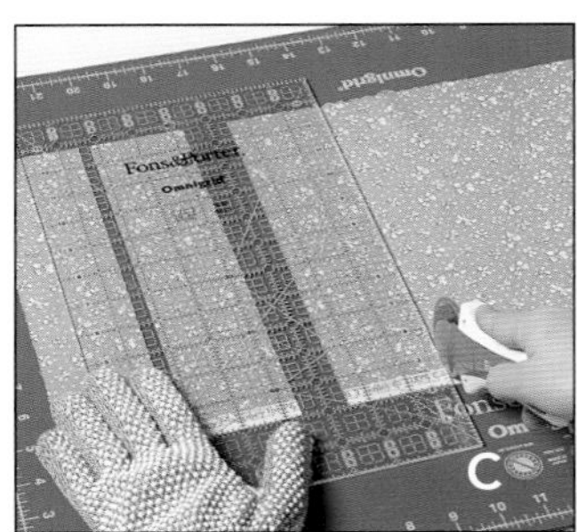

Setting up Your Sewing Machine

Sew Accurate ¼" Seams

Standard seam width for patchwork and quiltmaking is ¼". Some machines come with a patchwork presser foot, also known as a quarter-inch foot. If your machine doesn't have a quarter-inch foot, you may be able to purchase one from a dealer. Or, you can create a quarter-inch seam guide on your machine using masking tape or painter's tape.

Place an acrylic ruler on your sewing machine bed under the presser foot. Slowly turn handwheel until the tip of the needle barely rests atop the ruler's quarter-inch mark (*Photo A*). Make sure the lines on the ruler are parallel to the lines on the machine throat plate. Place tape on the machine bed along edge of ruler (*Photo B*).

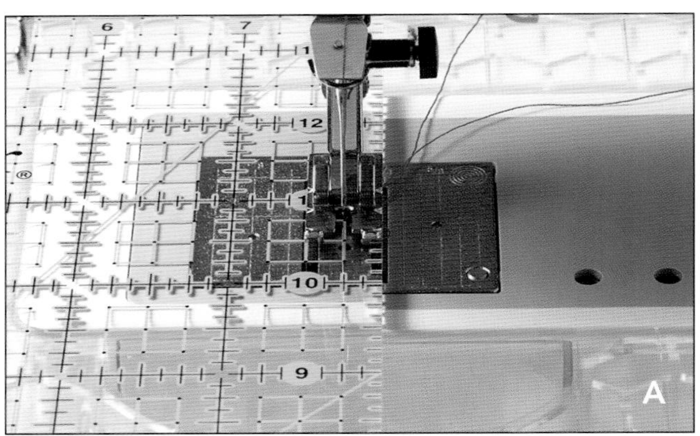

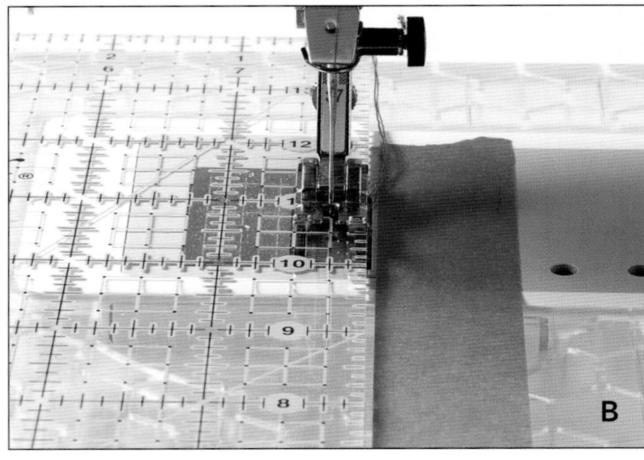

Take a Simple Seam Test

Seam accuracy is critical to machine piecing, so take this simple test once you have your quarter-inch presser foot on your machine or have created a tape guide.

Place 2 (2½") squares right sides together, and sew with a scant ¼" seam. Open squares and finger press seam. To finger press, with right sides facing you, press the seam to one side with your fingernail. Measure across pieces, raw edge to raw edge (*Photo C*). If they measure 4½", you have passed the test! Repeat the test as needed to make sure you can confidently sew a perfect ¼" seam.

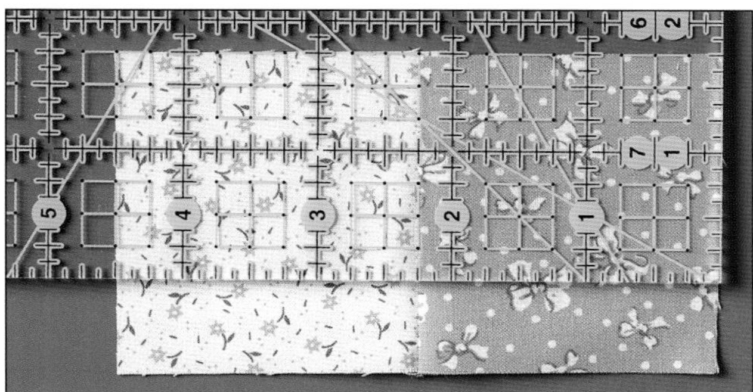

Sewing Comfortably

Other elements that promote pleasant sewing are good lighting, a comfortable chair, background music—and chocolate! Good lighting promotes accurate sewing. The better you can see what you are working on, the better your results. A comfortable chair enables you to sew for longer periods of time. An office chair with a good back rest and adjustable height works well. Music helps keep you relaxed. Chocolate is, for many quilters, simply a necessity.

Tips for Patchwork and Pressing

As you sew more patchwork, you'll develop your own shortcuts and favorite methods. Here are a few favored by many quilters:

- As you join patchwork units to form rows, and join rows to form blocks, press seams in opposite directions from row to row whenever possible (*Photo A*). By pressing seams one direction in the first row and the opposite direction in the next row, you will often create seam allowances that abut when rows are joined (*Photo B*). Abutting or nesting seams are ideal for forming perfectly matched corners on the right side of your quilt blocks and quilt top. Such pressing is not always possible, so don't worry if you end up with seam allowances facing the same direction as you join units.

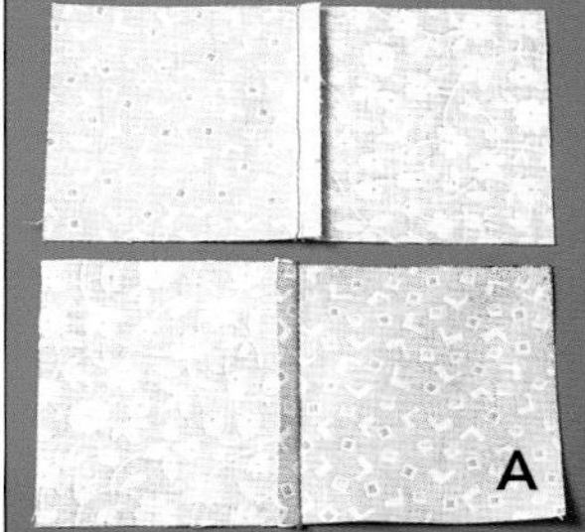

A

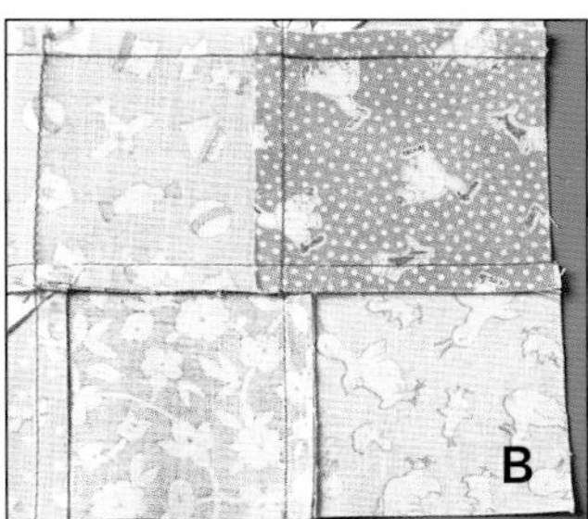

B

- Sew on and off a small, folded fabric square to prevent bobbin thread from bunching at throat plate (*Photo C*). You'll also save thread, which means fewer stops to wind bobbins, and fewer hanging threads to be snipped. Repeated use of the small piece of fabric gives it lots of thread "legs," so some quilters call it a spider.

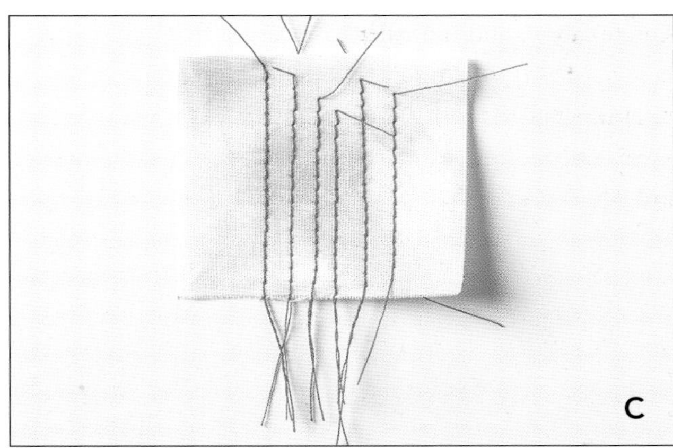

C

- Chain piece patchwork to reduce the amount of thread you use, and minimize the number and length of threads you need to trim from patchwork. Without cutting threads at the end of a seam, take 3–4 stitches without any fabric under the needle, creating a short thread chain approximately ⅛" long (*Photo D*). Repeat until you have a long line of pieces. Remove chain from machine, clip threads between units, and press seams.

D

- Trim off tiny triangle tips (sometimes called dog ears) created when making triangle-square units (*Photo E*). Trimming triangles reduces bulk and makes patchwork units and blocks lie flatter. Though no one will see the back of your quilt top once it's quilted, a neat back free of dangling threads and patchwork points is the mark of a good quilter. Also, a smooth, flat quilt top is easier to quilt, whether by hand or machine.

E

- Careful pressing will make your patchwork neat and crisp, and will help make your finished quilt top lie flat. Ironing and pressing are two different skills. Iron fabric to remove wrinkles using a back and forth, smoothing motion. Press patchwork and quilt blocks by raising and gently lowering the iron atop your work. After sewing a patchwork unit, first press the seam with the unit closed, pressing to set, or embed, the stitching. Setting the seam this way will help produce straight, crisp seams. Open the unit and press on the right side with the seam toward the darkest fabric, being careful to not form a pleat in your seam, and carefully pressing the patchwork flat.
- Many quilters use finger pressing to open and flatten seams of small units before pressing with an iron. To finger press, open patchwork unit with right side of fabric facing you. Run your fingernail firmly along seam, making sure unit is fully open with no pleat.
- Careful use of steam in your iron will make seams and blocks crisp and flat (*Photo F*). Aggressive ironing can stretch blocks out of shape, and is a common pitfall for new quilters.

F

Adding Borders

Follow these simple instructions to make borders that fit perfectly on your quilt.

1. Find the length of your quilt by measuring through the quilt center, not along the edges, since the edges may have stretched. Take 3 measurements and average them to determine the length to cut your side borders (*Diagram A*). Cut 2 side borders this length.

2. Fold border strips in half to find center. Pinch to create crease mark or place a pin at center. Fold quilt top in half crosswise to find center of side. Attach side borders to quilt center by pinning them at the ends and the center, and easing in any fullness. If quilt edge is a bit longer than border, pin and sew with border on top; if border is

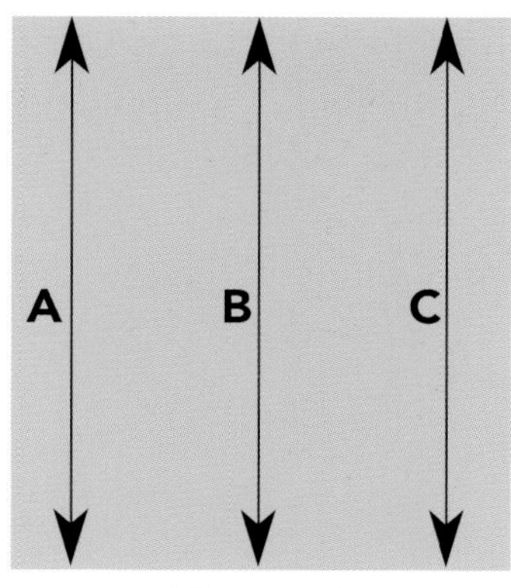

Diagram A

A ____________

B ____________

C ____________

TOTAL ____________

÷3

AVERAGE LENGTH ____________

> **HELPFUL TIP**
>
> **Use the following decimal conversions to calculate your quilt's measurements:**
>
> ⅛" = .125
> ¼" = .25
> ⅜" = .375
> ½" = .5
> ⅝" = .625
> ¾" = .75
> ⅞" = .875

slightly longer than quilt top, pin and sew with border on the bottom. Machine feed dogs will ease in the fullness of the longer piece. Press seams toward borders.

3. Find the width of your quilt by measuring across the quilt and side borders (*Diagram B*). Take 3 measurements and average them to determine the length to cut your top and bottom borders. Cut 2 borders this length.

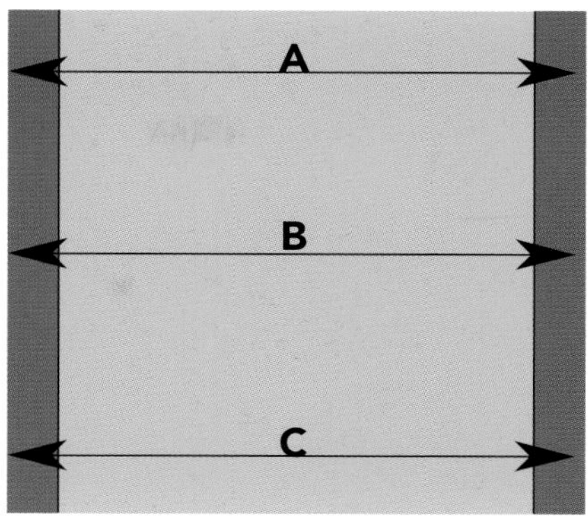

Diagram B

4. Mark centers of borders and top and bottom edges of quilt top. Attach top and bottom borders to quilt, pinnning at ends and center, and easing in any fullness (*Diagram C*). Press seams toward borders.

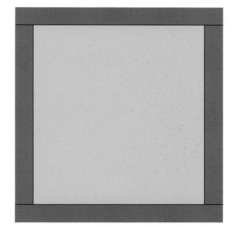

Diagram C

5. Gently steam press entire quilt top on one side and then the other. When pressing on wrong side, trim off any loose threads.

Joining Border Strips

Not all quilts have borders, but they are a nice complement to a quilt top. If your border is longer than 40", you will need to join 2 or more strips to make a border the required length. You can join border strips with either a straight seam parallel to the ends of the strips (*Photo A* on page 170), or with a diagonal seam. For the diagonal seam method, place one border strip perpendicular to another strip, rights sides facing (*Photo B*). Stitch diagonally across strips as shown. Trim seam allowance to ¼". Press seam open (*Photo C*).

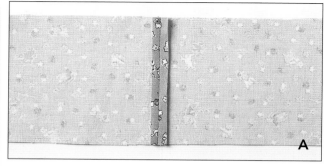

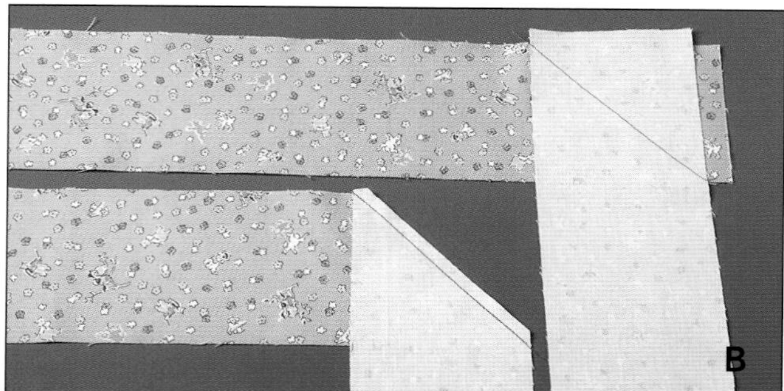

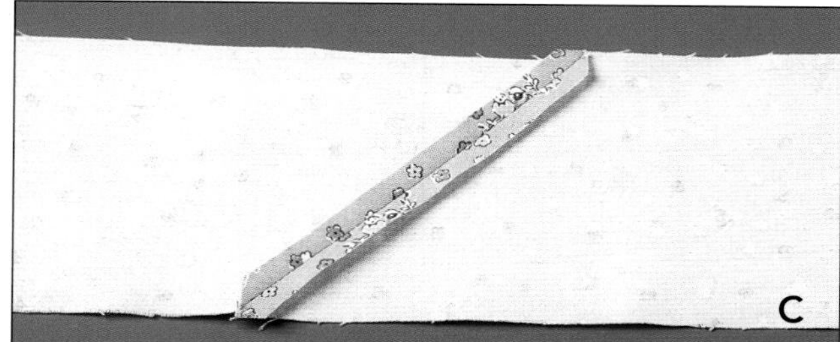

Quilting Your Quilt

Quilters today joke that there are three ways to quilt a quilt—by hand, by machine, or by check. Some enjoy making quilt tops so much, they prefer to hire a professional machine quilter to finish their work. The Split Nine Patch baby quilt shown at left has simple machine quilting that you can do yourself.

Decide what color thread will look best on your quilt top before choosing your backing fabric. A thread color that will blend in with the quilt top is a good choice for beginners. Choose backing fabric that will blend with your thread as well. A print fabric is a good choice for hiding less-than-perfect machine quilting. The backing fabric must be at least 3"–4" larger than your quilt top on all 4 sides. For example: if your quilt top measures 44" × 44", your backing needs to be at least 50" × 50". If your quilt top is 80" × 96", then your backing fabric needs to be at least 86" × 102".

For quilt tops 36" wide or less, use a single width of fabric for the backing. Buy enough length to allow adequate margin at quilt edges, as noted above. When your quilt is wider than 36", one option is to use 60"-, 90"-, or 108"-wide fabric for the quilt backing. Because fabric selection is limited for wide fabrics, quilters generally piece the quilt backing from 44/45"-wide fabric. Plan on 40"–42" of usable fabric width when estimating how much fabric to purchase. Plan your piecing strategy to avoid having a seam along the vertical or horizontal center of the quilt.

For a quilt 37"–60" wide, a backing with horizontal seams is usually the most economical use of fabric. For example, for a quilt 50" × 70", vertical seams would require 152", or 4¼ yards, of 44/45"-wide fabric (76" + 76" = 152"). Horizontal seams would require 112", or 3¼ yards (56" + 56" = 112").

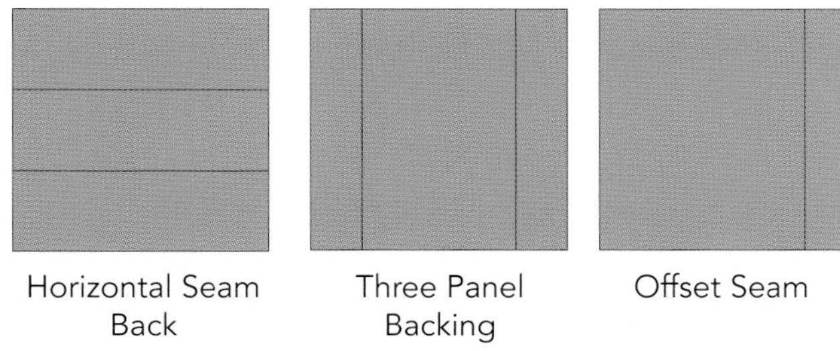

Horizontal Seam Back Three Panel Backing Offset Seam

For a quilt 61"–80" wide, most quilters piece a three-panel backing, with vertical seams, from two lengths of fabric. Cut one of the pieces in half lengthwise, and sew the halves to opposite sides of the wider panel. Press the seams away from the center panel.

For a quilt 81"–120" wide, you will need three lengths of fabric, plus extra margin. For example, for a quilt 108" × 108", purchase at least 342", or 9½ yards, of 44/45"-wide fabric (114" + 114" + 114" = 342").

For a three-panel backing, pin the selvage edge of the center panel to the selvage edge of the side panel, with edges aligned and right sides facing. Machine stitch with a ½" seam. Trim seam allowances to ¼", trimming off the selvages from both panels at once. Press the seam away from the center of the quilt. Repeat on other side of center panel.

For a two-panel backing, join panels in the same manner as above, and press the seam to one side.

Create a "quilt sandwich" by layering your backing, batting, and quilt top. Find the crosswise center of the backing fabric by folding it in half. Mark with a pin on each side. Lay backing down on a table or floor, wrong side up. Tape corners and edges of backing to the surface with masking or painter's tape so that backing is taut (*Photo A*).

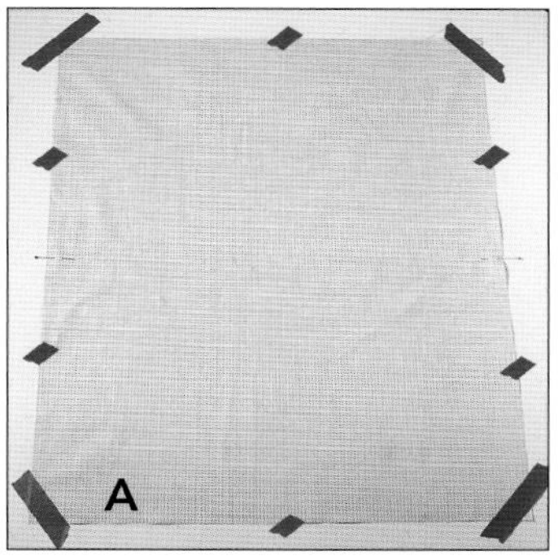
A

Fold batting in half crosswise and position it atop backing fabric, centering folded edge at center of backing (*Photo B*). Unfold batting and smooth it out atop backing (*Photo C*).

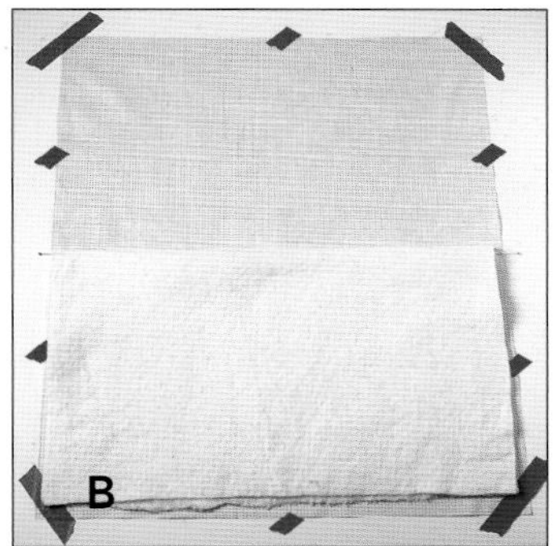
B

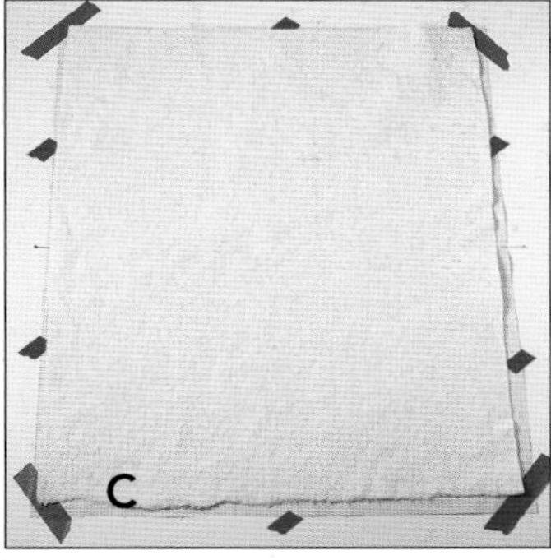
C

In the same manner, fold the quilt top in half crosswise and center it atop backing and batting (*Photo D*). Unfold top and smooth it out atop batting (*Photo E*).

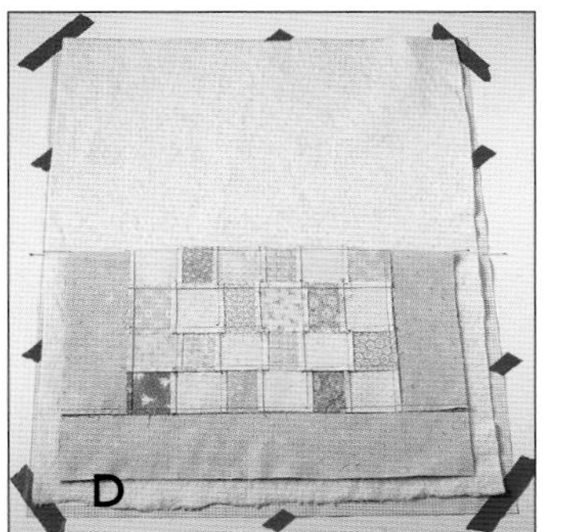
D

E

Use safety pins to pin baste the layers (*Photo F*). Pins should be about a fist width apart. A special tool, called a Kwik Klip, or a grapefruit spoon makes closing the pins easier. As you slide a pin through all three layers, slide the point of the pin into one of the tool's grooves. Push on the tool to help close the pin.

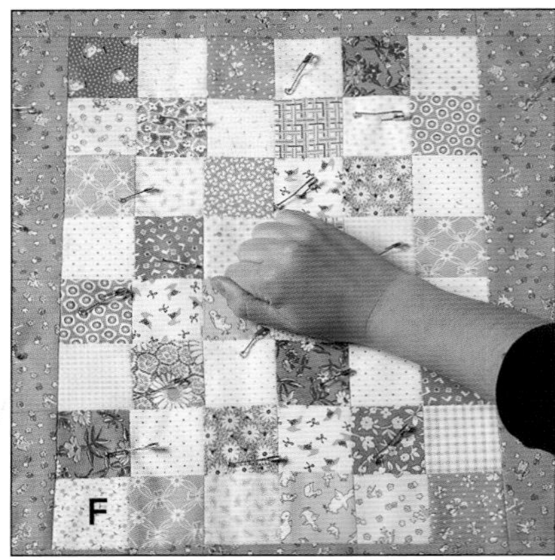

For straight line quilting, install an even feed or walking foot on your machine. This presser foot helps all three layers of your quilt move through the machine evenly without bunching.

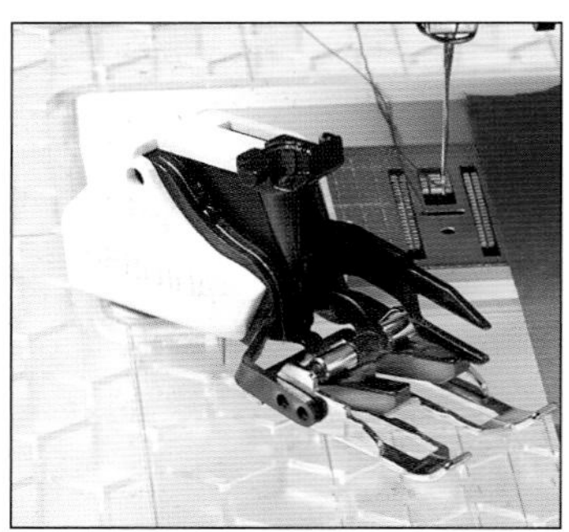

Walking Foot

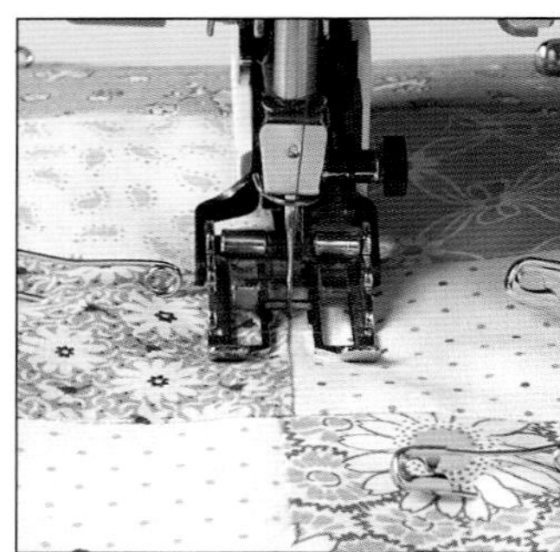

Stitching "in the ditch"

An easy way to quilt your first quilt is to stitch "in the ditch" along seam lines. No marking is needed for this type of quilting.

Binding Your Quilt

Preparing Binding

Strips for quilt binding may be cut either on the straight of grain or on the bias.

1. Measure the perimeter of your quilt and add approximately 24" to allow for mitered corners and finished ends.
2. Cut the number of strips necessary to achieve desired length. We like to cut binding strips 2¼" wide.
3. Join your strips with diagonal seams into 1 continuous piece (*Photo A*). Press the seams open. (See page 169 for instructions for the diagonal seams method of joining strips.)

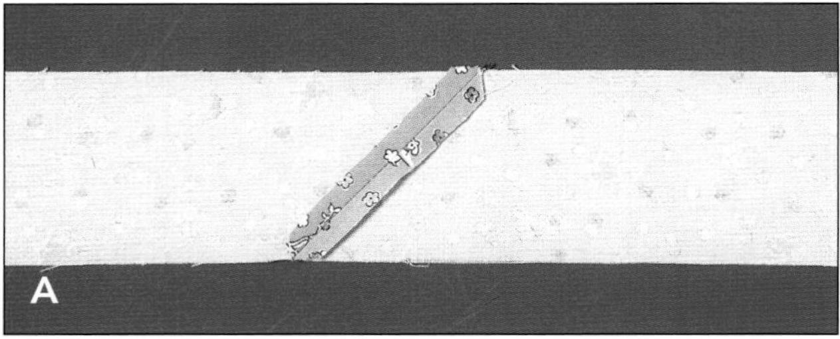

4. Press your binding in half lengthwise, with wrong sides facing, to make French-fold binding (*Photo B*).

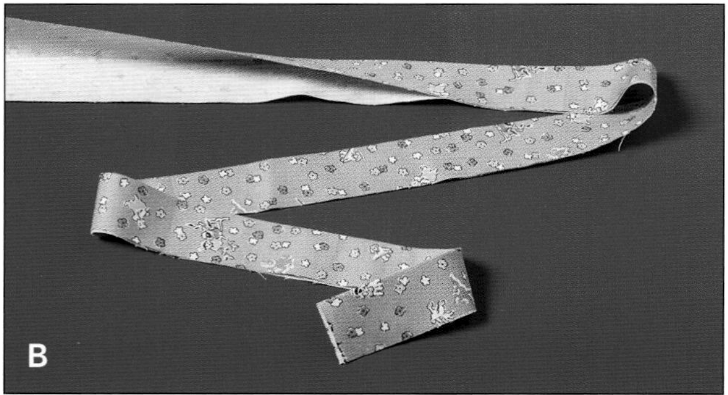

Attaching Binding

Attach the binding to your quilt using an even-feed or walking foot. This prevents puckering when sewing through the three layers.

1. Choose beginning point along one side of quilt. Do not start at a corner. Match the two raw edges of the binding strip to the raw edge of the quilt top. The folded edge

will be free and to left of seam line (*Photo C*). Leave 12" or longer tail of binding strip dangling free from beginning point. Stitch, using ¼" seam, through all layers.

C

2. For mitered corners, stop stitching ¼" from corner; backstitch, and remove quilt from sewing machine (*Photo D*). Place a pin ¼" from corner to mark where you will stop stitching.

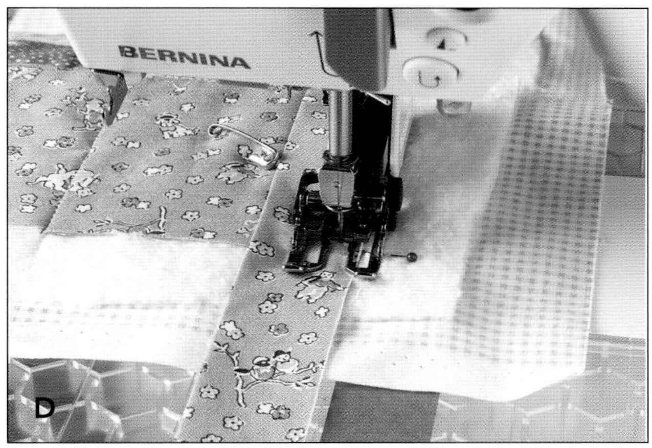

D

Rotate quilt quarter turn and fold binding straight up, away from corner, forming 45-degree-angle fold (*Photo E*).

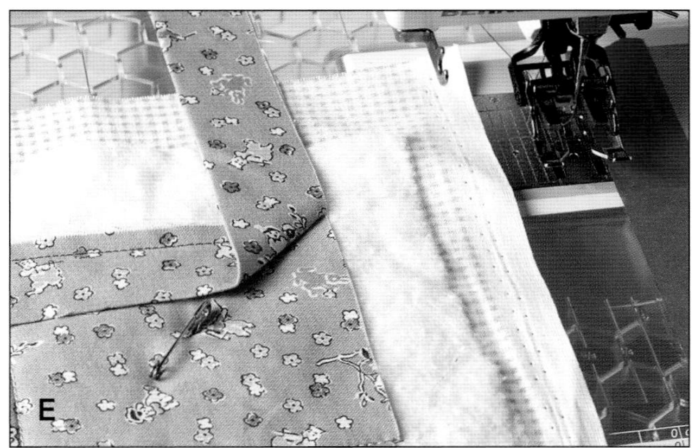
E

Bring binding straight down in line with next edge to be sewn, leaving top fold even with raw edge of previously sewn side (*Photo F*). Begin stitching at top edge, sewing through all layers (*Photo G*).

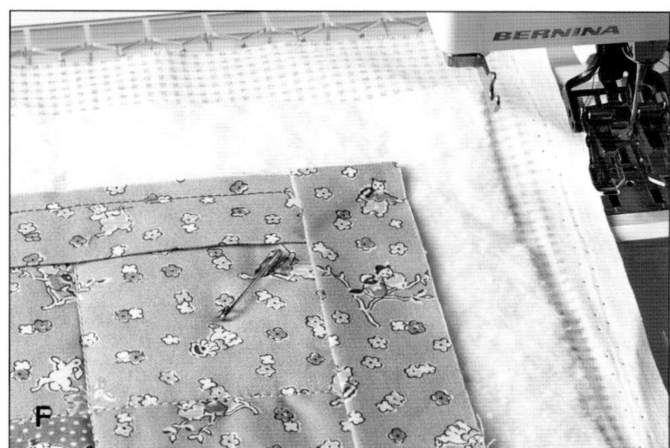

F

G

3. To finish binding, stop stitching about 8" away from starting point, leaving about a 12" tail at end (*Photo H*). Bring beginning and end of binding to center of 8" opening and fold each back, leaving about ¼" space

H

between the two folds of binding (*Photo I*). (Allowing this ¼" extra space is critical, as binding tends to stretch when it is stitched to the quilt. If the folded ends meet at this point, your binding will be too long for the space after the ends are joined.) Crease folds of binding with your fingernail.

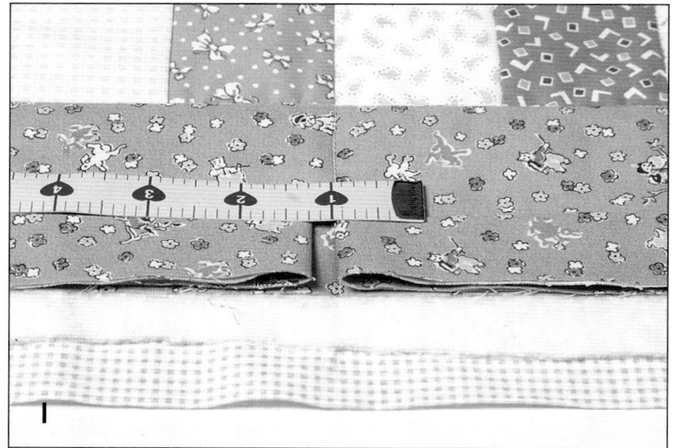

I

4. Open out each edge of binding and draw line across wrong side of binding on creased fold line, as shown in *Photo J*. Draw line along lengthwise fold of binding at same spot to create an X (*Photo K*).

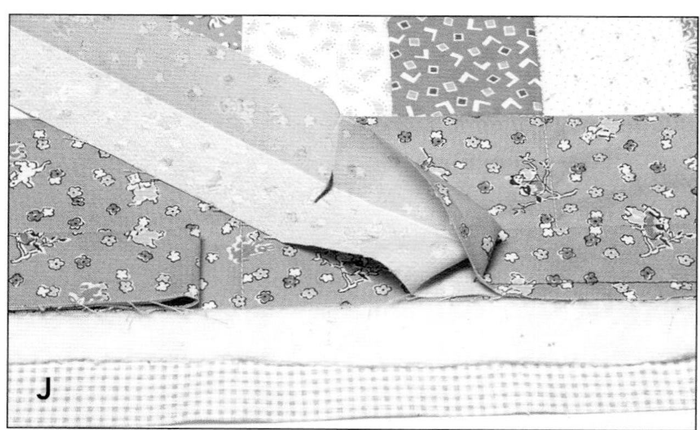

J

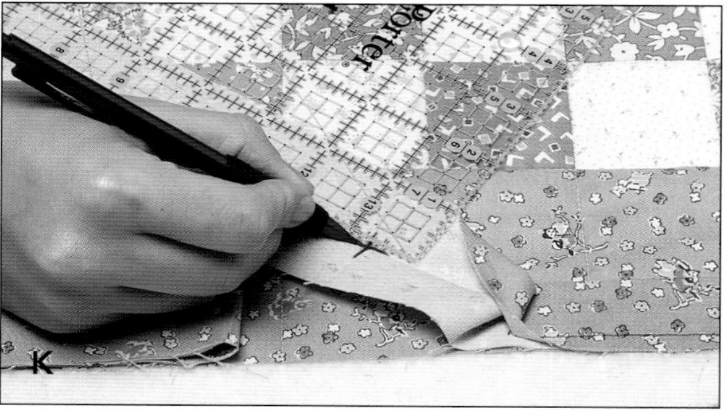

K

5. With edge of ruler at marked X, line up 45-degree-angle marking on ruler with one long side of binding (*Photo L*). Draw diagonal line across binding as shown in *Photo M*.

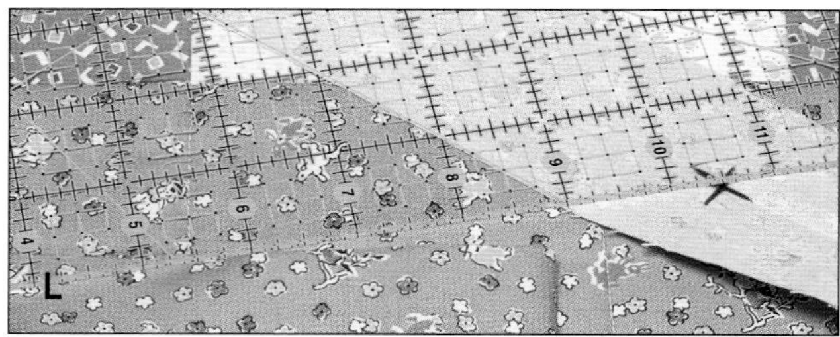

L

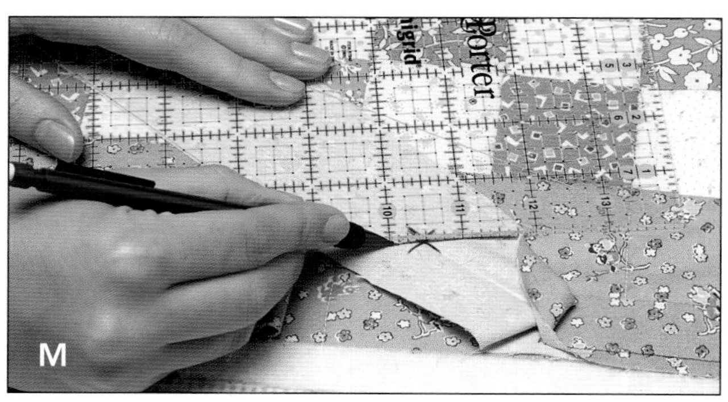

M

Repeat for other end of binding. Lines must angle in same direction (*Photo N*).

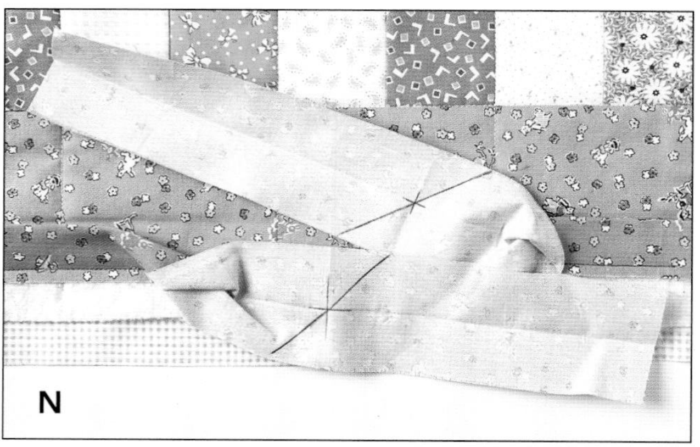

N

6. Pin binding ends together with right sides facing, pin-matching diagonal lines as shown in *Photo O*. Binding ends will be at right angles to each other. Machine-stitch along diagonal line, removing pins as you stitch (*Photo P*).

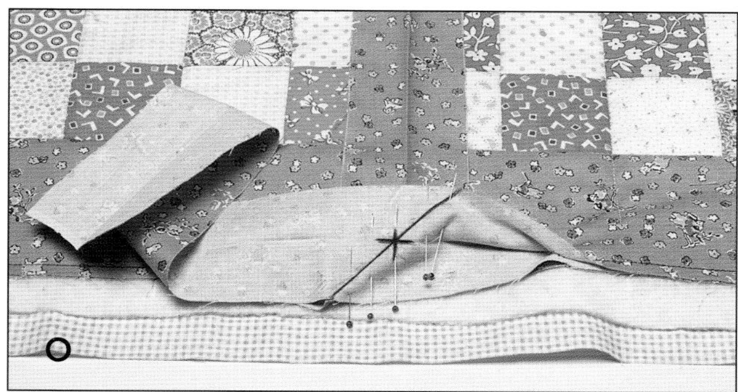

O

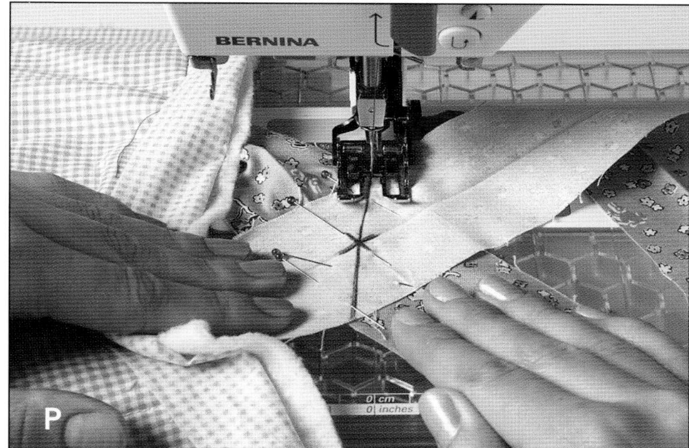

P

7. Lay binding against quilt to double-check that it is correct length (*Photo Q*). Trim ends of binding ¼" from diagonal seam (*Photo R*).

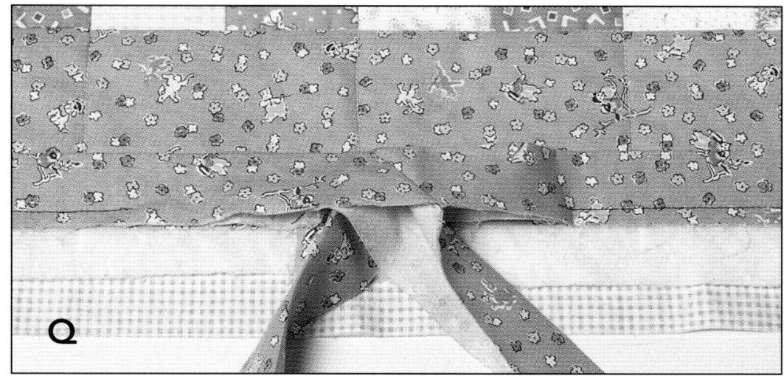

Q

R

8. Finger press diagonal seam open (*Photo S*). Fold binding in half and finish stitching binding to quilt (*Photo T*).

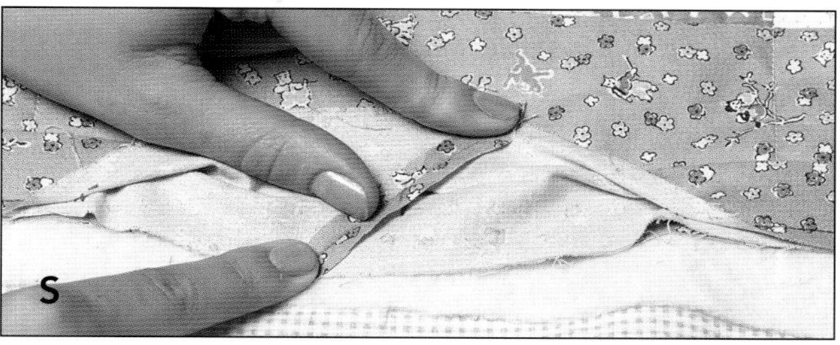

S

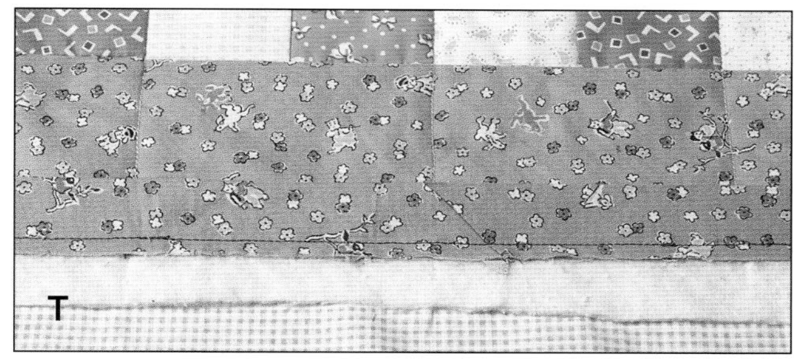

T

Hand Stitching Binding to Quilt Back

1. Trim any excess batting and quilt back with scissors or a rotary cutter (*Photo A*). Leave enough batting (about ⅛" beyond quilt top) to fill binding uniformly when it is turned to quilt back.

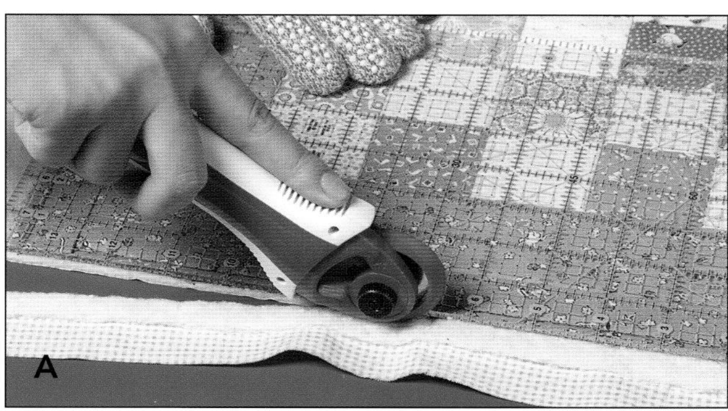

A

2. Bring folded edge of binding to quilt back so that it covers machine stitching. Blindstitch folded edge to quilt backing, using a few pins just ahead of stitching to hold binding in place (*Photo B*).

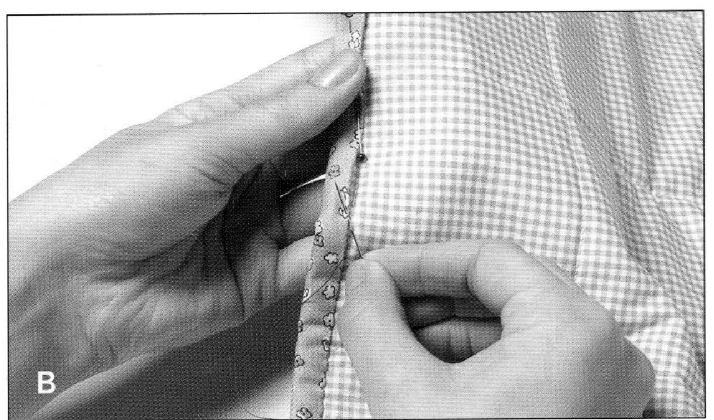
B

3. Continue stitching to corner. Fold unstitched binding from next side under, forming a 45-degree angle and a mitered corner. Stitch mitered folds on both front and back (*Photo C*).

C

Finishing Touches

- **Label your quilt so the recipient and future generations know who made it.** To make a label, use a fabric marking pen to write the details on a small piece of solid color fabric (*Photo A*). To make writing easier, put pieces of masking tape on the wrong side. Remove tape after writing. Use your iron to turn under ¼" on each edge, then stitch the label to the back of your quilt using a blindstitch, taking care not to sew through to quilt top.

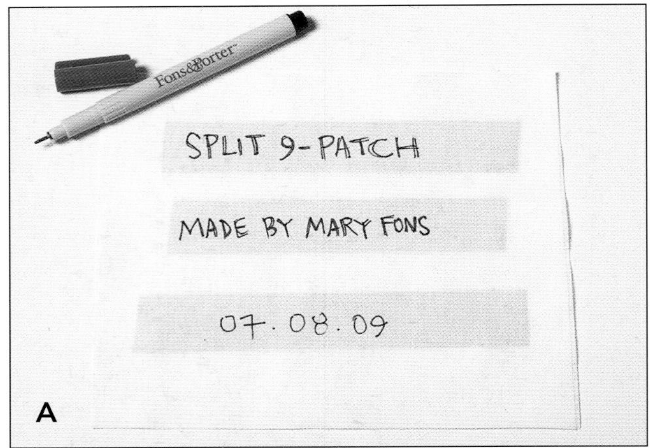

A

- **Take a photo of your quilt.** Keep your photos in an album or journal along with notes, fabric swatches, and other information about the quilts.
- **If your quilt is a gift, include care instructions.** Some quilt shops carry pre-printed care labels you can sew onto the quilt (*Photo B*). Or, make a care label using the method described above.

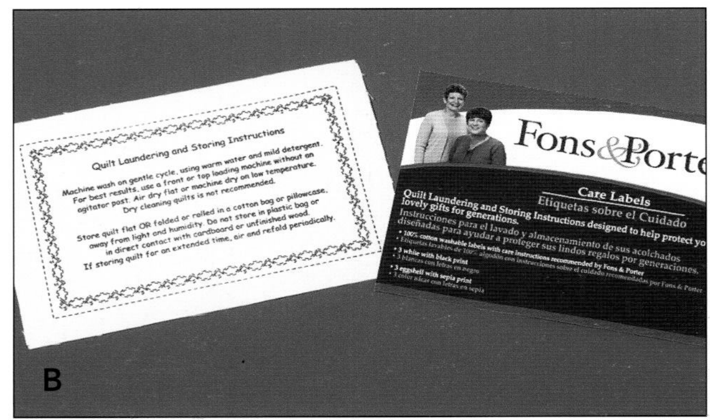

B